# Multidimensional Modelling with CA-SuperCalc for Windows

## Janet Swift

# I/O Press

First Published 1994
©I/O Press
Cover Design: Jane M Patience
ISBN 1 871962 26-9

British Library Cataloguing in Publication Data
A catalogue record for this book is available from the British Library

All Rights Reserved. No part of this publication may be reproduced, stored in a retrieval system, or transmitted in any form or by any means, electronic, mechanical, photocopying, recording or
otherwise, without prior written permission.

Products mentioned within this text may be protected by trade marks, in which case full acknowledgement is hereby given.

Although every effort has been made to ensure the correctness of the information contained herein neither the publisher nor the author accept liability for any omissions or errors that may remain.

Typeset by I/O Press

Printed and bound in Great Britain by Cromwell Press Limited,
Broughton Gifford, Wiltshire

# Contents

**Preface**

**Chapter 1    Models and Sheets                              1**

The sheet - what you should know; Why move on from a sheet?; Compete!; What can't models do?

**Chapter 2    Understanding Dimensions                       7**

Multidimensional?;A data table; Crosstabulation; A 2D model; Dimensions and items; Database and data table; 2D SCW sheets; Categorical data; 4D car sales; Sparse data; Using a model

**Chapter 3    Building Models                                21**

Building a new model; Assigning names; The right mouse button; Item names; Rotating the model; Deleting items; Adding items; Moving items; Inserting a dimension; Deleting a dimension; Save and Open; The education survey

**Chapter 4    Ranges                                        37**

Cell references; Simple arithmetic; Ranges; Using ranges in functions; Split ranges; Summary; Underspecification; Pointing; Pointing at a range; Summing education; Relative and absolute; Saying what you mean

**Chapter 5    Global Formulae                               53**

Functions and formulae; The trouble with copying; Scope; Creating a global formula; The scope of education; Applying scope; Applying education; Editing globals; Creating new globals from old; Which formula to apply?; Deleting globals; Using scope - a question of style

**Chapter 6    Formatting and Dimensionality    73**

Overview; Attributes - fonts,alignment,patterns; Format shortcuts; Styles; Selecting ranges in the visible dimensions; Formatting pages; Formatting slices; Ordering items; Formatting - a simple example; Multiple views; Column width and row height; Hidden items; Dimension styles; Formatting car sales; Format checklist

**Chapter 7    Page Models    99**

Pages; A 3D page model; Formatting pages; Using pivoting; Adding a summary page; Imported page models; More than 3D; Indexing dimensions; Large models

**Chapter 8    Structure, Range and Scope    113**

Absolute but self adjusting; Relative references; Relative pointing; Names; Formulae - range and scope; Inserting and deleting items; Surgery on models; Moving items can be harmful; Renaming items is safe; Duplicate item names; Updating the scope; Moving items and scope; Structure and scope; World sales

**Chapter 9    Crosstab Models    139**

Discrete data; Making categories; Discrete variables = dimensions; The Variables dimension; Sources of databases; The DBF format; Importing a DBF file into a sheet; Sheets to models; Importing DBF files to a model; The Staff model; Exporting DBF from a model; Repeated measures; Aggregation; Aggregation using a sheet; Fully crossed and nested models; Analysing crosstab models; Marginals; Marginals - an example; Deviations; A predicted table; Statistics; Missing data; Allocate; Advanced allocation; Self allocation

**Chapter 10    Functional Models    183**

A simple investment; The LABEL function; Using items in functions; Dealing with text labels; Index values; Index expressions; External lookup tables; A 3D example; Charts and models; Charting the investment data; Plotting row labels; Terms; Entering values using terms; Analysing a mailshot

**Chapter 11   Estimation and Prediction            211**

Curves and relationships; Simple curves; Inexact relationships; Practical estimation; Curve Builder; Estimation formulae; Specifying the curve; LogLinear and LogLog curves; Log curves using Curve Builder; A lookup table curve; S-shaped curves; Fixed and variable components; Two independent variables; Summary; Forecasting; The statistical functions; Curves and charts; Regression

**Chapter 12 What-if? Sheets, Links and Models      253**

Links; The mailshot example; Sheets and constants; Sheets for presentation; What-if tables; A one-input example; Two-input data tables; Tabulating a model; Goal seeking; Goal seeking mailshot

**Index**

**Other books of interest**

# Preface

Multidimensional modelling is an idea that can seem intimidating to some but in practice CA-SuperCalc for Windows' models are as easy as using a 2D spreadsheet. Given the increased power that you get by using models is it well worth spending some time finding out exactly how they work. I'm sure that the effort will quickly be repaid.

To avoid repeating material in the companion book *Mastering CA SuperCalc for Windows* I have assumed that the reader knows most of the basics of how to use sheets. However, the two books can be used independently of one another. Many of the examples used are deliberately small scale to make it possible to see what is going on. In practice the only difference between these models and real models is the amount of data involved!

In working on both my books about SCW I have repeatedly been impressed by how powerful this application is and how it has "extra" features and facilities that do not have equivalents in many other spreadsheets. I can therefore recommend SCW to anybody who is interested in what the spreadsheet is, as well as what it does. And I hope these books manage to convey some of my own enthusiasm.

Janet Swift
June 1994

## Companion Disk

All the examples discussed in this book - plus extra ones that could not be included due to limitations of space - are included on a 3.5" (720K) disk. This disk costs £5 (including VAT, if applicable, and postage) and can be ordered directly from I/O Press. Please enclose cheque, postal order or your VISA or Access details when ordering.

## Update Service

To keep you up-to-date with changes and revisions in SCW we plan to produce an update booklet as a service to readers of this book and Mastering CA SuperCalc for Windows. If you would like a free copy then send a self addressed envelope large enough to hold an A5 booklet stamped with postage for 100gms to:

**I/O Press (SCW Update Service)**

There is no need to include any proof of purchase. Your envelope will be kept on file until the update becomes available.

I/O Press,
Oak Tree House, Leyburn,
North Yorkshire DL8 5SE
Tel: (0969) 24402 Fax: (0969) 24375

# Chapter 1

# Models and Sheets

CA-SuperCalc for Windows has two major components, sheets and models. A sheet is what most users would recognise as a traditional spreadsheet and in nearly all cases they provide a starting point for using the entire package. Models on the other hand are more sophisticated and many users regard them as something that they will get round to using some time in the future. While it is true that models are more sophisticated they suit particular applications so much better than a simple two-dimensional sheet that they actually make the task easier. In this chapter we look briefly at the differences between models and sheets and what it is you should already know about using sheets.

## » The sheet - what you should know

This book is primarily about using SCW's Multi-Dimensional Models or MDMs. While it is completely self-contained it is obvious that it cannot cover the details of using sheets. It is therefore taken for granted that you already have most of the basic ideas concerned with using sheets. In particular, it is assumed that you know what a sheet, and more generally a spreadsheet, is and the sort of task you would use it for. If you discover that one of the later chapters mentions some aspect of using sheets that you are unfamiliar with then consult SCW's manuals, the on-screen help, or *Mastering CA-SuperCalc for Windows*, this volume's counterpart dedicated to explaining how sheets work and how they can be used.

Although it isn't possible to give an exhaustive list of the ideas that you should already have mastered, the most important are:

- » Using standard Windows mouse operations - click, double-click and drag.

- » Selecting menu commands using the left mouse button and displaying and using the pop-up menu associated with the right mouse button.

- » Standard column letter and row number cell references, e.g. A1, B20.

- » Corner to corner range references, e,g. A1:B10

- » Absolute and relative cell references, e.g. $A$1 as opposed to A1.

- » Entering data and formulae into cells, moving around a sheet and editing data and formulae.

- » Modifying row height and column width by dragging.

- » Formats and formatting.

It is also assumed that you know very general things like how to save a file and maintain a coherent directory structure. If you need any help with any of these topics then see the on-screen help or read the manual.

## » Why move on from a sheet?

When you first start using SCW there is no doubt that the sheet is the easiest and most attractive option. The reason is that sheets allow you to work in an ad-hoc manner. You can enter some data in one area, move to another and enter some formulae. If you want some intermediate results then you can find yet another area and enter more formulae and data. In other words the sheet is the ideal "scratch pad" or electronic "back of the envelope"!

There is nothing wrong with using a sheet in this way and it is infinitely preferable to using a pocket calculator and paper. The only danger is that the ad-hoc sheet may become more useful than you ever imagined and then it is important to attempt to convert it into an organised template that reduces the chances that you will make mistakes.

So the sheet provides the freedom to work in an ad-hoc manner but it can also be organised to produce reusable templates - where then does the model fit in? The key characteristic of the model is that it takes on the structure of the data. Instead of having arbitrary areas in a sheet where particular data can be entered, a model has no such "unallocated" areas. Every cell in a model is designed to hold particular data from the moment that the model is created. This means that if you have very little idea of the structure of the data you are working with then you will find a model difficult to get started. In a sheet you might store the data somewhere, enter some formulae and then decide that it's all wrong and move it somewhere else! In a model you have to prepare the areas where the data will be stored before you enter the data and making changes is not quite as easy. However, after a little practice you very quickly become able to identify the sort of data that suits a model and then getting started is no more difficult than with a sheet.

Notice that this implies that unless you are prepared to learn something about models first you are unlikely to start using them spontaneously. Your ability to identify situations that would benefit from a model depends on you knowing what a model is in the first place! The surprise that is waiting for you is that more data than you would expect is crying out to be stored and analysed in a multidimensional model!

## » Compete!

Don't expect to be able to use an MDM for every task that you tackle. Computer Associates could have decided to restrict SCW to just models. In principle you can do nearly everything you can do in a sheet in a model. In fact SCW is based on an earlier program, Compete!, which supported models but not sheets. If you are familiar with Compete! then you will find that upgrading to SCW is quite easy - but you need to take into account the availability of sheets and when they might be more suitable for a particular task. If you have existing Compete! models you can import them into SCW simply by opening their files.

## » What can't models do?

There are some specific restrictions on the commands that you can use within models. If you are familiar with sheets you may find some of these restrictions worrying. In most cases the reason for the restriction is that the facility makes little sense when used in connection with a model. In all cases the fact that the facility is available in a sheet means that you can still use it to create a combined sheet/model system using links.

The major restriction is that you cannot make use of any of the Data commands. This means that you cannot set up a database within a model or use the data form to enter data. It also means that you cannot use the other commands that are included in the Data menu - Sort, Series, Table, Parse, Matrix, Distribution and Regression. However, do not be misled into thinking that these facilities are therefore irrelevant to models. There are situations when combining these facilities, accessed via links to a sheet, with a model produces a powerful analytical tool - but we will return to that idea in the final chapter of this book.

You can make full use of SCW's charting facilities and all of the commands on its other menus with only a few modifications to take account of the differences between sheets and models.

## Key points

» It is assumed that you already know something of how Windows, SCW and sheets work. This book is about using SCW's Multi-Dimensional Models or MDMs.

» Models are more sophisticated and structured than sheets and this makes it more difficult to get started with them.

» Sheets remain ideal for ad-hoc calculation and analysis although they can be organised for long term use.

» Not all tasks are best tackled by constructing a model and it is only after you have seen some examples of models that you can learn to recognise when they are going to be useful.

# Chapter 2

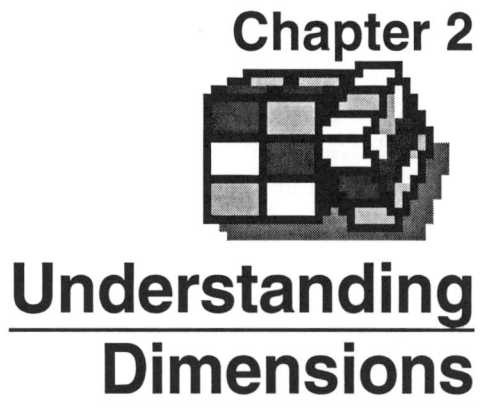

# Understanding Dimensions

In this chapter we take a look at the type of data and models that SCW can work with. The emphasis is on understanding the data and the models and no explanations are given of how the models were constructed or any other details of using SCW. The next chapter deals with details of 'how'. This chapter is about 'why'.

## » Multidimensional?

The most obvious difference between SCW and other spreadsheets is its ability to work with multidimensional data. The use of the word 'multidimensional' can sound intimidating but in practice a great deal of data used in ordinary spreadsheets is multidimensional and we have to find ways of accommodating it within the 2D spreadsheet's limited framework. In short, if the data is naturally multidimensional then it is much easier to recognise this fact and work with it in its natural form rather than force it into an inappropriate mould. Indeed, many of the stranger contortions of standard spreadsheet use can be blamed on multidimensional data which fights very hard against being flattened out onto a 2D worksheet!

Of course not all data is multidimensional and it is important to be able to identify the type of data that you are working with. SCW has an excellent 2D worksheet facility so there isn't any need to switch applications if the data would better fit into a traditional 2D design. However, it is important to realise that even when working with 2D data there are still differences between a 2D worksheet and a 2D SCW model. An SCW model integrates the data into its structure in a way that can be quite confusing at first. As we shall see, what is treated as data in a worksheet often becomes the structure of a model.

At the moment this talk of data, structure and models is very abstract and before we get any deeper it is time to find out exactly how it all works by way of a small example.

## » A data table

A small survey has been conducted to discover if gender has any influence on how far a student progresses through the education system. The data collected on each subject was coded so that it reduced to M or F for Male or Female gender and High, Medium, and Low as scores of educational experience. If you were to be asked to enter this data into a spreadsheet you would most probably produce something very similar to that shown below.

| | A | B | C |
|---|---|---|---|
| 1 | Record | Education | Gender |
| 2 | 1 | High | F |
| 3 | 2 | Low | M |
| 4 | 3 | Medium | F |
| 5 | 4 | Medium | M |
| 6 | 5 | Low | M |
| 7 | 6 | Low | M |
| 8 | 7 | Medium | F |
| 9 | 8 | High | F |
| 10 | 9 | Low | F |
| 11 | 10 | Medium | F |
| 12 | 11 | Low | M |
| 13 | 12 | Medium | M |
| 14 | 13 | Low | F |
| 15 | 14 | High | M |
| 16 | 15 | High | F |
| 17 | 16 | High | F |
| 18 | 17 | Medium | F |
| 19 | 18 | High | M |
| 20 | 19 | Low | M |
| 21 | | | |

*EDU1.MDS : Window1*

Notice that the headings 'Education' and 'Gender' are included along with the 'real' data in the worksheet. Also notice that the rows and columns of the worksheet are numbered and lettered in the usual spreadsheet style. If you want to refer to any particular item of data then you have to supply its 'co-ordinates' as in cell B3 or C10.

## » Crosstabulation

The data table does record the data values quite well but in terms of analysing or working with the data this simple listing is almost useless. What we really need is a count of how many people fall into each of the possible categories - Male/Low, Male/Medium etc.. A table of categories and counts is usually referred to as a 'Crosstabulation' or crosstab for short. (It is also known by the more classical name of contingency table.) How to go about constructing a cross tabulation is something that will be discussed further in later chapters but for the moment let's just assume that the number in each category has been arrived at by some method - manual counting is entirely reasonable with so few measurements.

|   | A | B | C | D | E |
|---|---|---|---|---|---|
| 1 |   |   |   |   |   |
| 2 |   | Education |   |   |   |
| 3 | Gender | Low | Medium | High |   |
| 4 | Male | 5 | 2 | 2 |   |
| 5 | Female | 2 | 4 | 4 |   |
| 6 |   |   |   |   |   |
| 7 |   |   |   |   |   |
| 8 |   |   |   |   |   |

EDU2.MDS : Window1

As you can see, there are six cells containing the data in the form of counts. What is more interesting is the way that some of the data in the original data table has been transformed into labels in the cross tabulation. For example, the categories Low, Medium and High were listed as educational experience data values in the original data table. This is an example of what happens when you use the structure of the data to build a model. Notice that it would be more reasonable to refer to any cell in the cross tabulation using the headings rather than the usual cell references A3 and so on. As we shall see this is exactly what an SCW model allows us to do.

## » A 2D model

Entering the same cross tabulation as an SCW model results in a slightly different appearance but you should also be able to see the similarities.

|        | Low | Medium | High |
|--------|-----|--------|------|
| Male   | 5   | 2      | 2    |
| Female | 2   | 4      | 4    |

EDU3.MDL : Window1

How this model was constructed will be explained and discussed in some detail later. What is important for the moment is that you understand clearly how the model relates to the data as it was presented in earlier steps. Now labels have replaced the meaningless A,B,C and 1,2,3 and in a sense part of the data has become part of the structure of the model. Now when you want to refer to a particular cell you have to specify the categories that it corresponds to. For example, in this model Male.Low is the cell that in a standard spreadsheet would be referred to as A1. If you are familiar with the idea of writing formulae using standard, A1 style, cell references then you will be pleased to know that you can now work in the same way but you can use meaningful cell names.

The change in the role of the category labels is fairly obvious but just as important is the way that the sets of categories have replaced the usual concept of rows and columns.

Now there are two dimensions - Gender, listed down the rows and Education, listed along the columns. We could just as easily swap the roles and have Education listed down the rows, and Gender listed down the columns. SCW makes this sort of table rotation very easy indeed. All you have to do is drag the first category of one dimension to the other using the right mouse button.

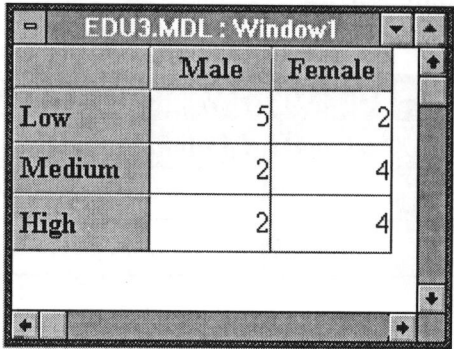

The most important point is that the identification of one of the dimensions with rows and the other with columns is just a way of presenting the table. The realities are the Education dimension and the Gender dimension and how they categorise the data - not an arbitrary assignment to rows and columns.

## » Dimensions and items

The survey example does demonstrate the basic ideas of constructing a model but it is only a 2D model. In general a model can have any number of dimensions up to the limit that SCW can work with. Each dimension of the model corresponds to some categorical property of the data. In the survey example the dimensions were Gender and Education. Each dimension has a number of categories or in SCW's jargon 'items'. Gender has two items - Male and Female and Education has three - High, Low and Medium.

Although an SCW model can have many more than two dimensions and a much larger number of items on each dimension, you should regard this as just 'more' and not 'different'. Most of the characteristics of a model with many dimensions can be seen, and often understood, better in a small two dimensional example. So if you find yourself puzzling about some aspect of a complicated model try to concentrate on two, or at most three, dimensions.

## » Database and data table

The stages that the survey data went through - from a data table to a cross tabulation and then to an SCW model - are entirely general. Whenever you have a table of data it is possible to convert it into a multidimensional model. Whether this model is meaningful, or in any sense appropriate, is another question - but it can be done. Another name for a data table is a database and this means that almost any database of information you may have can be converted into an SCW model. In traditional database jargon the columns of the table are called 'fields' and each row corresponds to a 'record' which stores data values for each field. When you convert the database it is the fields that determine the structure of the model. That is, they translate into the dimensions and the data values that they record become the items on that dimension. One, and only one, of the fields will converted into the data actually recorded in the body of the model.

This link between database and model is important not only for theoretical reasons but for practical ones. Later we will see how it is possible to perform this conversion automatically and use database tables as an intermediate step in model construction. The link is also two-way because you can also automatically convert any model into a database table.

## » 2D SCW sheets

If you are familiar with traditional spreadsheets such as SuperCalc you may already know about the database facilities that they offer. Essentially you construct a data table much like the one earlier but there are additional commands to allow you to work with the table - to search for particular data records, to extract records that meet specific criterion etc.. SCW offers the same range of facilities but not as part of a multidimensional model but within a separate 2D spreadsheet - a sheet.

You can open as many sheets as you need and work with them alongside a multidimensional model. Sheets are used to perform both the data manipulation necessary to construct a model and for calculations based on the data in a model. You can of course also use a sheet for any of the traditional tasks that a 2D spreadsheet would be used for!

## » Categorical data

In the survey example we started from a database of measurements and proceeded to make a cross tabulation of counts. Although the reduction of data using cross tabulation is a common enough method of creating a model, it is worth examining some of the other possibilities. Some types of data present themselves almost in a ready made multidimensional model. Much financial data is of this type. Usually there is a time dimension divided up into months, quarters, years, or whatever interval is appropriate. In many cases there is also a budget dimension which is divided into actual and forecast. Thus even the simplest of financial data often starts out with two dimensions and quickly adds some more corresponding to the financial entities within the organisation, products, production methods, sales type and so on. For this sort of data no preprocessing is required and the categories for the model are immediately obvious.

## » 4D car sales

As an example of a model using data in which the categories are immediately obvious consider the sales volumes for two car showroom sites. Roving Cars operates two showrooms - one in town and one out of town. It also sells four different types of car - Popular, Family, Pickup and Van. So far the data appears to have two dimensions - Showroom with two items and Type with four - but there is also a time dimension and a budget dimension to add bringing the total to four.

You can see the resulting model below.

| | Year | | Showroom | | Budget | |
|---|---|---|---|---|---|---|
| | Type | | City | | Actual | |
| | 1990 | 1991 | 1992 | 1993 | 1994 | 1995 |
| Popular | 12345 | 14343 | 15000 | 18087 | | |
| Family | 92345 | 100232 | 130332 | 120233 | | |
| Pickup | 23244 | 32344 | 56421 | 30545 | | |
| Van | 2343 | 10755 | 18930 | 15864 | | |

In this view the Type and Time dimensions are arranged to produce a 2D table. You can see that the Time dimension has six items corresponding to years 1990 to 1995. The remaining two dimensions Showroom and Budget aren't included in the tabulation of the data in quite the same way - they are the 'fixed dimensions'. Whenever an SCW model has more than two dimensions one pair are selected as the visible dimensions to form the 2D table and the remaining dimensions become fixed dimensions. The reason that they are called fixed dimensions is simply that all of the data in the 2D table on display corresponds to the values of the fixed dimension selected and displayed at the top of the model. The area at the top of the model where the fixed dimensions are displayed is called the 'Model bar' and the values selected are the 'fixed items'.

You can see that the data on display all corresponds to the City showroom and Actual budget. You can select which category or item of any of the fixed dimensions is used by simply picking it from a drop down list that appears when you click on the arrow to the right of the fixed dimension's box.

For example, you can select Out of Town from the drop down list associated with the Showroom dimension to display the sales for that particular showroom.

| | | CARS1.MDL : Window1 | | | | |
|---|---|---|---|---|---|---|
| Year | | Showroom | Budget | | | |
| Type | | Out of town | Actual | | | |
| | 1990 | 1991 | 1992 | 1993 | 1994 | 1995 |
| Popular | 19922 | 23455 | 25434 | 14665 | | |
| Family | 82333 | 120000 | 143553 | 132348 | | |
| Pickup | 15230 | 32344 | 54675 | 20677 | | |
| Van | 0 | 8455 | 14656 | 4343 | | |

The idea of fixed dimensions and the changes that you can make to the displayed data by altering the fixed items is relatively straightforward. Rather more difficult to grasp is the result of changing which dimensions are fixed and which are visible. You can make any fixed dimension visible by the simple and quick operation of dragging it (using the right mouse button) from the model bar to the visible dimension you want it to replace. However, the speed and magnitude of the change to the visible part of the model is so great that it is easy to become confused. It almost takes a moment to see what you are looking at. Changing the visible dimensions is referred to as a 'rotation' of the model.

For example, you can rotate the model by swapping the Showroom dimension with Type.

You can see that the look of the model has changed dramatically and this impression is more so when it happens in a split second when using SCW. However, this said, once you have taken time to look at the model you should be able to understand its new appearance with little difficulty. In most cases selecting an appropriate view of the model can make understanding the data or making comparisons easier. You can use this view to compare the sales of each model at the two showrooms by simply changing the fixed item on the Type dimension.

| | | | Year | | Type | | Budget | | |
|---|---|---|---|---|---|---|---|---|---|
| | | | Showroom | | Popular | | Actual | | |
| | | 1990 | 1991 | 1992 | 1993 | 1994 | 1995 |
| City | | 12345 | 14343 | 15000 | 18087 | | |
| Out of town | | 19922 | 23455 | 25434 | 14665 | | |

Clearly, part of making good use of any model is the selection of appropriate views.

## » Sparse data

In practice there are a number of problems that can arise with multidimensional data. The most common and obvious is simply a shortage of values to fill the model! As the number of dimensions increases the number of cells in a model increases very rapidly. For example, a two-dimensional model with four items on each dimension has 16 cells. Adding one more dimension with four items increases this to 64. Making the model four-dimensional with four items in each dimension gives 256 cells, five dimensions increases this to 1024 cells and so on.

Each time a dimension is added the total number of cells in a model is multiplied by the number of items on the dimension and this rapidly becomes a very large number. For example, a 12-dimensional model, the largest number of dimensions that SCW can handle, with only four items on each dimension has a staggering 16,777,216 cells!

Even when the model isn't quite so extreme, supplying enough data to fill all of the cells can be a time consuming exercise. In many cases a model will contain missing values - empty cells - for one reason or another. How these missing values should be treated for analysis or presentation is discussed in Chapter 9 but it is worth saying that SCW has some commands and functions designed to help manage this problem.

There are a number of other problems that you will encounter in converting data to a multi-dimensional model. In particular there is the issue of hierarchical data and the need to aggregate multiple measurements. These will be dealt with in later chapters after you have become more familiar with the basic model.

## » Using a model

Constructing the model is one aspect of using SCW but it is worth asking what value the model has once it is finished? Often the act of constructing the model is sufficient to reveal information of interest. Being able to look at the data in a number of rotations is also helpful. You can also produce graphs and charts which summarise the message in the data.

In more complex situations you may need to test the assumptions that there are patterns in the data by working out deviations from what you would expect. For example, if you have assumed a 10% growth in the sales of a particular product you could work out the difference between actual and predicted sales. In this case it is not just a matter of entering data into a model but formulae that work out results. In some cases a model may be almost nothing but formulae that can be used to explore the way a system or situation works.

In other words, an SCW model can not only be used as a way of presenting data in an accessible form but as a way of working out trends, deviations and predictions. There is much to say about how to work out results based on the data in an SCW model and this topic is taken up in many of the later chapters. However, it is worth saying that while SCW makes such calculations easy to perform it is still the user's task to understand and interpret the results.

# Key points

» There is a close relationship between a database data table and an SCW multidimensional model. It is often possible to convert one into the other without loss of information.

» In an SCW model some of the measurements are treated as dimensions to categorise the data of interest.

» The values of a dimension are referred to as its items.

» At any moment two of the dimensions of a model are visible and the rest are fixed. The visible dimensions are used to create a 2D table of values corresponding to the selected items on the fixed dimensions.

» Swapping a fixed and a visible dimension produces a rotation of the model and allows you to see the data in a new way.

» The number of cells in a multidimensional model increases very rapidly and often there will be a problem in obtaining or entering all of the data that a model needs.

» The purpose of building a model may be to inspect or present the data but it is also possible to analyse and predict using SCW's computational facilities.

# Chapter 3

# Building Models

In this chapter the focus falls on using SCW to construct simple multidimensional models. You should have a clear idea of what you are trying to do from Chapter 2 and now it is time to find out exactly how to do it.

The first step in constructing any model is to add and remove dimensions and rename them from their default labels AA,BB and so on by substituting meaningful names. After that you need to be able to manipulate the items on each dimension - add, delete and rename are the basic operations which complete the model.

## » Building a new model

When you create a new model it has a default number of dimensions and items. Each dimension and item has a default name. Clearly the early stages of building a model is going to be concerned with adding and deleting dimensions and assigning meaningful names. It is worth restating that it is assumed that you already know the basic elements of using Windows via a mouse.

To show you the steps in building a model it is easier to start with the second example introduced in Chapter 2. The reason is that this apparently more complex 4D model is closer to the structure of the model that is provided as a default.

The first step in building any model is to create a new default model either by selecting the File,New command or clicking on the 'New' icon in the tool bar.

The dialog box that appears allows you to select the type of object that you are trying to create.

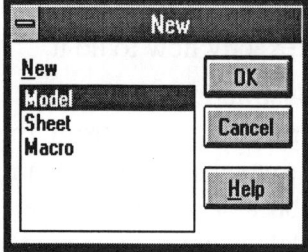

The alternatives to Model, i.e. Sheet and Macro, are discussed in greater detail in *Mastering CA-SuperCalc for Windows*. Sheet is a 2D spreadsheet similar to that provided by SuperCalc 5 and Macro is a way of creating an automatic procedure. Sheets and macros are used in later chapters.

## Upgrade Info

Compete, the forerunner of SCW's multidimensional models, created default models with three dimensions called Dim1, Dim2 and Dim3. The default items names were also different and less regular. Dim1 had items A through E and Dim2 had items 1 to 10. This gave the appearance of a standard 2D spreadsheet with numbered rows and lettered columns. Dim3 had items Z1 to Z5 which rather spoiled the pattern.

If you added new dimensions the default naming was continued with Dim4, Dim5 and so on. When adding new items no default name was assigned.

If you select Model and click on the OK button a default model is created. The default model has four dimensions called AA, BB, CC and DD. Each dimension has five items called A1 to A5, B1 to B5 and so on. Be careful not to confuse an item name like A1 with a traditional spreadsheet cell reference. In the default model A1 is an item not a cell.

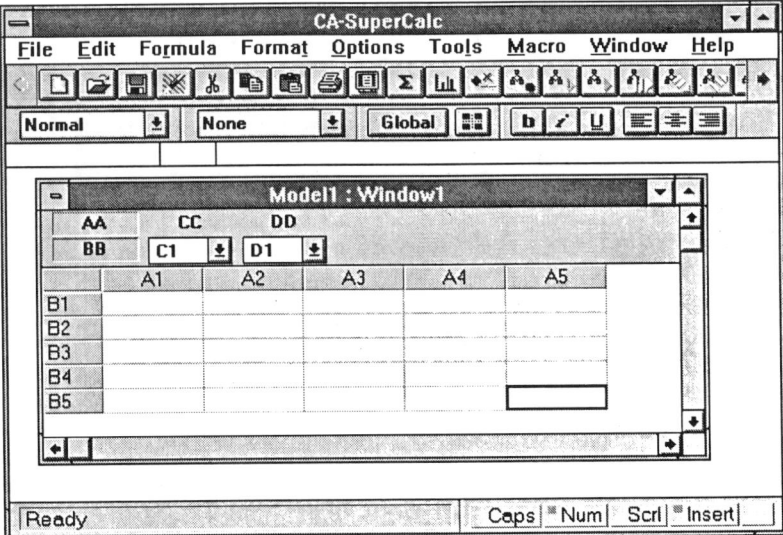

Initially the model is displayed so that AA and BB are the visible dimensions. Also notice that the tool bar and the menus have changed. The range of commands you have access to depends on the type of object - model, sheet or macro - with which you are working.

## » Assigning names

The default dimension and item names are usually not particularly useful and it makes sense to replace them with meaningful names. In the case of the car sales data introduced in Chapter 2 the dimension names need to be changed to - Type, Showroom, Budget and Time. You can change the name of a dimension by using the command Edit,Rename. This produces the Rename dialog box.

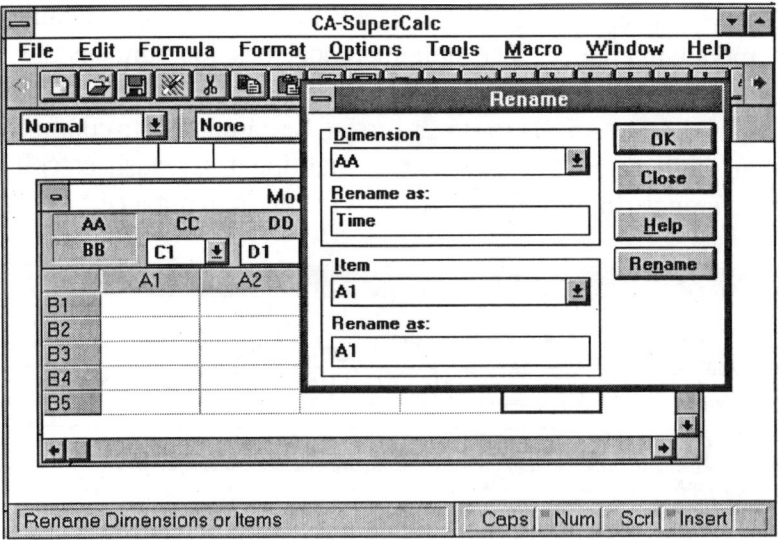

You can use this to rename any dimension or any item on a dimension. In practice there is an easier way of naming items so the Rename dialog box's main use is in giving names to dimensions.

Select any of the dimensions from the drop down list that appears when you click on the down arrow at the right of the text box. You can then type in a new name in the text box below. If you then click the OK button you will have changed the name of a single dimension. If you want to change the name of a number of dimensions then you have to click the Rename button after each one. The most common mistake is to forget to click the Rename button after each change of name with the result that only the last change of a set is actually recorded. Another common error is to press Enter at the end of typing in a new name and this has the effect of closing the Rename dialog box forcing you to reopen it to change another name.

To create the 4D car sales model change the name of dimension AA to Time, BB to Type, CC to Showroom and DD to Budget. It actually doesn't matter which dimension you give each name to. The dimensions are sorted into alphabetical order by name and which pair are the visible dimensions can be almost instantly changed.

## » The right mouse button

If you click on something with the right mouse button then what happens depends on the type of object that you have clicked on. In most cases, however, a pop-up menu will appear that lists frequently used commands that apply to the object. For example, if you click on any of the dimension names listed at the top of the model a menu that includes the Rename option appears. It is often faster to use the shortcut menu than return to the main menu bar.

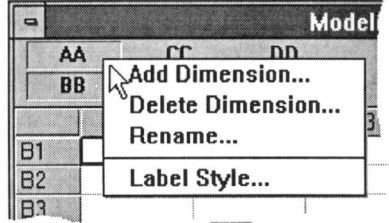

## » Item names

You could use the Rename dialog box to rename each of the items on each dimension. This works in exactly the same way as for renaming the dimensions, except that you use the Item text boxes just below the Dimension text boxes. However, it is easier simply to enter the new names directly into the visible dimensions. To do this you simply double click on the item name that you want to change. This changes the appearance of the item name so that it displays an editing cursor. You can now simply type over or edit it to produce the new name.

To construct the car sales model you should enter the items 1990 to 1994 in the Time dimension and Popular, Family, Pickup, Van in the Type dimension.

## » Rotating the model

You cannot enter new items on the fixed dimensions simply by typing them over the existing names - only the visible dimensions can be altered in this way. You could resort to the Edit,Rename command but it is usually easier to rotate the model so that you can see the dimension you want to change. Rotating the model is often used to make modifications to the model easier so it is worth explaining exactly how to do it.

To change a fixed dimension into a visible dimension all you have to do is click, using the right mouse button, on the fixed dimension's box in the model bar and while holding the right button down, drag it to the visible dimension that you want it to replace. As you move the dimension around the screen the cursor will change to a circle with a diagonal bar - a "prohibited" sign - when the position to which you are trying to drag it would be illegal. When you don't see the circle with a diagonal bar you can drop the dimension and it will swap with one of the visible dimensions.

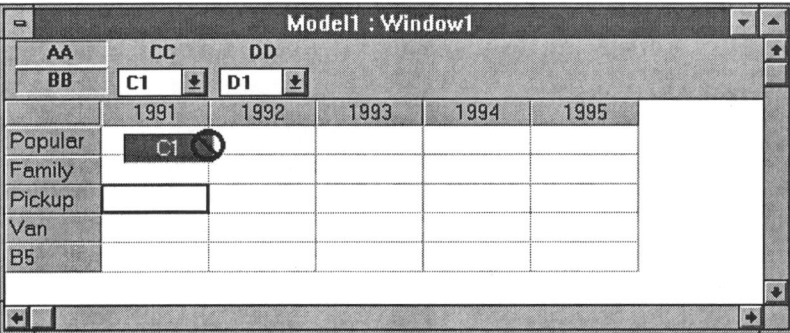

To complete the renaming of the car sales model you can either make CC and DD into the visible dimensions and enter the new labels in one go or, if you find this confusing, change just one of the visible dimensions at a time. In either case enter City and Out of town as items on the Showroom dimension and Actual and Forecast on the Budget dimension.

## » Deleting items

Now we have all of the dimension and item names changed to suitable values but the structure of the model still isn't complete. Some of the dimensions have too many items and the Time dimension is one short! SCW allows you to delete items using the Edit,Delete Items command. However, this command is only available after you have selected the items that you want to delete.

To select an item simply click on its name in one of the visible dimensions and it will change to reverse or highlight display. You can select multiple items to delete in one of a number of ways. If the items are next to one another then you can drag across the item names to highlight them. Alternatively you can click on a second item name while holding down the shift key (i.e. shift-click). When you are happy with your selection the Edit,Delete Items command will remove it from the model.

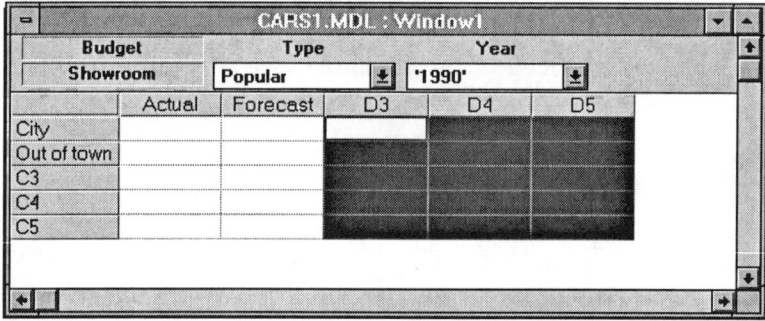

Notice that you can access the Edit,Delete Items menu option using the right mouse button while items are selected. If you click on an item with the right mouse button while it is not selected then you will not see the pop-up menu but "pick up" the item instead. Picking up an item with the right mouse button can be used to move it to a new location.

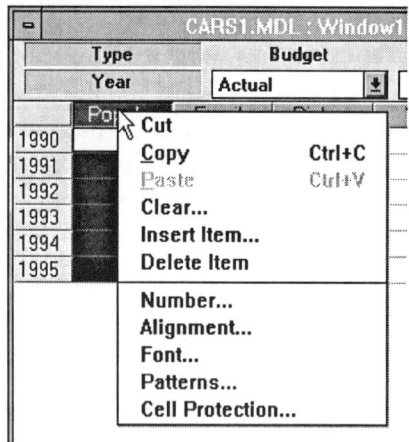

In the car sales data model you should delete items D3 to D5 in the Budget dimension, C3 to C5 in the Showroom dimension and B5 in the Type dimension. Notice that you have to make these dimensions visible to delete their items.

## » Adding items

When it comes to the Time dimension then the problem is the opposite in that there is one item too few. To insert a single item simply select the item to the left, i.e. the one that comes immediately before the new item, and then select the command Edit,Insert Item. This produces the Insert Item dialog box which you can use to enter the item's name. New items are given a default name based on the numbering of the existing items. If the new item is to follow a numeric item then it will be given a default name obtained by adding one to the existing name. Thus in the car sales example the default name is 1995, i.e. one more than 1994, the item it follows.

If the new item is to follow a non-numeric item name the default name is obtained by writing 1 next to it. For example, if the new item is to follow an item called Van it would be given the default name Van1.

In the case of the car sales model the item 1995 has to be inserted to follow 1994 in the Time dimension.

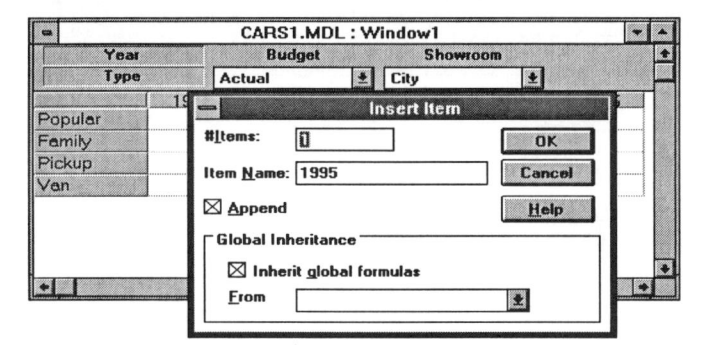

If you want to insert multiple items then you can by entering the number in the #Items box in the Insert Item dialog box. In this case the items are given default names numbered sequentially from the starting name. You can make use of this auto naming feature to avoid having to enter sequences of item names. For example, an alternative way of entering the six date items 1990 to 1995 would have been to insert six new items with the first default name entered as 1990. You can also enter sequences of item names like Van1, Van2 and so on in the same way.

An even easier way of adding new items is to drag one of the cells on the "edge" of the model using the left mouse button.

If you click and hold the left mouse button on one of the cells at the edge of the model then you will first see the cursor change to a multiple arrow pointing in the direction in which you can drag new items. If you click and hold on the cell at the bottom right hand corner of the model you will see horizontal and vertical arrows indicating that you can drag new items on both visible dimensions. If you drag in the direction of the arrows then new items will appear as you move the mouse. Each time you move the mouse far enough to accommodate a new item one appears in ghostly grey. If you move the mouse back it disappears.

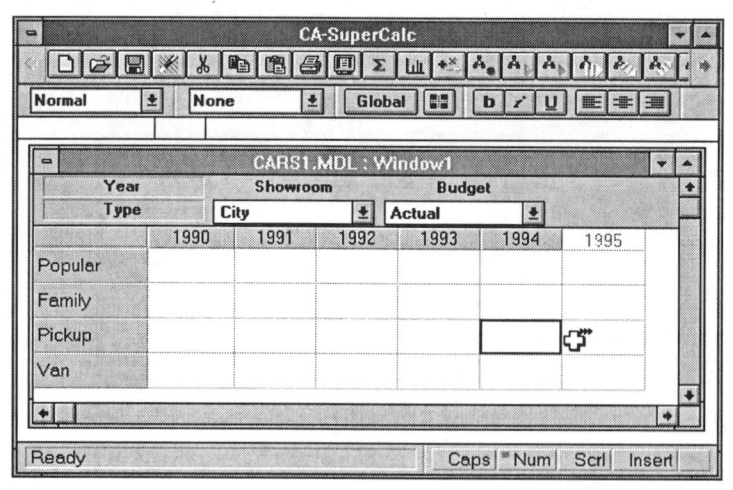

When you have dragged the correct number of items into existence simply release the mouse button to end the drag operation and the items shown in grey change colour and are added to the model.

## » Moving items

If you find that the order in which items are listed on one of the visible dimensions doesn't correspond to the natural or desirable order then you can move items. The simplest way to move an item is to drag it to its new position using the right mouse button. This works in exactly the same way as dragging a dimension to rotate the model only now you are dragging items within a single dimension. Notice that if you drag an item from one visible dimension to another then they change places.

An alternative way of moving an item is to use the Edit, Move Item command. First select the item to be moved, give the command and then select the item position to which it is to be moved using the dialog box that appears.

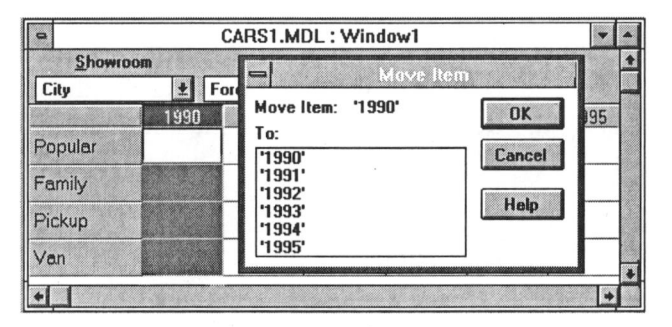

## » Inserting a dimension

If you need an additional dimension in a model you can add it using the Edit,Add Dimension command. This produces the Add Dimension dialog box which you can use to give the dimension a name and specify the number of items it should have. The dimension will be given a default name like AA,BB and so on according to the number of dimensions already in the model and this will happen even if you have changed the existing dimension names.

The items that are created along with the dimension are given a sequence of default names obtained by adding 1, 2, 3 etc.

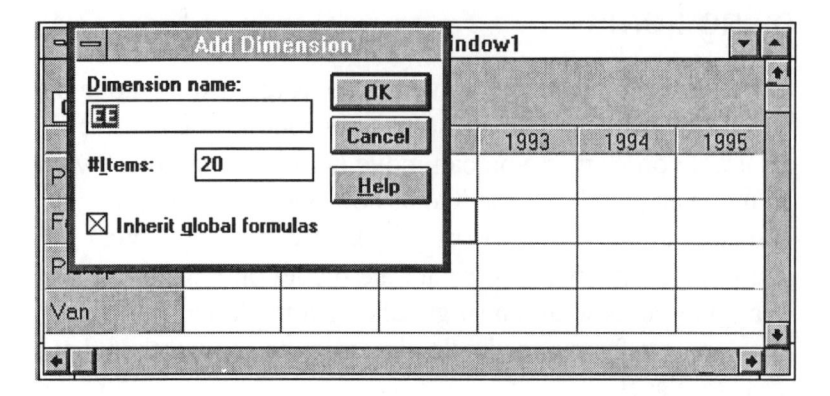

to the dimension name. So, for example, if you call a dimension Time and create 5 new items they will be given the names Time1, Time2, Time3 and so on. Similarly, if you call the new dimension Showroom and create 5 items they will be called Showroom1, Showroom2 and so on.

Adding a dimension with a name that will generate the correct sequence of item names and then changing the dimension name using the Rename command is one shortcut to model creation.

## » Deleting a dimension

If you want to delete one of the fixed dimensions all you have to do is use the Edit,Delete Dimension command and select the name of the dimension that you want to delete.

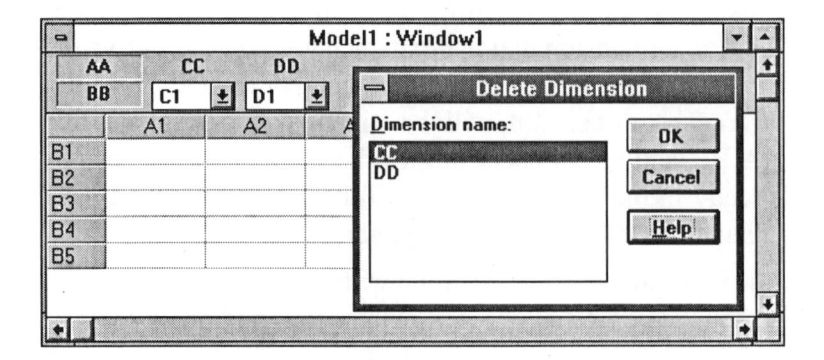

## Clicking and dragging

When working with a model there are a range of shortcut operations that depend on the use of the left and right mouse buttons. At first it is easy to become confused and use the wrong button. To save you from wondering why a click or drag operation doesn't work as you expect it is worth summarising the mouse operations - even though some of them are described in more detail later.

In the body of the model clicking and dragging with the left mouse button selects a cell or a range respectively. The right mouse button displays an appropriate pop-up menu.

Dragging a cell on the edge of the model with the left mouse button extends the items on one or both of the visible dimensions.

Clicking with the left mouse button on an item in one of the visible dimensions selects that item and dragging selects a range. Clicking with the right mouse button picks up the item so that you can drag it - however, if the item is selected then a pop-up menu appears instead. That is, you cannot drag an item while it is selected. Dragging an item can be used to re-order the items on the dimension or to pivot the model.

For the fixed dimensions the left mouse button is used to select items from the drop down lists and the right mouse button is used to drag the dimensions to pivot the model. As with the visible dimensions, you have to drag an item with the right mouse button to pivot the model. If you click with the right mouse button on a dimension name then a pop-up menu with commands relevant to adding, deleting or renaming dimensions appears instead.

A common mistake is to click with the left mouse button when you are trying to drag an item on a visible dimension - this often results in an accidental change to the row height or column width.

If you want to delete one of the visible dimensions you can either rotate the model so that it becomes one of the fixed dimensions and delete it in the usual way or you can adopt a two stage process. First you have to delete all of the items on that dimension except one and then use the Edit, Delete Dimension command - which will allow you to delete any dimension with only one item. Notice that no matter how hard you try you cannot delete dimensions so as to produce a 1D model! There are always at least two dimensions.

## » Save and Open

After you have gone to so much trouble to create a model it is worth saving it on disk using the command File,Save. You can reload any model saved to disk using the command File,Open. Saving and opening model files is just the same as in any Windows application. However, you might like to make one modification to the setup of SCW to make sure that your data is safe. Use the command Options,Workspace and in the dialog box that appears select the box labelled Create Backup. If this box is checked (i.e. shown with a cross) then a backup of the existing file will be created each time you save a model. Only one backup is kept and it has the same name as the model but the three letter extension .BAK.

If you have been following the construction of the 4D car sales model save it as CARS1.

## » The education survey

To consolidate the model building techniques introduced so far you might like to implement the simple 2D model of the education survey data introduced in Chapter 2. There are a number of possible ways of completing the task and all that really matters is that you can find some combination that works.

The steps involved are:

» Create a new - i.e. default model using File,New
» Delete the CC and DD dimensions
» Rename dimension AA as Education
» Rename dimension BB as Gender
» Rename items A1, A2 and A3 as Low, Medium and High
» Delete items A4 and A5
» Rename items B1 and B2 to Male and Female
» Delete items B3,B4 and B5
» Enter the data and save the model under the name EDU3.

Of course it doesn't matter if you delete and rename different dimensions to the ones named above. All that matters is that your final model has a dimension called Gender with items Male and Female and a dimension Education with items Low, Medium and High. You can always rotate the model and/or move items to make it look like the model in Chapter 2.

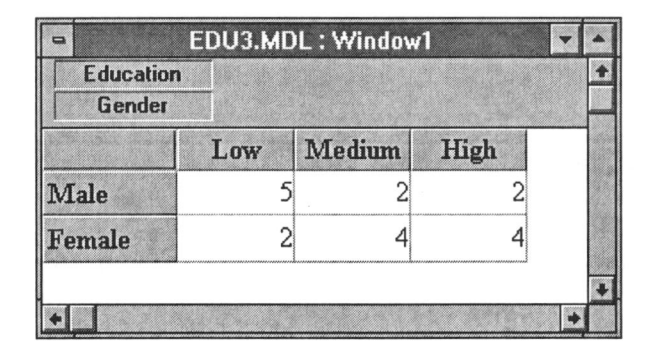

| Education / Gender | Low | Medium | High |
|---|---|---|---|
| Male | 5 | 2 | 2 |
| Female | 2 | 4 | 4 |

# Key points

» Creating a model is a matter of starting from the default four-dimensional model that File,New creates and editing it.

» You can rename dimensions using the Edit,Rename command.

» The easiest way of renaming items is to type over the item names in one of the visible dimensions, but you can also use the Edit,Rename command.

» You can delete items using the Edit,Delete Item command.

» To delete a visible dimension you either have to rotate the model so that it becomes fixed or delete all but one of its items and select Edit,Delete Dimension with the remaining item selected.

» You can insert a new dimension using Edit,Add Dimension.

» New items created either by the Insert Item or Add Dimension command are given sequential names. This fact can be used as a way of automatically generating item names.

» A model can be rotated by dragging an item, using the right mouse button, to the dimension it is to replace.

» You can re-order items by dragging them using the right mouse button or by using the command Edit,Move Item.

» Before moving on to the next chapter make sure that you can add and delete items and dimensions, rotate a model and move items.

# Chapter 4

# Ranges

Being able to specify and work with cell ranges is vital to a confident understanding of how models work. In the previous chapters it has been sufficient to use the mouse to point at cells. However, the simple techniques of clicking and dragging are insufficient when it comes to dealing with multidimensional selections. In practice they aren't even practical when it comes to selecting a large 2D range. In this chapter we look at how to specify which cells you want to make use of in operations and calculations.

## » Cell references

Any cell in a model can be specified precisely by giving the items on each dimension that correspond to it. You can think of this as a sort of "map reference" for cells. By quoting an item on each of the dimensions you can "pin down" exactly the cell you are referring to.

For example, in the 4D car sales model any cell can be specified by giving a value of Type, Time, Showroom and Budget. You write such a cell reference with full stops between each item to act as punctuation. For example, Popular.'1990'.City.Actual specifies a single cell in the model.

Notice that to make it clear that 1990 is an item name rather than a number you have to surround it by single quotes. The same is true for any item name that could be mistaken for something else. However, you don't have to enclose names that contain spaces with single quotes. For example, you would use Popular.'1990'.Out of town.Actual. If in doubt, though, you can always use single quotes to make it clear that you are using an item name.

Notice that a model cell reference is very similar to one in a traditional 2D spreadsheet but in this case the columns are lettered A, B and so on and the rows numbered 1,2,3 etc.. Using this system of naming a cell is specified by just giving its column letter and row number as in A2, B56 and so on without full stops as punctuation.

If you are working with the default item names in a SCW model i.e. A1,A2.., B1,B2.., C1,C2.. and D1,D2.. on dimensions AA, BB, CC and DD - then make sure that you don't become confused by traditional 2D cell references. In the default model a cell reference can be something like A1.B2.C5.D3 which looks like a set of 2D cell references - it isn't! Each letter and number combination is of course an item on a dimension.

That is,

» in a sheet A1 is a cell

» in a model A1 is an item on the AA dimension

If constructing a cell reference seems very tricky and tedious then it is worth saying now that in most cases you don't actually have to type in cell references - they can be entered automatically by pointing with the mouse. However, you do still have to understand the way that they work because you often have to check and edit cell references.

## » Simple arithmetic

As in the case of a sheet, you can enter any arithmetic expression that you want evaluated. To indicate that you want the expression worked out you have to precede it by an equals sign. If you forget the equals sign then the arithmetic is stored as text and displayed as you entered it. If you use a cell reference within an arithmetic expression then the value stored in the cell is retrieved and used.

For example, if you open a new (default) model and enter the formula
    =A1.B1.C1.D1-A2.B1.C1.D1

into A3.B1.C1.D1 then SCW will work out the difference between the contents of the two cells specified.

|    | A1 | A2 | A3 |
|----|----|----|----|
| B1 | 3  | 2  | =A1.B1.C1.D1-A2.B1.C1.D1 |
| B2 |    |    |    |
| B3 |    |    |    |

As will be explained later it usually isn't necessary or desirable to write out cell references in full in this way - but if you want to, it does work!

## » Ranges

Being able to specify a single cell is just a special case of being able to specify a set of cells or 'range' within the model. The simplest sort of range is just a 2D rectangle of cells. In the case of traditional spreadsheets this is the only type of cell range provided but in the case of multidimensional models we need something a little more sophisticated. It is important to master SCW's methods of range references because they are the key to understanding calculation within models.

To make understanding range specifications easier at first it is better to consider a 2D example. The ideas introduced, however, apply in any number of dimensions.

If you were asked to specify the 2D shaded area in the model shown below then there are two possible ways of doing it.

|    | A1 | A2 | A3 | A4 | A5 |
|----|----|----|----|----|----|
| B1 |    |    |    |    |    |
| B2 |    |    |    |    |    |
| B3 |    |    |    |    |    |
| B4 |    |    |    |    |    |
| B5 |    |    |    |    |    |

You could give the locations of two opposite corners - A2.B2 and A4.B3 for example. Giving opposite corners fixes the rectangle precisely and it is an entirely unambiguous specification of the range. If this is the way that you first thought of then the chances are that you are an existing 2D spreadsheet user because the 'corner-to-corner' approach is the standard method of defining a range.

*A2.B2:A4.B3*

In SCW a corner-to-corner range is written by quoting the cell references of the two corners separated by a colon for punctuation. In the example shown above the range reference would usually be quoted as A2.B2:A4.B3 but A2.B3:A4.B2 or any other order that gives two opposite corners is just as good.

The second method of specifying the range is unique to SCW and so you are unlikely to have seen it used before. Instead of giving the cell references of the corner cells you can specify the item ranges on each of the dimensions. In this case the range would be written (A2:A4).(B2:B3) and you can see how this marks out the range in the figure below.

*(A2:A4).(B2:B3)*   *(A2:A4)*

*(B2:B3)*

This is type of range reference is known as an "intersection range" because of the way that the item ranges on the dimensions intersect to define the range. Notice that an intersection range looks like a cell reference. The dot always separates dimensions and the colon specifies a range. For example, A1.B1 is a single cell and (A1:A3).B1 is part of a row.

|    | A1 | A2 | A3 | A4 | A5 |
|----|----|----|----|----|----|
| B1 |    |    |    |    |    |
| B2 |    |    |    |    |    |
| B3 |    |    |    |    |    |
| B4 |    |    |    |    |    |
| B5 |    |    |    |    |    |

The intersection range is the standard way of working in models. So much so that if you enter a range as a corner to corner reference it will be automatically converted into intersection format. For example, if you use A2.B2:A4.B3 within a formula it will be converted to (A2:A4).(B2:B3).

So what exactly is the advantage of an intersection range? The most immediate advantage is that it generalises to more than two dimensions in a way that the corner-to-corner reference does not. For example, in a 3D model an intersection range like (A2:A4).(B2:B3).(C2:C3) defines a cube of cells in the region where the three item ranges intersect.

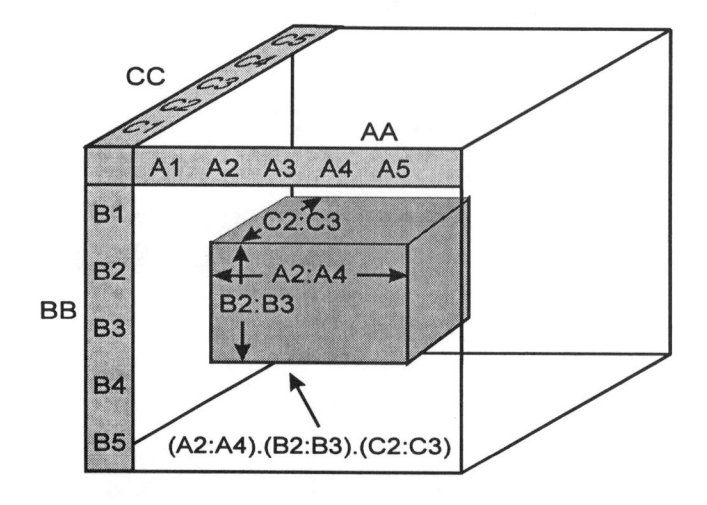

This is exactly analogous to the intersection of two item ranges defining a 2D area and it is the same in four, five, and in fact any number of dimensions - although imagining what a range looks like beyond 3D is impossible!

It might be worth pointing out that to define a 2D range in a multidimensional model you can still use an intersection range by setting all but two of the item ranges to a single item. For example, (A2:A4).(B2:B3).C1 is a 2D range in a 3D model.

## » Using ranges in functions

As well as simple arithmetic there are a number of functions that operate on the values stored in a range of cells. The best known and most commonly used of these is the SUM(*range*) function which will add up all of the values in the cells specified by *range*. If you are familiar with the SUM function from its role in SCW's sheets or a traditional 2D spreadsheet then all that really needs to be added is the fact that it also works with a multidimensional range as is appropriate to a model. For example, SUM((A2:A4).(B2:B3)) will sum the 2D range used in the earlier examples.

## » Split ranges

There is another big advantage to using intersection ranges in that it is possible to define areas that are not simple rectangles. The basic idea of defining item ranges on each dimension still holds but the notation is extended to allow not only simple item ranges but lists of items and multiple item ranges.

For example, the four corner-to-corner ranges marked out in the 2D model that follows can be specified by the single intersection range

(A1:A3,A6:A7).(B3:B5,B8:B10)

|    | A1 | A2 | A3 | A4 | A5 | A6 | A7 | A8 |
|----|----|----|----|----|----|----|----|----|
| B1 |    |    |    |    |    |    |    |    |
| B2 |    |    |    |    |    |    |    |    |
| B3 | ■ | ■ | ■ |    |    | ■ | ■ |    |
| B4 | ■ | ■ | ■ |    |    | ■ | ■ |    |
| B5 | ■ | ■ | ■ |    |    | ■ | ■ |    |
| B6 |    |    |    |    |    |    |    |    |
| B7 |    |    |    |    |    |    |    |    |
| B8 | ■ | ■ | ■ |    |    | ■ | ■ |    |
| B9 | ■ | ■ | ■ |    |    | ■ | ■ |    |
| B10| ■ | ■ | ■ |    |    | ■ | ■ |    |

Each of the item's ranges is separated by a comma but apart from that the notation is the same. To see how much simpler this is try specifying the same range using the corner-to-corner method.

After a while the intersection range method of specifying which cells you want to include in a calculation becomes second nature. This is not just a practice effect because there is something very direct and natural about making lists of the items that qualify data for inclusion in a calculation.

## » Summary

Although there are some other conventions, such as using a dimension name to mean all of the items on that dimension, we have now met all the fundamental rules. These are:

> » If you use the dimension's name then all of the items on that dimension are to be included. For example, using the default model, AA means all of the items on the AA dimension.

> » A single item means that item and no others on that dimension. For example, A1 means just item A1 on dimension AA.

» A list of items separated by commas and enclosed in brackets means just the items listed on that dimension. For example, (A1,A3,A5) means items A1, A3 and A5 on dimension AA.

» A range of items can be indicated using the familiar *start:stop* notation. For example, (A1:A3) means A1, A2 and A3 on dimension AA.

» You can mix lists and ranges of items within brackets. For example, (A1:A3,A5) means A1,A2, A3 and A5.

Using this notation you can easily specify which items on a dimension are to be included in the range - even if you have to resort to listing them one by one!

Some examples of intersection ranges using the default 4D model with AA and BB visible may help. The descriptions in terms of "rows" and "columns" all refer to the visible cells with AA as the column dimension and BB as the row dimension:

| **Range** | **Refers to** |
| --- | --- |
| AA.BB.CC.DD | The entire model |
| AA.B1.C1.D1 | The entire first row |
| (A1:A3).B1.C1.D1 | First 3 cells in first row |
| (A1:A3).(B1:B2).C1.D1 | 3x2 square in top left-hand corner |
| (A1:A3).BB.C1.D1 | First three cells in each row |

## » Underspecification

'Underspecification' is a technique that SCW uses both to simplify the entering of ranges and to make them more flexible. Look back at the example in the previous section of performing simple arithmetic where the formula

=A1.B1.C1.D1-A2.B1.C1.D1

was entered into A3.B1.C1.D1. You will notice that most of the items in the cell references are unchanged - B1.C1.D1 is common to all three and only the item on the AA dimension changes.

To make entering cell references easier, and to make formulae easier to read, SCW uses the rule that if you underspecify a cell reference then it will fill in the items on the missing dimension. In other words an underspecification is simply a cell reference that doesn't have an item specified for each dimension. The missing items are filled in by using those items from the cell that the reference is stored in. This may sound a little tricky but in fact it is perfectly natural.

For example, if you enter the cell reference A1 into the cell A3.B1.C1.D1 then this incomplete reference is expanded to A1.B1.C1.D1. That is, as you didn't specify the items on the BB, CC and DD dimensions they were assumed to be the same as for the cell where the reference is stored.

The rule is that any items that are in common between the cell being referenced and the cell that the reference is stored in need not be quoted. This turns out to fit in with the sort of formulae that you want to enter most of the time. Cells that you need to reference are usually in the same column or the same row on the visible dimensions and of course this means that you almost never need to enter the items corresponding to the fixed dimensions. For example the subtraction formula

=A1.B1.C1.D1-A2.B1.C1.D1

stored in A3.B1.C1.D1 can be written as

=A1-A2

because it is in the same row and the same fixed dimension items as the two cells being subtracted.

The only disadvantage of this scheme is that you need to know the cell where the formula is stored to make complete sense of it. With the actual model in front of you this is never a serious problem and, as we shall see, the very fact that a formula is underspecified can tell you a lot about its intent.

There is one exception to the underspecification rule and that is when a formula contains a reference to its own cell, that is the cell in which it is stored, the entire specification has to be given. This self reference is a rare occurrence and is usually the result of a mistake!

Under specification works with corner-to-corner range references and with intersection range references.

Remember, the rule is:

» any dimension not specified within a cell reference or within an intersection range implicitly takes the same value as the cell that it is stored in.

As will become apparent there are other good reasons for using this scheme as well as just reducing the amount of typing.

## » Pointing

In addition to the use of underspecification, the use of pointing in place of typing makes entering cell references very easy indeed. Most cell references can be entered simply by pointing at the cell that contains the value required. If you open a default model, place the cursor on cell A3.B3.C1.D1. (i.e. the cell in the middle of the visible dimensions) and type equals on the formula input line you can see the cell references that SCW constructs for you by simply clicking on any other visible cell.

If the cell that you click on is in the same row then only the column dimension is entered. If it is in the same column then only the row dimension is entered. If you click on any other cell then both the row and column items are entered. Of course the fixed dimension items are never entered because these are the same for every visible cell. You can see the cell references for the eight cells around A3.B3.C1.D1 below.

|  | A1 | A2 | A3 | A4 | A5 |
|---|---|---|---|---|---|
| B1 |  |  |  |  |  |
| B2 |  | A2.B2 | B2 | A4.B2 |  |
| B3 |  | A2 |  | A4 |  |
| B4 |  | A2.B4 | B4 | A4.B4 |  |
| B5 |  |  |  |  |  |

## » Pointing at a range

You can also enter a range by pointing. All you have to do is click on the first corner of the range and then drag to define the opposite corner. The highlighted area is selected and will be used as the subject of any command that you use. If you are entering a formula then the equivalent range will be inserted on the formula entry line.

Even though you might think about this operation as dragging from corner to corner the range reference is entered as an intersection range. Also notice that the range reference will be underspecified and so its exact form will depend on the cell that the range is being stored in.

## » Summing education

After this discussion you should now find the example of summing the values in the education survey model very easy. The formula entered into the cell Low.Row Totals is

SUM(Male:Female)

You can see that this is an instruction to sum the range Low.Male:Low.Female but the Low item can be left out because of the cell that the formula is stored in i.e. Low.Row Totals.

Now consider what happens if we copy the formula from Low.Row Totals into each cell in the Row Totals dimension. This is quite easy to do. Select the cell that contains the formula and copy it to the clipboard using Edit,Copy. Next select the cells to which you want to copy the formula and use Edit,Paste. The formula will be duplicated in each of the selected cells and evaluated in each of its new positions. I say 'in each of its new positions' because the formula as it stands does mean something slightly different in each of the cells.

As the formula is underspecified, i.e. as Male:Female, the missing dimension, i.e. the underspecified dimension, is taken from the cell it is stored in. This means that when it is stored in Low.Row Totals it sums Low.Male:Low.Female. When it is stored in Medium.Row Totals it sums Medium.Male:Medium.Female and in High.Row Totals it sums High.Male:High.Female. In other words it sums each of the columns of the spreadsheet according to the cell into which it is copied. This is because the original formula did not specify which column to sum.

| EDU6.MDL : Window1 | | | | |
|---|---|---|---|---|
| Education | | | | |
| Gender | | | | |
| | Low | Medium | High | Col Totals |
| Male | 5 | 2 | 2 | 9 |
| Female | 2 | 4 | 4 | 10 |
| Row Totals | 7 | 6 | 6 | 19 |

Underspecification was used to make the formula read 'sum this column from Male to Female' and so the formula sums whichever column it finds itself in!

Of course this is exactly the behaviour we want. In general when you specify a formula by pointing you will find that it has this 'self adjusting' property.

So to summarise:

» underspecification makes formulae self adjusting when they are copied.

## » Relative and absolute

*A note for 2D spreadsheet users*

If you are familiar with traditional 2D spreadsheets you will by now be thinking that this self adjusting behaviour is similar to the use of relative cell references. It is similar but it isn't the same. In this case the relative nature of the cell reference comes about because of underspecification and not because of the choice between a relative or absolute cell reference.

As will be explained later, there is a separate facility for specifying a relative or absolute cell reference.

If you want to think in traditional terms, and it can be helpful, then the best you can do is to imagine that the items that are included in an underspecified cell reference are absolute and the items that are not included are relative.

## » Saying what you mean

Underspecification has a slightly more important role to play in building a model than simply providing a way of entering a formula just once - when it is actually needed many times. Indeed as will be explained copying a formula using

Edit,Copy and Edit,Paste is to be discouraged - we have better ways of controlling a model!

Underspecification actually corresponds more closely to what you are trying to say. For example, SUM(Male:Female) seems to be saying that you want to sum the Gender dimension from Male to Female over all other dimensions. In other words, the underspecification almost tells you the range that you would like the formula to apply to.

This idea of using underspecification as a more accurate way of describing what you want to calculate will recur time and time again in later chapters. For the moment all that is necessary is to draw your attention to the fact that it is more than just a simpler way of entering a formula.

# Key points

» Most models require calculated results that involve other cells in the model.

» To refer to a cell use a cell reference which specifies an item on each dimension separated by dots, e.g. A1.B3.C5.D4

» To refer to a set of cells you use a range reference. SCW supports two types of range reference - the traditional corner-to-corner range reference and a multidimensional intersection range reference.

» The corner-to-corner reference works by specifying the cell reference of a pair of opposite corners of a rectangle of cells separated by a colon, e.g. A1.B1:A3.B5.

» An intersection range is defined by a list of items on each of the dimensions.

» An item list can consist of a pair of brackets () containing item ranges of the form start:stop and individual items each separated by commas, e.g. (A1:A3,A4,A6:A5).

» You can use a dimension name to mean all of its items and a single item name to mean just this item.

» In a formula any dimensions that are not specified are said to be underspecified and are taken by default to be the same as the corresponding items of the cell in which the reference is stored.

» Underspecification produces automatic adjustment of a formula when it is moved or copied to a new location.

» Underspecification often corresponds more closely with the intended meaning of a formula, i.e. where it is to be applied, than a complete specification does.

# Chapter 5

# Global Formulae

In this chapter we begin to look more closely at the subject of performing calculations within an SCW model. Although there are many similarities to using spreadsheet functions and formulae, many subtle differences make the model more powerful.

Although in some cases it may be sufficient to enter data into a model and then use the model to examine and draw conclusions from it, in most cases the data will need to be processed. This means that you will almost certainly want to perform some calculations on the data - form sub-totals, sums, compare differences and so on. The first stage in mastering this aspect of SCW is to discover how formulae are entered and controlled. In a later chapter we will look more closely at how the wide range of functions and advanced tools can be used to analyse the data.

## » Functions and formulae

As we have already seen, you can construct formulae and use functions within a model just as you would within any 2D spreadsheet. All of the familiar and obvious spreadsheet range functions, SUM, MAX, MIN, etc., can be used. You will find a full description of all of these in the on-screen help and in Chapter 8 of Mastering CA-SuperCalc for Windows. In later chapters we will meet the few functions which are model specific and look at functions which are central to data analysis and modelling in the wider sense.

The only difference in the way that functions and formulae are used in models is the adoption of intersection ranges to make the specification of multidimensional ranges possible and allow the use of underspecification to make intersection ranges easier to define. However, as mentioned at the end of the last chapter, these changes bring with them the possibility of doing things a little differently.

## » The trouble with copying

When you enter a formula into a spreadsheet or model the same formula is usually required in more than one location. Put simply, if you want to sum one column in a model view then the chances are you will want to sum the rest! The fact that the same calculation is needed repeatedly is as much part of the structure of the model as the data itself.

The standard spreadsheet approach to the need for repeated calculations is to provide a copy command and some facilities for adjustment of the formula being copied to take account of its new position. That is, you can use the command Edit,Copy to make a single copy of a formula on the Windows Clipboard and then make multiple copies of it by selecting the area into which you want to paste it and using the command Edit,Paste.

As has already been explained, you can continue to use this traditional copy and paste approach but there is a better way.

## » Scope

The copy and paste method has a number of disadvantages. The first is that when the formula is created the user probably has an clear idea of where it will be used in the model. This is referred to in SCW's jargon as the formula's 'scope'. The standard approach forces the user to copy the formula into this scope after entering a single correct example. This results in no trace of the intended scope being stored or recorded along with the model. To discover the scope of any formula you have to examine the model to discover which cells contain copies.

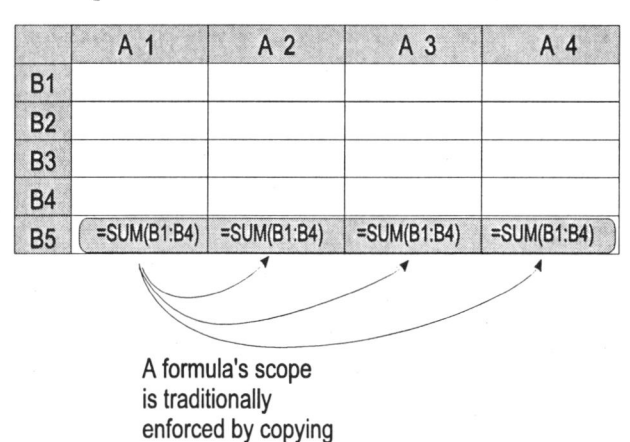

|    | A 1 | A 2 | A 3 | A 4 |
|----|-----|-----|-----|-----|
| B1 |     |     |     |     |
| B2 |     |     |     |     |
| B3 |     |     |     |     |
| B4 |     |     |     |     |
| B5 | =SUM(B1:B4) | =SUM(B1:B4) | =SUM(B1:B4) | =SUM(B1:B4) |

A formula's scope is traditionally enforced by copying

The second disadvantage is that all sense of this being a single formula which applies to a range of cells is lost in that changing any one instance of the formula doesn't update the copies. To keep a formula up-to-date you have to change one instance and then copy this throughout the scope. Of course if the scope has been forgotten or is unclear then this might be difficult.

For these and other reasons its seems more reasonable to recognise the idea of a 'global formula', i.e. one that can be applied to more than one cell. So instead of using copying to define where a formula applies, a global formula has its scope stored along with it as an explicit range reference.

|    | A 1        | A 2 | A 3 | A 4 |
|----|------------|-----|-----|-----|
| B1 |            |     |     |     |
| B2 |            |     |     |     |
| B3 |            |     |     |     |
| B4 |            |     |     |     |
| B5 | =SUM(B1:B4)|     |     |     |

An alternative to copying a formula is to allow it to work out results in cells that are within its scope

Scope= (A1:A4).B5

Global formulae are perhaps the most radical part of SCW's approach to spreadsheet modelling. It takes a little time to get used to but the advantages make it well worth the effort.

## » Creating a global formula

When you first enter a formula into a cell it is technically a 'cell level' formula. This means that it applies only to the cell in which it is stored and the only way to extend its action to other cells is to make copies of it in the other cells. You can convert any cell level formula into a global formula, which does not need to be copied to apply to other cells, very simply. Once converted to a global formula you can convert it back to a cell level formula but you need to be aware that this may not delete the global formula that you have applied to other cells. This idea is explained in more detail later.

To convert a cell level formula to a global formula you select the cell that contains it and then use the command Formula,Set Scope or click on the Global button in the middle of the toolbar.

## Creating a global formula

In either case the Set Scope dialog box is displayed.

```
┌─────────────── Set Scope ───────────────┐
│ Formula:                      ┌────────┐│
│ ┌─────────────────────────┐   │   OK   ││
│ │ =SUM((B1:B4))           │   └────────┘│
│ └─────────────────────────┘   ┌────────┐│
│ Scope:                        │ Cancel ││
│ ┌─────────────────────────┐▲  └────────┘│
│ │ A1.B5.C1.D1|            │   ┌────────┐│
│ │                         │▼  │  Edit..││
│ └─────────────────────────┘   └────────┘│
│                               ┌────────┐│
│                               │  Help  ││
│ ☐ Apply formula to scope      └────────┘│
└─────────────────────────────────────────┘
```

This shows the formula that you are about to make global and its current scope. By default a formula's current scope is just the cell in which it has been stored - i.e. A1.B5.C1.D1 in this case. If you click on the OK button at this point the formula will be converted from a cell level to a global formula. Of course unless you have changed the default scope you will notice very little difference! You will find that a global formula is, by default, displayed in a different colour and you will not be able to move or copy the formula. If you try Edit,Copy followed by Edit,Paste you will see the following message box appear.

```
┌─────────────── CA-SuperCalc ───────────────┐
│                                            │
│  (!)  Cannot apply Global Formula outside its scope. │
│                                            │
│              ┌────┐                        │
│              │ OK │                        │
│              └────┘                        │
└────────────────────────────────────────────┘
```

This isn't an error or an accident. From the previous discussion you should be able to see that copying a global formula is unnecessary and liable to confuse the situation. As you will discover later, you can copy a global formula but for the moment it is best to ignore this possibility.

You can use the Set Scope dialog box to edit the global formula, i.e. to change what it computes in all of the cells that it applies to - but its most common and standard use is to alter a global formula's scope. This can be done by directly editing or entering the scope specification in the Scope text box displayed. To do this you simply have to work out the range reference of the cells to which you want the formula applied and type this in.

Of course making up a range reference in this way can be tedious and is error prone so a better way is to construct the scope by interactively selecting from a list of dimensions and items. To do this simply click on the Edit button to display the Edit Scope dialog box.

```
┌─────────────── Edit Scope ───────────────┐
│ Dimensions:      Items:         ┌──────┐ │
│ ┌──────────┐    ┌──────┐        │  OK  │ │
│ │ AA       │    │ A1   │        └──────┘ │
│ │ BB       │    │ A2   │        ┌──────┐ │
│ │ CC       │    │ A3   │        │Cancel│ │
│ │ DD       │    │ A4   │        └──────┘ │
│ │          │    │ A5   │        ┌──────┐ │
│ └──────────┘    └──────┘        │ Help │ │
│                                 └──────┘ │
│ Scope                                    │
│ ┌──────────────────────────┐    ┌──────┐ │
│ │ A1.B5.C1.D1              │    │Append│ │
│ │                          │    └──────┘ │
│ └──────────────────────────┘    ┌──────┐ │
│                                 │Replace││
│                                 └──────┘ │
└──────────────────────────────────────────┘
```

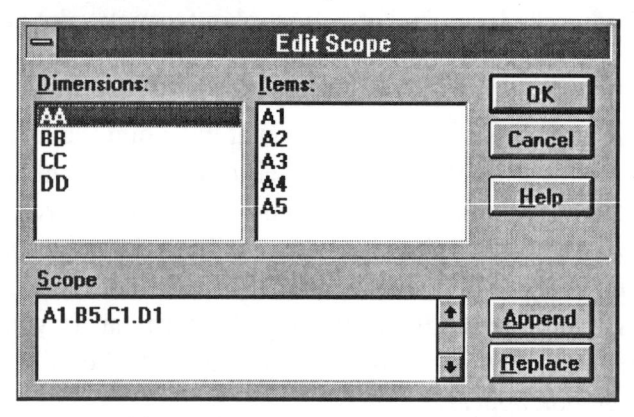

You can use this to define or expand the scope of a formula by simply clicking on lists of dimensions and items. A scope is specified as an intersection range and how easy you find it to define or edit a scope depends very much on whether you feel at home with such range specifications.

The way that the Edit Scope dialog box works might seem a little confusing at first. You can select any of the available dimensions and you will be shown a complete list of its items.

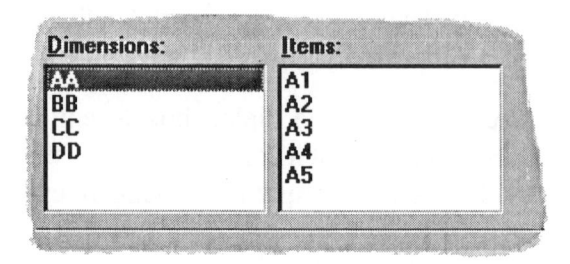

```
Dimensions:      Items:
┌──────────┐    ┌──────┐
│ AA       │    │ A1   │
│ BB       │    │ A2   │
│ CC       │    │ A3   │
│ DD       │    │ A4   │
│          │    │ A5   │
└──────────┘    └──────┘
```

## Creating a global formula

From this list of items you can select a continuous or discontinuous range. To select a continuous range simply click on the first item and then drag to the last item. Alternatively click on the first item in the range and Shift click, i.e. hold down the Shift key while clicking on the last item in the range. To select individual items to be added to the selection Ctrl click, i.e. click while holding down the Ctrl key, on each item you want to add. For example, to select the item range (A2:A3,A5) you would first click on A2 and drag to A3 then you would Ctrl click on A5.

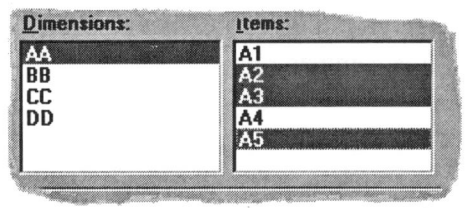

Once you have highlighted the items from a particular dimension you can either append these to the existing range for that dimension or you can replace it. Clearly if the current scope is more or less what you want and you just need to add some additional items then use the Append option. If the existing scope is a long way from what you want then use the Replace option to build it from scratch. Notice that whether you append or replace only the items belonging to the currently selected dimension are affected.

To add the items to the scope click on the Append button. To replace all of the items click on the Replace button. Each time you click on Replace the current items are replaced by the selected items and each time you click on Append they are added. You can use this fact to correct mistakes.

Notice that a scope range specification consists of an item range for each dimension in the model. This is because, in general, a scope can apply the formula to any cell in the model and this means that it must have the same dimensions as the model. If you leave out a dimension in a scope specification then the entire range of items is assumed to apply. That is,

(A2:A3,A5).B5.C1

where the specification for the DD dimension is missing, is the same as

(A2:A3,A5).B5.C1.(D1:D5)

Similarly, if you use the dimension name in place of an item range, all of the items on the dimension are included. That is,

(A2:A3,A5).B5.C1.DD

is the same as

(A2:A3,A5).B5.C1.(D1:D5)

## » The scope of education

In the education model the existing scope of the SUM formula is Low.Row Totals, i.e. the single cell that it was entered into.

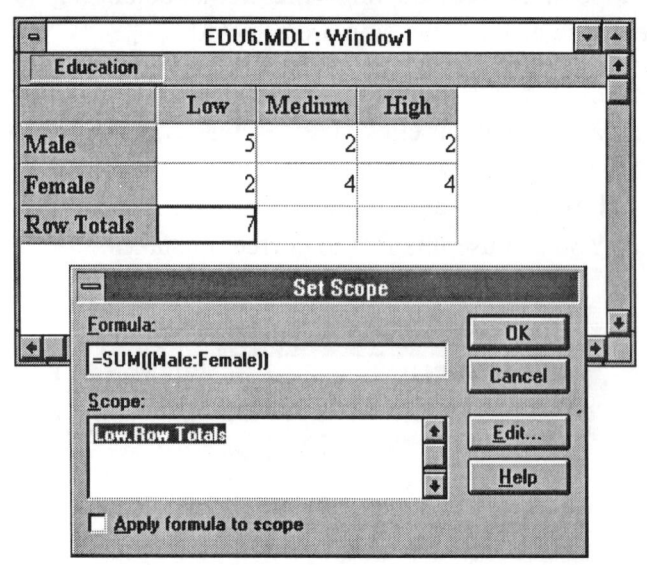

| Education | Low | Medium | High |
|---|---|---|---|
| Male | 5 | 2 | 2 |
| Female | 2 | 4 | 4 |
| Row Totals | 7 | | |

Set Scope

Formula: =SUM((Male:Female))

Scope: Low.Row Totals

☐ Apply formula to scope

In practice we would like this formula calculated on all of the Education items and so its scope should be (Low:High).Row Totals or equivalently Education.Totals since the item range (Low:High) is the complete Education dimension.

To create this new scope you can either type in the intersection range Education.Row Totals or you can use the Edit Scope dialog box to select Education or equivalently Low, Medium and High in the item box. When you click on the Replace button the Education dimension part of the scope is changed to Education - meaning the Education dimension in its entirety. If you had only wanted the formula worked out on Low and Medium you would have selected just these two items and the scope would have been amended to (Low:Medium).Row Totals. You can alter the scope interactively by selecting items and dimensions and seeing how the scope is altered.

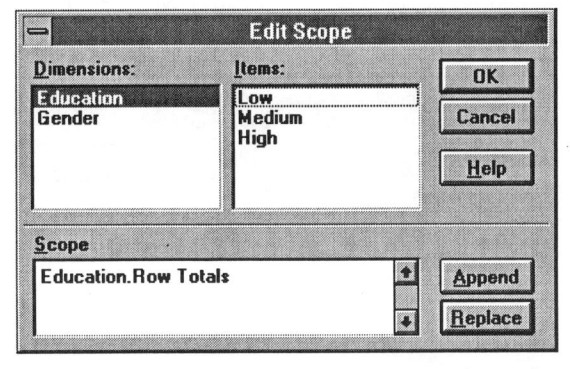

![Edit Scope dialog box showing Dimensions list with Education selected and Gender; Items list with Low, Medium, High; Scope field showing Education.Row Totals; buttons OK, Cancel, Help, Append, Replace]

Once you have selected or entered the correct scope for the formula you can click on OK in the Edit Scope dialog box and then in the Set Scope dialog box. When you return to the model you might be surprised to discover that the SUM hasn't been worked out in each of the columns. In fact the only visible change is that the result of the SUM function is shown in a different colour. The reason for this is that as well as defining a formula's scope you also have to give the OK or apply the formula to the range that you have specified. The reason for this two-step procedure is to make it less likely that you will overwrite existing values or formulae by specifying an inappropriate scope and to increase the flexibility of the scope method of controlling where a function is calculated.

## » Applying scope

As we have seen in the Education example, setting a formula's scope isn't the same as applying it to the selected range. In SCW a formula's scope governs the possible range in which it can be used. It is up to you to take an extra step and actually apply it to that range.

To apply a formula to its scope all you have to do is click on the Apply formula to scope box in the Set Scope dialog box. In this case when you click on OK the formula will be calculated and the results shown for each cell specified by the scope.

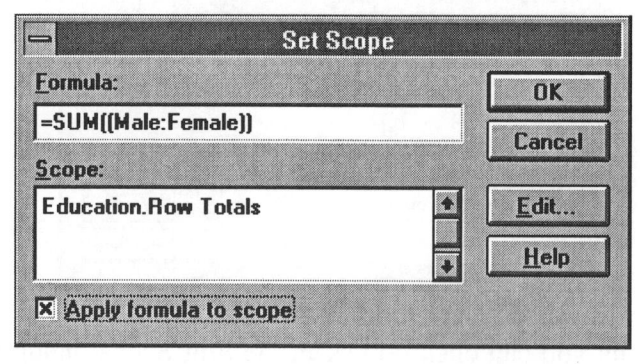

[Set Scope dialog box showing Formula: =SUM([Male:Female]), Scope: Education.Row Totals, with Apply formula to scope checked, and OK, Cancel, Edit..., Help buttons]

When a global formula is applied to its scope every cell in that range is overwritten by the formula. In this respect it really does act like a copy operation. However, because a scope is by its nature multidimensional, applying a formula to its entire scope is potentially more damaging. It is quite possible to modify parts of the model that are currently not on display. With such power also comes a concomitant danger! To try to protect you from making mistakes SCW automatically clears the Apply formula to scope check box every time you use the Set Scope dialog box. This can be frustrating if you keep on changing the scope of a formula and repeatedly forget to check the Apply formula to scope box before you click on OK.

## » Applying education

The SUM formula entered into the Education model has the correct scope but at the moment it isn't doing anything. If you apply the formula to its new scope, Education.Row Totals, the result is exactly what you would expect - in fact it is apparently no different from copying the formula into the same range. If you examine one of the cells that the formula has been applied to you will find that it even appears to contain a copy of the formula.

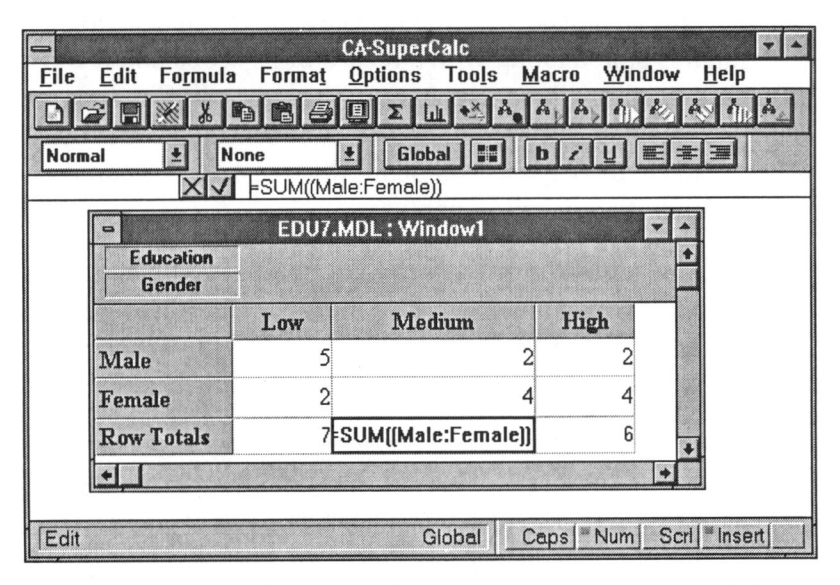

|  | Low | Medium | High |
|---|---|---|---|
| Male | 5 | 2 | 2 |
| Female | 2 | 4 | 4 |
| Row Totals | 7 | =SUM((Male:Female)) | 6 |

The only visible differences between a cell level and a global formula are its default colour and the fact that the word Global appears on the status line at the bottom of the SCW window when the current cell contains a global formula.

A global formula is stored centrally
and applied to the cells that need it

| Global formula | Scope |
|---|---|
| SUM(B1:B4) | (A1:A4).B5 |

|    | A 1 | A 2 | A 3 | A 4 |
|----|-----|-----|-----|-----|
| B1 |     |     |     |     |
| B2 |     |     |     |     |
| B3 |     |     |     |     |
| B4 |     |     |     |     |
| B5 | =SUM(B1:B4) | =SUM(B1:B4) | =SUM(B1:B4) | =SUM(B1:B4) |

## » Editing globals

If a global formula looks just like a copied cell level formula what is the advantage of using it? The answer is that a global formula is stored along with a record of its scope and it can be changed throughout its scope with a single edit. To change its scope is easy enough. Simply use the Formula,Set Scope command to display the Edit Scope dialog box. Then edit the scope and, if appropriate, apply it.

Editing the global formula itself is even easier. All you have to do is edit one of its instances in the model, i.e. the formula as stored in any of the cells that it is applied to. When you have completed the edit and try to enter the new formula you will see a dialog box which gives you a choice of how the formula changes should be treated.

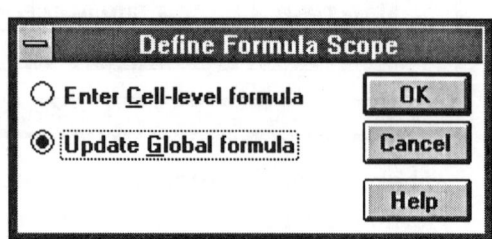

Define Formula Scope

○ Enter Cell-level formula
◉ Update Global formula

OK
Cancel
Help

You can either choose to enter the new version of the formula as a cell level formula or as a change to the global formula. If you select Enter Cell-level formula then the edited version is stored in the cell and loses any association it had with the global formula. In this case the global formula isn't altered in any way. Its scope also remains unchanged and if you apply the global formula to its scope it will overwrite the new cell level formula you have just entered.

If you select the Update Global formula option then the edited version of the global formula replaces the original. The change to the global formula affects all of the cells that it has been applied to. This instant change to all cells using the formula is of course one of the advantages of making a formula global in the first place. It avoids the need to re-copy a cell level formula into its scope - a very error prone procedure even if you can remember what its scope was supposed to be!

For example, if you should want to change the SUM formula in the Education model to a MAX formula, i.e. find the maximum value in each column, all you would have to do is edit any of its instances. When you try to enter the edited formula the Define Formula Scope dialog box appears. If you click on OK without changing the default selection of Update Global Formula then all of the instances of the formula are changed. If you select the alternative Enter Cell-level formula then the formula will be entered as a cell level formula and will not affect the other instances of the global formula.

Notice that only cells where the global formula has been applied are affected by the change. An alternative method of editing a global formula is to edit it in the Set Scope dialog box that appears when you click on the Global button - see the next section.

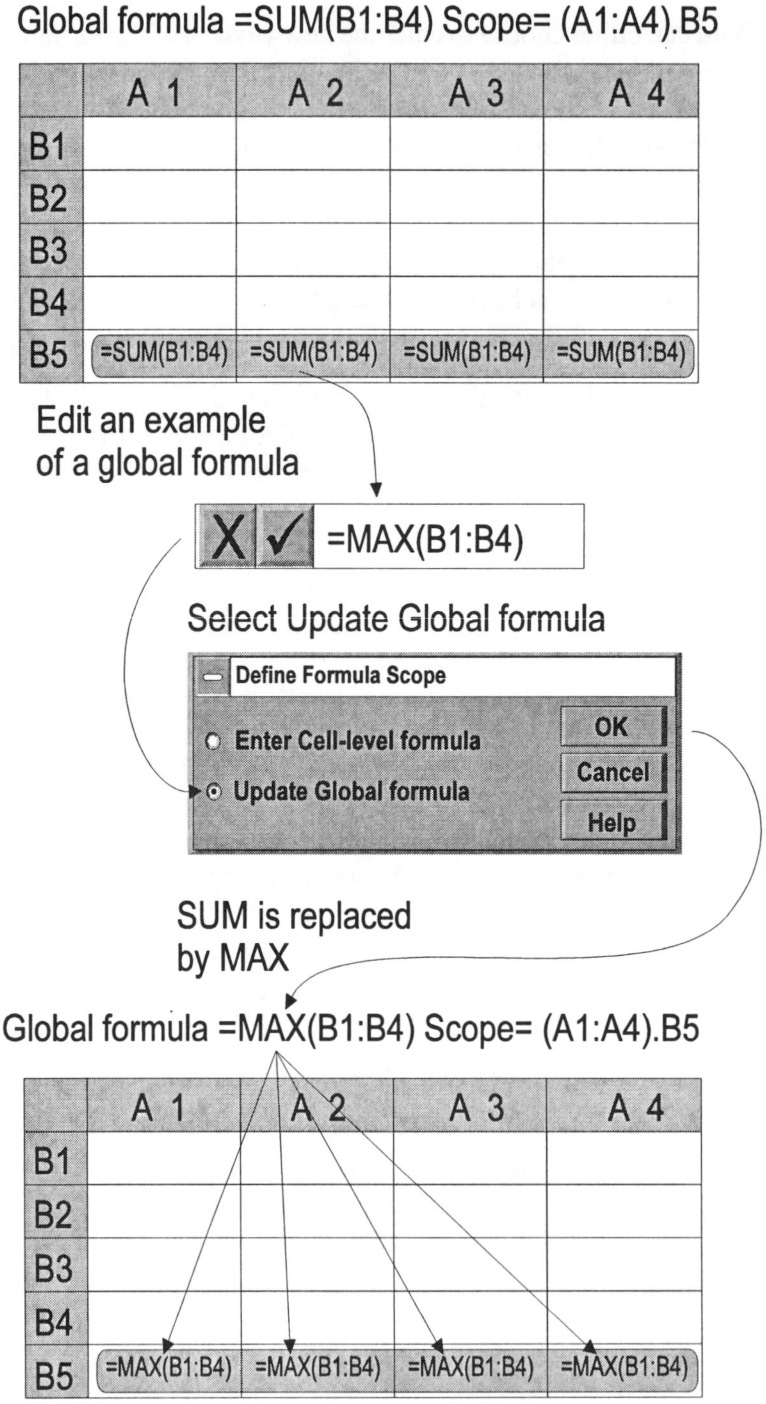

Global formula =SUM(B1:B4) Scope= (A1:A4).B5

|    | A 1 | A 2 | A 3 | A 4 |
|----|-----|-----|-----|-----|
| B1 |     |     |     |     |
| B2 |     |     |     |     |
| B3 |     |     |     |     |
| B4 |     |     |     |     |
| B5 | =SUM(B1:B4) | =SUM(B1:B4) | =SUM(B1:B4) | =SUM(B1:B4) |

Edit an example of a global formula

X ✓ =MAX(B1:B4)

Select Update Global formula

**Define Formula Scope**

○ Enter Cell-level formula
⊙ Update Global formula

[ OK ]
[ Cancel ]
[ Help ]

SUM is replaced by MAX

Global formula =MAX(B1:B4) Scope= (A1:A4).B5

|    | A 1 | A 2 | A 3 | A 4 |
|----|-----|-----|-----|-----|
| B1 |     |     |     |     |
| B2 |     |     |     |     |
| B3 |     |     |     |     |
| B4 |     |     |     |     |
| B5 | =MAX(B1:B4) | =MAX(B1:B4) | =MAX(B1:B4) | =MAX(B1:B4) |

You can see that using a global formula allows you to make sweeping but consistent changes throughout a model. Compare this to updating a cell level formula that has been copied into a range. After modifying a copy of the formula you have to make sure that you copy it into the same range and because this range is not obvious errors are very likely.

The only error that you are likely to make is that you enter an intended change to a global formula as a local formula. In this case you should be able to notice the mistake by the change in display colour in going from a global to a local formula and the lack of any change to the results displayed by the global formula. The solution is to reapply the global to the cell and edit it again.

## » Creating new globals from old

There is another way of editing a global formula but it doesn't produce the same effect as editing an instance. You can edit the global formula using the Formula text box in the Set Scope dialog box. If you select an instance of the formula and click on the Global button you will see the Set Scope box. You can then place the the text cursor in the Formula text box and edit the definition of the global formula. This may look as if you are editing, and so making changes to, the global formula but in fact what you are doing is adding a new global formula to the model. If you click on OK then the new version of the formula will be applied to the cell that you selected but it will not change the cells in the scope of the original formula.

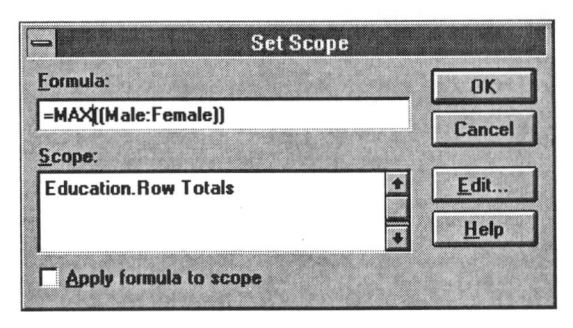

```
┌─────────────── Set Scope ───────────────┐
│ Formula:                                │
│ ┌─────────────────────────┐   ┌──────┐  │
│ │ =MAX([Male:Female])     │   │  OK  │  │
│ └─────────────────────────┘   └──────┘  │
│ Scope:                        ┌──────┐  │
│ ┌─────────────────────────┐   │Cancel│  │
│ │ Education.Row Totals    │   └──────┘  │
│ │                         │   ┌──────┐  │
│ │                         │   │ Edit…│  │
│ │                         │   └──────┘  │
│ │                         │   ┌──────┐  │
│ └─────────────────────────┘   │ Help │  │
│                               └──────┘  │
│ ☐ Apply formula to scope                │
└─────────────────────────────────────────┘
```

The new version of the global formula becomes another global formula in its own right. It inherits the original's scope so if you click on the Apply formula to scope check box before clicking on OK it will appear to update the original formula - but it actually replaces it. The original formula is still stored as a global formula that you can apply at any time in the future.

Also notice that you can apply the new formula to a range of cells by selecting this range before you click on the Global button. After editing the global formula it will be applied to the range that you have selected - which of course must be contained within its scope.

## » Which formula to apply?

It is obvious that there may be, and usually are, many global formulae within a model. This causes us no difficulty but it may be that a given cell will be within the scope of more than one global formula - and the question is which one applies. The solution is that it is the last formula to be applied to a cell which determines its result.

For example, the Education survey model can be extended to show both row and column sums. The scope of the row sum is Education.'Row Totals' and the scope of the column sum is Gender.'Col Totals'. You can see that the cell 'Row Totals'.'Col Totals' is in the scope of both global formulae and which one applies depends on which global scope was most recently applied.

| | | Low | Medium | High | Col Totals |
|---|---|---|---|---|---|
| Education | | | | | |
| Gender | | | | | |
| Male | | 5 | 2 | 2 | 9 |
| Female | | 2 | 4 | 4 | 10 |
| Row Totals | | 7 | 6 | 6 | 19 |

EDU8.MDL : Window1

## Which formula to apply? 69

In this case both global formulae give the same result anyway - i.e. the sum of the whole table. Also in this case there are only two global formulae to choose between for the whole of the model. In a more complicated, and realistic, case there would be many more formulae and their scopes would overlap in more than one cell. Sorting out which global formula applies at each overlap, by applying each to its entire range, would be difficult and in some cases impossible.

One solution to this problem is to restrict the scope of the global formulae so that they don't overlap and so that each one covers exactly the range that you want to use the formula in. This is the ideal but sometimes it is quicker and simpler to explicitly choose which of a number of possible formulae applies to a particular cell. After all SCW already makes a distinction between the scope of a formula and the range of cells to which it is actually applied.

To choose which global formula applies you use the Formula, Apply Formula command (or use the F11 key). This produces the Apply Formula dialog box.

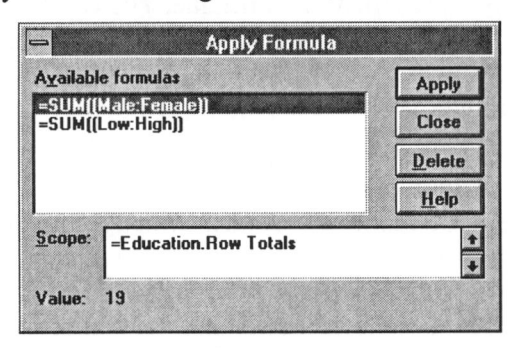

```
┌─────────────────── Apply Formula ───────────────────┐
│ Available formulas:                      ┌─────────┐│
│ ┌──────────────────────────────────────┐ │  Apply  ││
│ │ =SUM((Male:Female))                  │ └─────────┘│
│ │ =SUM((Low:High))                     │ ┌─────────┐│
│ │                                      │ │  Close  ││
│ │                                      │ └─────────┘│
│ │                                      │ ┌─────────┐│
│ │                                      │ │ Delete  ││
│ │                                      │ └─────────┘│
│ │                                      │ ┌─────────┐│
│ │                                      │ │  Help   ││
│ └──────────────────────────────────────┘ └─────────┘│
│ Scope:  ┌──────────────────────────────────────┐   │
│         │ =Education.Row Totals                │   │
│         └──────────────────────────────────────┘   │
│ Value:  19                                          │
└─────────────────────────────────────────────────────┘
```

This displays a list of global formulae that could be applied to the cell - i.e. all of those for which the cell is in scope - and you can examine and select which one to apply. Once you have done this you should of course avoid applying the other formula to its entire scope.

## » Deleting globals

You have already seen that it is possible to convert a global formula back into a cell level formula simply by performing a token editing, i.e. without actually make any changes to it, and then selecting Enter Cell-level formula in the Define Formula Scope dialog box that appears. To delete a global formula from the model completely you have to use the Apply Formula command - even though you may not actually want to apply a new formula to the cell in question. When the Apply Formula dialog box appears select the formula that you want to delete and click on the Delete button. Following this all of the cells that the formula was applied to will show as blank.

## » Using scope - a question of style

The idea of applying a formula to cells within its scope on an ad-hoc basis gives you a great deal of freedom but it also re-introduces many of the problems associated with the copy and paste style of replicating formulae. You can always check up on a formula's scope and re-apply it in one operation if necessary. However, if you adopt the policy of applying global formulae ad-hoc then there is no way of knowing exactly where any given formula has actually been applied!

Using this method of working you would define a formula's scope as a sort of maximum range in which it could be needed and then go through and select the cells in which you actually want it and apply it. The Apply Formula command will work with a range of cells selected and will apply the global formula to all of them - so this task isn't time consuming. Applying global formulae in this way does give you some advantages. In particular, updating a global formula doesn't change the range of cells it applies to - so we still have the benefit of centralised update. Also there is no chance that the formula can be applied outside its scope. In this sense the scope acts like a protective fence keeping the formula under control.

The alternative to applying formulae ad-hoc is to use exact scopes and always apply formulae to their entire scopes. To minimise the risk of losing data some SCW users advise NEVER applying a global formula to its entire scope but to always use the Apply Formula command to verify which cells the formula is applied to. Personally I think that this misses most of the advantages of the global formula method. It is much better to always define scopes that are exact. Think of a scope as the area of the model which you would like to copy the global formula into and there should be no problem. If you do this then applying the formula to its entire scope is a single operation.

You should be convinced by now that the use of global formulae complete with scope and application is a good way to work. In fact it is even better than you might think! If you build your models appropriately then they are self extending. What this means is that when you insert new items, and even new dimensions, the model will automatically adjust itself to be correct. If you compare this behaviour with the work that traditional 2D spreadsheets need when you insert even a single new row it is yet another reason to prefer the model. However, these ideas need us to take an even closer look at ranges and scope - which we do in the next chapter.

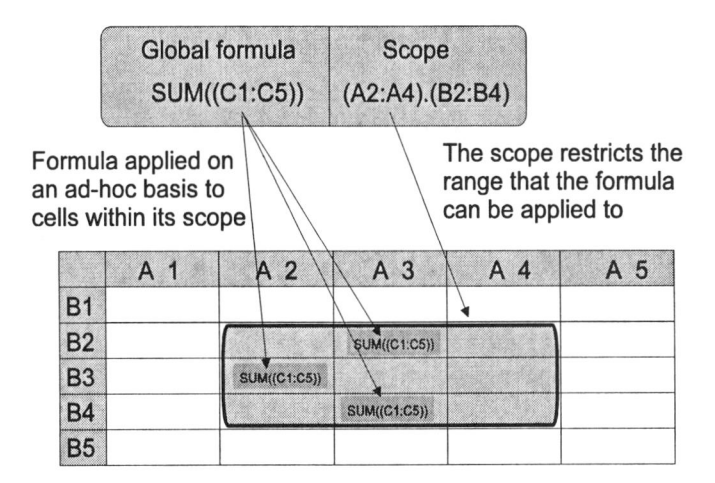

| Global formula | Scope |
|---|---|
| SUM((C1:C5)) | (A2:A4).(B2:B4) |

Formula applied on an ad-hoc basis to cells within its scope

The scope restricts the range that the formula can be applied to

|    | A 1 | A 2 | A 3 | A 4 | A 5 |
|----|-----|-----|-----|-----|-----|
| B1 |     |     |     |     |     |
| B2 |     |     | SUM((C1:C5)) |     |     |
| B3 |     | SUM((C1:C5)) |     |     |     |
| B4 |     |     | SUM((C1:C5)) |     |     |
| B5 |     |     |     |     |     |

## Key points

» Traditionally formulae have been applied to multiple cells by copying but this is an error prone method which leaves no trace of where the formulae are active within a sheet.

» A global formula is associated with a scope - a range reference - that defines the cells that it can be applied to.

» Applying a global formula to a cell within its scope has the same effect as copying it to that cell in that the result of the formula is evaluated at its new location.

» If you edit a global formula you have the option of converting it into a local formula or accepting it as a change to the global formula as applied to the cells within its scope.

» It sometimes happens that a cell will be in the scope of more than one global formula. In this case you can select which formula to apply to the cell.

» There are two approaches to making the best use of the scope facility:
The first is to use the scope as a guard zone which limits the formula's use.
The second is to treat the formula's scope as the range to which it is applied.

» Applying a formula to its entire scope has the advantage that you always know exactly where the formula is active.

# Chapter 6

# Formatting and Dimensionality

In this chapter we look at some of the aspects of presentation which make a model easier to use and easier to understand. Formatting isn't a difficult idea and it applies to sheets as well as models. The formatting of sheets is fully described in Chapter 4 of *Mastering CA SuperCalc for Windows*. To avoid repetition the emphasis in this chapter is specifically on how formatting applies to multidimensional models. If you require a more detailed introduction to formatting in general then see the aforementioned book.

## » Overview

If you have used a traditional 2D spreadsheet under MS-DOS then you will already know something about formatting but you might be surprised just how much control you have over the look of a model. On the other hand if you have used almost any Windows application then it will not come as so much of a shock! You can apply fonts, colours, patterns and numeric formats.

If you are familiar with sheets the only real surprise is that you cannot use the Border command to add rulings to form a table. If you want to create a 2D ruled table then the solution is to link the data to a sheet - see Chapter 12 - and format the table in the sheet.

When you apply formats and styles to the cells within a model this is very like formatting a 2D sheet for presentation purposes. However, there are considerations which are unique to multidimensional models. For example, you can make use of particular formats to make different views readily identifiable. There is also the question of how you format an entire model and not just one particular view and how do you produce a report from a model? Sadly in the first version of SCW you can only apply formats to the ranges selected in the visible dimensions - but with one very important exception. You can also apply any format to a slice through the model. A slice is a special form of multidimensional range. So being able to format a slice isn't quite as powerful as being able to format an arbitrary multidimensional range but in nearly all practical applications it is all you need.

Before moving on to examine how formatting applies to a model it is worth examining what is available.

## » Attributes - fonts, alignment, patterns

There is a range of attributes that you can apply to any range of cells in the visible dimensions, or to a slice of the model, to make the data in them look different or stand out. Most aspects of using this facility are easy enough to understand and are well explained elsewhere so only a brief discussion is included here:

- » **Number** - You can assign any numeric, date or time format to any 2D range of cells on the visible dimensions. A selection of predefined formats is available and these are often all that are required. If you want to create your own formats then this is a relatively simple matter.

- » **Alignment** - Values stored in cells can be left aligned, right aligned or centred using the Format,Align command which displays the Alignment dialog box. In addition to these alignments you can also alter the way text is treated within a cell. If you select the Fill option any text in a cell is repeated until it fills the current width of the cell. If you check the Wrap Text box then lines of text will be broken to start new lines at the cell width.

- » **Fonts** - You can select any of the available Windows fonts using the Format,Fonts command. You can select typeface, point size and effects such as bold, italic etc.. If you restrict your choices to TrueType fonts your models will print out on almost any type of printer without changing the way that they look.

- » **Patterns** - You can fill any selected area with a hatched pattern or a solid colour using the command Format,Patterns which displays the Patterns dialog box. You can select both foreground and background colours. The only tricky part of using Patterns is that they are always shown in black and white in the dialog box. All you have to remember is that the black part of the pattern will show in the selected foreground colour and the white part in the selected background colour.

Using fonts, alignment and patterns you can differentiate different areas of the model corresponding to different types of data or results. You can also assign different colours to different views of the model to help you identify more positively what you are looking at.

As well as these attributes, all of which affect the appearance of data, there is a cell protection attribute which determines if the contents of the cell can be seen or altered. This is discussed in more detail later.

## » Format shortcuts

If you click the right mouse button while any cell or range of cells is selected a pop-up menu appears which allows you to set any of the attributes listed above. This is usually the quickest way to apply attributes to a range.

You can also use the bold, italic and underline buttons in the ribbon bar to set or alter these characteristics of the currently selected cells. The left, centre and right justify buttons can also be used to set the alignment of the currently selected cells.

## » Styles

Using attributes isn't difficult but it is very easy for a model to become chaotic in its appearance because of the range of different attributes used. It is much better to define a named style which groups together numeric format, alignment, font, pattern and even protection.

If you already know how to use styles in connection with sheets then there is very little new in using them with models. However, notice that the borders attribute is missing. As already mentioned, you cannot apply the borders attribute to a model.

## Styles 77

For example, if you use the command Format, Style or click with the right mouse button on the Style box at the left of the ribbon bar, you will see the Style dialog box.

You can select the style that you want to examine or apply and its description appears in the box below. Not all styles include all of the possible attributes within their definition and applying a style to a selected area only changes those attributes defined by the style.

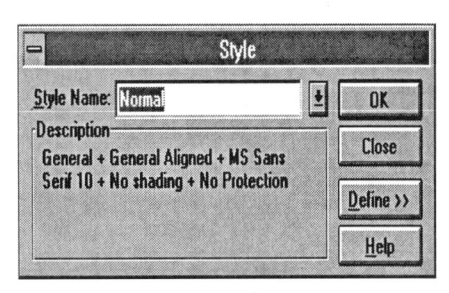

Having selected an area of the model, you can apply a style either by using the command Format,Style and the Style dialog box or by selecting the style name from the drop down list at the left-hand corner of the toolbar. The name on view changes to show the style of the currently selected area.

To define a new style or edit the definition of an existing one all you have to do is click on the Define button and fill in the extended dialog box that appears.

You can use this to enter a new style name and then to make selections for format, alignment etc.. Any attributes that are not selected are not part of the style specification. Notice that certain attributes are interdependent. For example, if you apply a style which specifies background colour and then subsequently apply a style which doesn't specify a pattern then the existing colour will not be changed.

The important points about using styles are:

» If you change a style's definition then all of the cells that have that style will also change - without the need to reapply the style.

» Any individual attributes that you apply before a style are altered if the style includes them within its control. For example, if you set a cell to bold and then apply a style that specifies an italic font the cell will display in italic.

» Any individual attributes that you set after applying a style will be honoured even if the style controls the attribute. For example, if you apply a style that specifies percentage display and then format the cell as general the cell will display the number in the manner you have entered it rather than as a percentage. Notice, however, that formats can be additive. For example, if you apply a style that specifies a bold font and then set the cell to italic it will display in bold italic.

» Reapplying a style will override any attributes that it controls which have been individually set. Doing this removes any added settings. For example, reapplying the bold style to the cell that had also been formatted toitalic to show in bold italic causes it to revert to "plain" bold.

What all this means is that if you want to define a basic style and then make deviations from it you should make sure that the style does not control those attributes that you want to change. For example, if you want to apply a single style to the body of a model but highlight some items by setting them to bold it is better not to include any font effects in the style.

Defining characteristic styles for various views and for parts of the model, such as results tables, can make a model much easier to understand. Rather than applying individual attributes on an ad-hoc basis you should try to organise attributes into named styles as you are building a model.

## » Selecting ranges in the visible dimensions

Applying formats to parts of the model brings us to the topic of selecting specific areas. Selecting ranges in the visible dimensions is exactly like selecting ranges in a 2D sheet. To recap you can select:

- » any rectangular area by simply clicking on one corner and then dragging to define the other corner.

- » an entire column by clicking (once) on the item name.

- » any entire row by clicking (once) on the item name.

- » the entire visible part of the model by clicking on the top left-hand corner of the border.

Notice that when clicking on item names you should be careful not to click more than once. If you do you will be offered the chance to edit the item name - which is probably not what you wanted to do!

You can also select a set of adjacent rows or columns by dragging the selection across all the rows or columns that you want to include. Another way of making the same selection is to click on the first row or column and then Shift-click on the final row or column.

To select individual rows or columns to add to the existing selection simply click on the desired row or column while holding down the Ctrl key. You can also use Ctrl-click to select discontinuous ranges within the models. As long as you hold down the Ctrl additional areas that you select are added to the existing selection.

The general rule is:

» Shift-click to extend a selection

» Ctrl-click to add to a selection

A few minutes practice and experimentation soon makes all this seem obvious.

## » Formatting pages

By selecting a 2D area on one of the visible dimensions you can format a model as a sequence of 2D slices. For example, in the case of the default model you could first format the AA, BB view for CC equals C1 and DD equals D1. You could then repeat this for CC equal to C2 and DD equal to D1 and so on until you had formatted all views of the model. Even for the default model this represents a lot of work. With two fixed dimensions and five default items on each you have 25 2D slices to format individually.

The situation is a little easier to imagine in the case of a 3D model with dimensions AA, BB and CC. In each case you have to format a range like AA.BB.C1, then AA.BB.C2 and so on. In the case of a 3D model you can see that you effectively have to format a set of 2D pages that are "page numbered" by the fixed dimension.

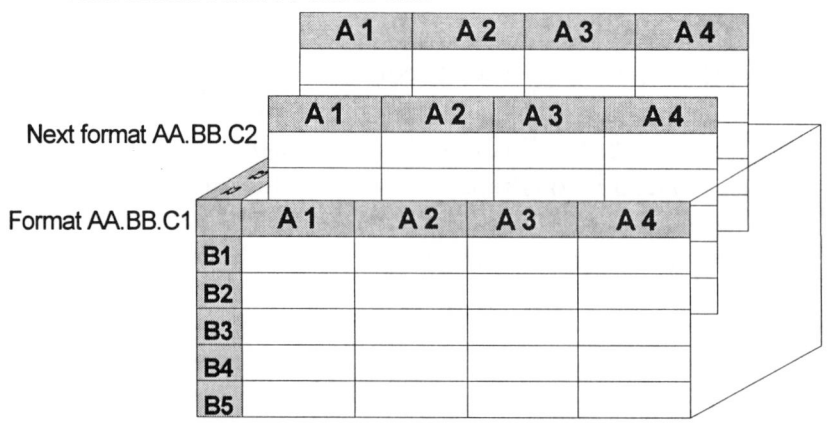

## » Formatting slices

A more powerful way of formatting larger chunks of a model in one operation is to select an item range on one of the visible dimensions and then, before you apply the formatting command, press and hold the Shift key. If you do this the Format menu changes to the Format All menu. Notice that you don't have to hold down the Shift key while selecting the item range - only while you are selecting the menu. The pop-up menu also changes to "format all" if you click the right mouse button while holding down the shift key. If the format items in the Format All menu are greyed out this is because you haven't selected an item range to which they can be applied.

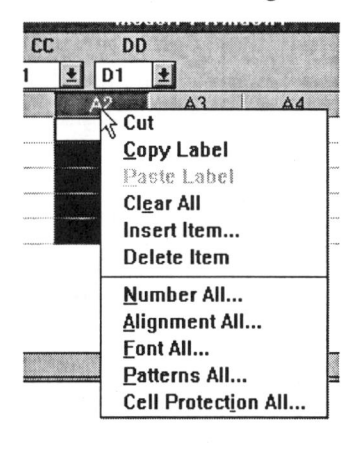

The effect of Format All is to apply the attributes to cells corresponding to the selected items on one of the visible dimensions and all of the fixed dimensions. For example, if you select item A1, i.e. the first column, in the default model and use the Font All option to set the font to Arial 10 point

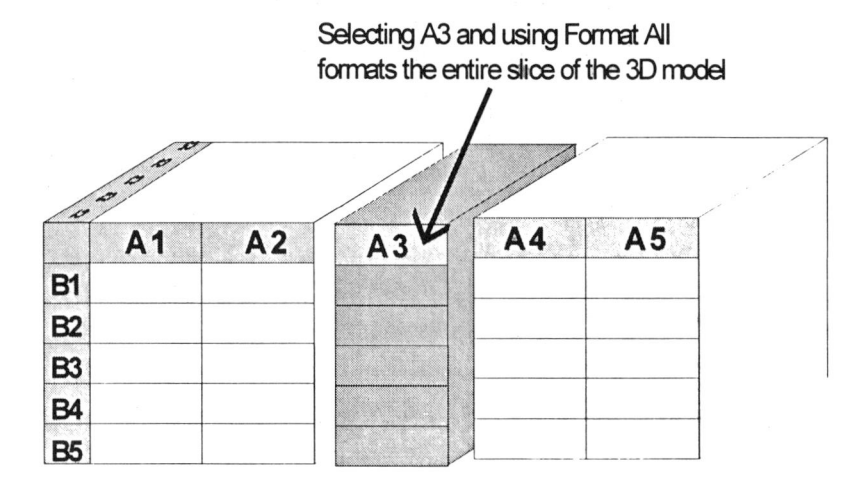

Selecting A3 and using Format All formats the entire slice of the 3D model

then the range A1.BB.CC.DD will be affected. In other words, every cell in the model with A1 in its reference is set to Arial 10 point.

Again, this idea is easier to visualise in the case of a 3D version of the default model. If you select A3 say and use Format All then the entire slice A3.BB.CC is formatted in one go.

You can select continuous item ranges and discontinuous item ranges when you are using Format All. This means that you can quickly build up a pattern of formatting throughout the model. For example, if columns A1 and A4 are to display as percentages irrespective of the values of the other dimensions you could select A1 and then select A4 while holding down the Ctrl key. Applying the Format All command results in A1.BB.CC and A4.BB.CC being set to the desired format.

You can also assign a style to a slice in the same way but notice that you have to use the Style All option in the Format menu. The pull down list of styles on the toolbar doesn't work in this mode.

## » Ordering items

The Format All option is clearly powerful but how exactly should you use it? One way to organise its use is to realise that it assigns a single format or style to a single item. What this means is that as long you choose items that determine the data's type then Format All is appropriate.

For example, if you select an item called Cost then presumable any cell corresponding to this item e.g. Cost.Now, Cost.Predicted, Cost.Historic etc. will contain a monetary value. In this case selecting Cost and applying a currency format to the corresponding slice makes good sense.

Compare this to the situation with applying a format to an item such as Predicted. In this case the data stored in cells corresponding to "Predicted" will not all be of the same type. Indeed the data type will change according to what is being predicted and clearly applying a single format to Predicted isn't a good idea. What this means is that you should try to identify items that determine the type of data stored in a cell irrespective of other dimensions.

Of course there is nothing stopping you from applying a format to a slice and then overriding it by applying another format to cells where it is inappropriate. For example, if you apply a currency format to Cost then an item such as Cost.Ratio may not fit into the pattern. In this case simply apply a suitable format, percentage say, to the Ratio item.

Notice that it is important that the currency format is applied to Cost first and then a percentage format applied to Ratio. This is because the item "Ratio" modifies whatever quantity it is applied to and so has a higher priority in determining the type of data stored in a cell. Usually a small number of qualities and modifiers can be identified and applying formats to items in the correct order results in a model which needs no individual adjustment.

It can be difficult to work out exactly what the effect of applying a sequence of formats to different slices is. For example, using the default model, if you select A1 then any format you apply to it affects A1.BB.CC.DD. If you next select item B1 the format you apply affects AA.B1.CC.DD. The question is what range does the first format now apply to? The answer is clearly A1.(B2:B5).CC.DD. That is, it applies to all cells that have the A1 item in their reference except for those that also have the B1 item. You can continue in this way applying formats to items on other dimensions.

» The rule is that each time you apply a format to an item then it affects this item on all dimensions and restricts earlier formatting to their current ranges less the item.

If this seems complicated and confusing then in practice I have to admit that it is easy to lose track of what you have done. Often you can format a model using a particular view only to be quite surprised at the way it looks when pivoted to a new view! With a little practice and understanding of the principles such surprises slowly but surely become less frequent.

## » Formatting - a simple example

Starting from a new default model select item A1 and apply a solid pattern in foreground green while holding down the Shift key. This sets the range A1.BB.CC.DD to green as you can check by changing the fixed dimensions and by pivoting

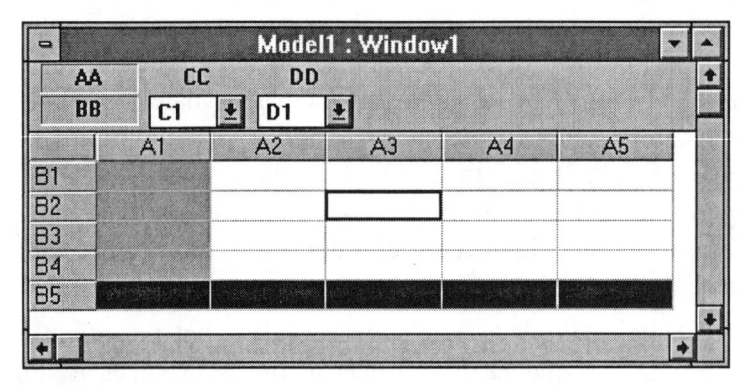

the model.

Using the standard visible dimensions, that is AA horizontally and BB vertically select item B5 and apply a solid pattern in foreground red while holding down the Shift key. This sets AA.B5.CC.DD to red. In the default view of the model, i.e. with visible dimensions AA and BB the result is that the left-hand column and bottom row are coloured differently. Given the way that the formats were applied this is true no matter what items you select on the fixed dimensions.

Now pivot the model so that CC replaces BB - but before you do this ask yourself what you expect to see?

The answer is that you see a single green column A1 with no trace of red.

The reason is, of course, that the red colour was applied to item B5 and there is no trace of this in the display. Now set the fixed dimension BB to B5. Again, before you do this work out what you expect to see. The answer is that the whole of the visible 2D spreadsheet is coloured red. Why? Because every cell on display has a reference that has B5 on the BB dimension. It's easy once you get used to associating the appearance of the item or items you have formatted with the use of that format.

Finally, just to make sure you understand the way that the formatting has been applied to the model pivot DD so that it replaces AA as the horizontal visible dimension. Now you should have little trouble in working out when you should see green and when you should see red. If there is an A1 selected in the fixed dimension AA then all of the cells on display will be green. If there is a B5 in the fixed dimension BB then all of the cells will be red. Easy but now for the tricky question. What happens if you select A1 on the AA dimension and B5 on the BB dimension? Will the cells display as red or green? The answer is that they will display as red because this format was applied to B5 after the green format was applied to A1. The rule is that the last format applied takes precedence.

## » Multiple views

You may feel that being restricted to a single two-dimensional view of your model, no matter how flexible and customisable, is not sufficient. In fact you can construct multiple views of a model. Each view shares the basic formatting of the model but you are free to select different fixed items in each view and pivot the model to choose different visible dimensions.

To create a new view all you have to do is use the command Window,New Window. This "clones" the current view of the model in a newly created window. To help you keep track of what each view is supposed to show you can name any window. Simply select the window and use the command Window,Name Window.

For example, the default model formatted as described in the previous example using red and green can be viewed on all four of its dimensions simultaneously by creating a single new window and pivoting the model.

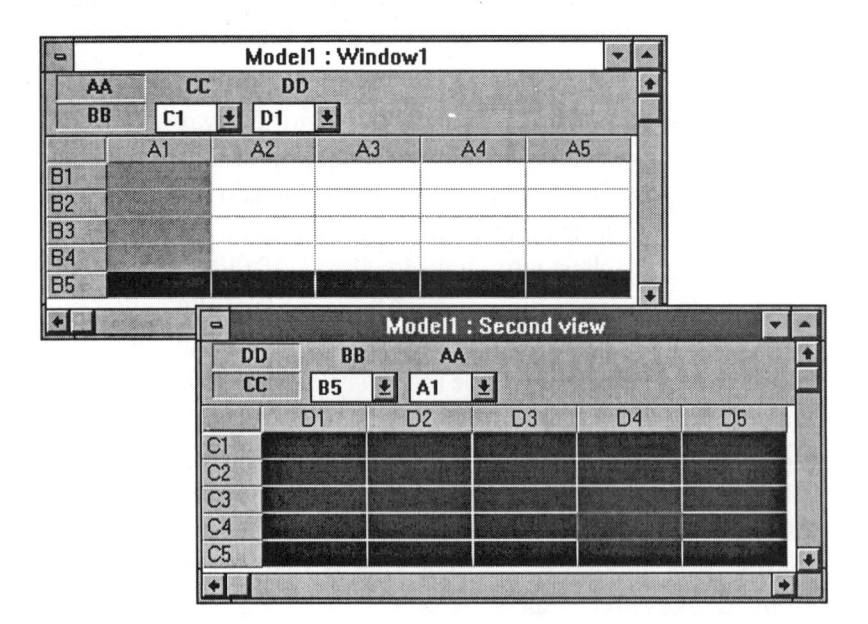

When you save a model all of its windows, including their current size and position, are saved along with it. What this means is that when you open the model again all the windows are restored just as they were before you last saved it.

Finally it is worth stating that any changes that you make to the model in one window will be immediately shown in any other window in which it should be visible.

## » Column width and row height

An important part of making any model usable is setting appropriate column widths and row heights. If a numeric value needs more space than is available it displays as a string of asterisks. Text that is too big will either spill over into the next cell (if it is left justified and the next cell is empty) or it will be truncated.

To alter the width of a column you can either drag the column dividers interactively in the column headings or use the Format,Column Width command. If you drag the column dividers then you can size a single column at a time. If you use the Format,Column Width command the size that you enter affects all of the currently selected columns.

In the same way, when you want to alter row height, you can drag the row dividers in the row labels or you can use the Format,Row Height command and enter the desired height for a selection of rows.

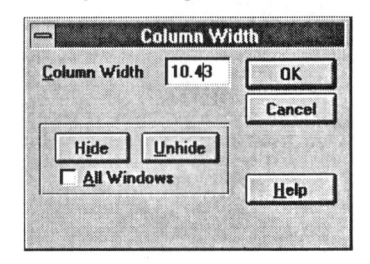

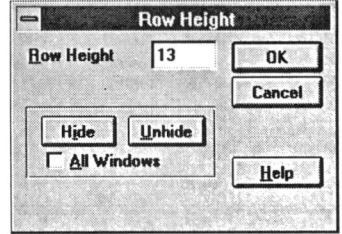

So far this discussion applies equally to sheets or models - but there are some differences in the way that row height and column width settings work in the two environments. The most obvious is that there is no "Best Fit"option for column width in models while there is in sheets. The reason is that column width and row height are associated with items when they are on the visible dimension. For example, if you set the column width of item A1 in the default model then this column width will be used no matter what values the fixed dimensions are set to. As long as the AA dimension is the horizontal visible dimension A1 will be shown with the assigned column width. This means that to set a best fit width SCW would have to search through every possible combination of fixed dimensions for the data item that needed the largest column width - a difficult task.

What matters most is that you understand that column width and row height are properties that you assign to particular items and that they are used whenever the item finds itself playing the role of a column or a row respectively.

The best way to make this clear is by way of a simple example. Starting from a new default model set the column width of A1 to 20 and the row height of B1 to 25. Now if you select alternative items on the CC and DD fixed dimensions you will see that the column width and row height do not change. However, if you pivot the model so that AA becomes the vertical visible dimension and BB the horizontal you will see that the column widths and row heights are returned to their defaults. This is entirely reasonable as you have not set the column width of B1 nor the row height of A1.

If you pivot the model back to its original state then you will again see the column width and row height you set. No matter how you pivot the model you will see the column width applied to A1 whenever it plays the role of a column heading and the row height applied to B1 whenever it plays the role of a row heading.

If you have more than one window open onto the model you will see the same column widths and row heights in each. A model has only one set of row heights and column widths associated with it, used in all windows as appropriate.

## » Hidden items

The column width and row height dialog boxes also control another aspect of the way that items display - or rather don't display! You can set any item or range of items to "Hidden" either as row or as columns. Items hidden as "rows" do not display when their dimension is the vertical visible dimension and items hidden as "columns" do not display when their dimension is the horizontal visible dimension. In other words, an item can be told to "hide itself" when it plays the role of a row or when it plays the role of a column in the visible dimensions.

Notice that you cannot hide an item when its dimension is one of the fixed dimensions. Also rows and columns can be hidden either in all windows or just in the window that is active at the time you use the Format,Column Width command or the Format,Row Height command. That is, unlike the other item attributes, column width and row height, it can be different in each window that you create.

To unhide a hidden item you have to select the items on either side of it and then use the Format,Row Height or Format, Column Width commands as appropriate.

You can use item hiding to present simplified views of models. For example, you can remove intermediate data or the steps in the calculation of a final figure.

## » Dimension styles

As well as being able to set styles for the data in the body of the model you can also specify a style for each or all of the dimensions. If you use the command Format,Label Style the Label Style dialog box appears. You can use this to select an alignment, font and pattern which determines how the items are displayed when the dimension is one of the visible dimensions.

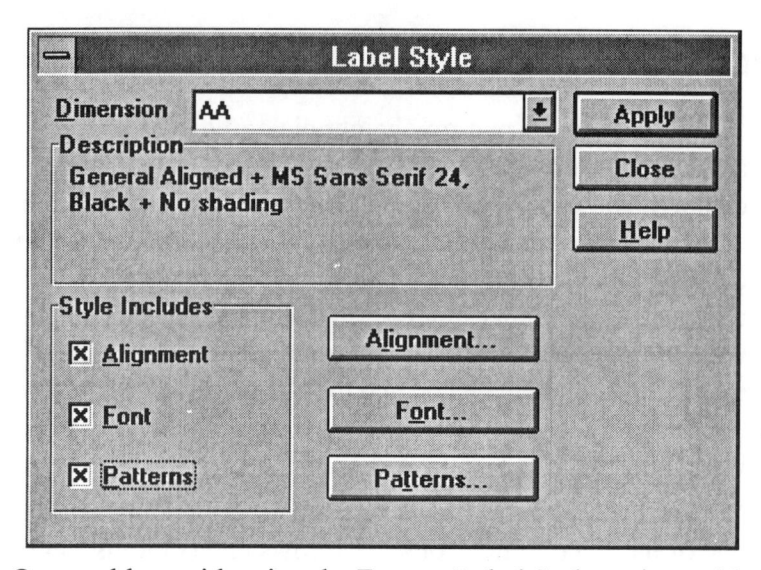

One problem with using the Format,Label Style command is that you can set a font size that is too big to be displayed in the default space. To set the row height and column width of the item labels in most cases it is simpler to drag the edge of the label bar to make it larger or smaller interactively. In other words, the row that contains the column labels and the column that contains the row labels behaves in exactly the same way as any row or column as far as setting width and height are concerned.

However, if you do need to change these sizes accurately you may need to use the Format,Label Row Height or Format,Label Column Width commands. These commands are only available in the Format All menu that appears when you select Format while holding down the Shift key. This displays the usual width and height dialog boxes which you can use to specify the width and height of the item labels.

Changing the width of the vertical labels and the height of the horizontal labels in the visible dimensions is a lot like changing the width and height of the rows and columns in the body of the model - but there is an important difference. The height of the row labels is fixed for all dimensions. This means that if you set the row height then it stays the same for all dimensions no matter how you pivot the model. However, the width of the column of labels is set for each dimension. That is, if you pivot the model and change the vertical visible dimension the space allocated to show its item labels will change.

The different treatment of the vertical and horizontal labels may seem a little odd and over complicated at first but it does fit in with what you usually want to do. The height needed to accommodate labels is governed by the point size of the font you use and this usually changes little - if at all. On the other hand the width needed for labels usually does vary according to the dimension - some dimensions being characterised by short item names and some by long item names.

Notice that you can also hide and unhide the entire label row or column on the visible dimensions. There are very few situations where this is necessary or a good idea. A quicker way to hide both the row and column labels on all visible dimensions is to use the command Options,Display and then select the Row and Column headings option in the dialog box that appears.

To control the way that the fixed dimensions are displayed you need to use the command Options,Model bar which displays the Model Bar dialog box.

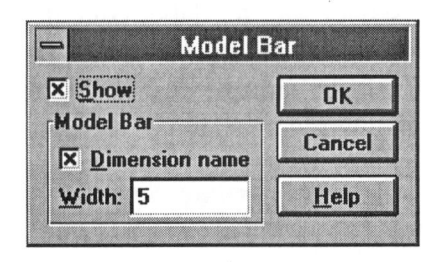

If you deselect the Show option then the fixed dimension items are not displayed. Clearly this is only useful if you want to hide the complexity of a model during a presentation. After selecting this option you cannot change the fixed dimensions in any way and the model looks and behaves much like a standard 2D spreadsheet.

Selecting the Dimension name box will result in the name of the fixed dimension being displayed above the fixed item. You can change the amount of space allocated to displaying the fixed dimension name and item box by entering a value for Width. Notice that this value sets the size allocated to each of the fixed dimensions. What this means is that you have to set the width so that the largest item name is not truncated - and remember this includes the visible dimensions which may at any moment be swapped to become new fixed dimensions.

## » Formatting car sales

If you look at the car sales model that was built in Chapter 3 you will see that it has a number of minor formatting problems.

The most obvious is the narrowness of the label column showing the car types. This is easily solved by dragging the dividers between the labels. However, if you pivot the model so that Type becomes the vertical visible dimension you will discover that the label column width returns to its default value which is still too small for "Out of Town". You have to set the column width and the row height for each dimension as required.

|  | \multicolumn{2}{c}{Year} | \multicolumn{2}{c}{Showroom} | \multicolumn{2}{c}{Budget} |
|---|---|---|---|---|---|---|
|  | \multicolumn{2}{c}{Type} | \multicolumn{2}{c}{City} | \multicolumn{2}{c}{Actual} |
|  | 1990 | 1991 | 1992 | 1993 | 1994 | 1995 |
| Popu | 12345 | 14343 | 15000 | 18087 |  |  |
| Famil | 92345 | 100232 | 130332 | 120233 |  |  |
| Picku | 23244 | 32344 | 56421 | 30545 |  |  |
| Van | 2343 | 10755 | 18930 | 15864 |  |  |

By default the labels in the model are in MS Sans Serif 10. Using Format, Label Style and then clicking on the Font... button in the Label Style dialog allows you to change this to any of the fonts you have available in a wide range of point sizes. Having accessed the Label Style dialog remember to use the Dimension drop-down list to select All Dimensions before clicking the Font... button. Then select the typeface and the point size required. Clicking on OK in the Font dialog returns you to the Label Style dialog. Click on the Apply button before closing this dialog box.

In this example we have used Arial 12 for the labels which spoils their column width adjustment and makes it necessary to adjust the row height. The width of the label column needs to be altered for each dimension but its row height only has to be set once. Both these modifications can be done interactively by dragging on the label cell dividers. Remember that when you want to make a number of columns the same width or rows the same height you have to select the range you want to adjust. A single change will then be repeated throughout the highlighted selection.

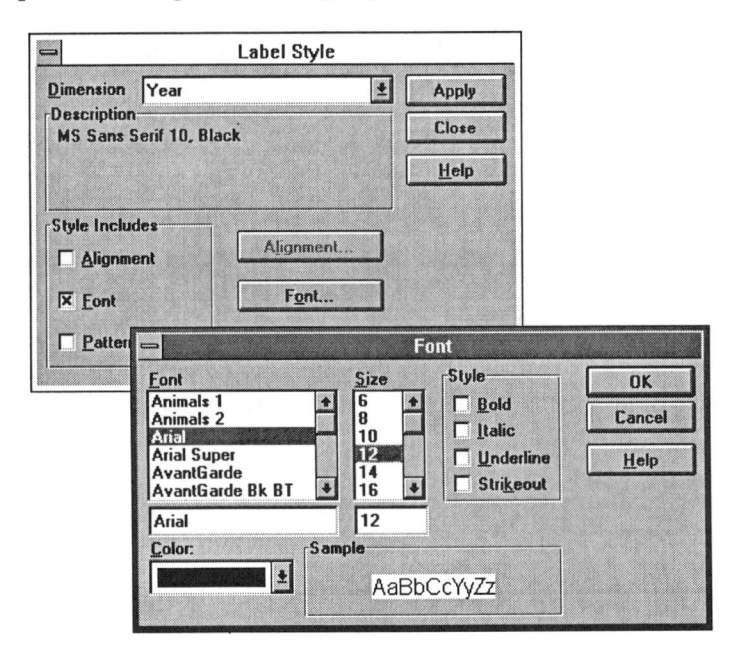

After setting the label column width and the label row height the next job is to set the column width and the row heights in the body of the model. Notice that here too the size of the item labels influences your choice. For example, all the numeric values in the model will fit into the default column widths but items names such as Popular and Out of Town don't. To solve this problem you have to manually adjust column widths with each dimension in turn acting as the horizontal visible dimension.

All the data in the model are currency values and so a currency numeric format applied to the entire model seems appropriate. To do this you simply select the entire visible portion of the model - by clicking on the corner between the row and column labels - and then use the Format All command - by clicking on the Format command while holding down the Shift key. From the Format All menu select the Number All command and finally a suitable currency format from the dialog box. Because the Format All command was used the number format is applied to the entire model and not just the visible dimensions.

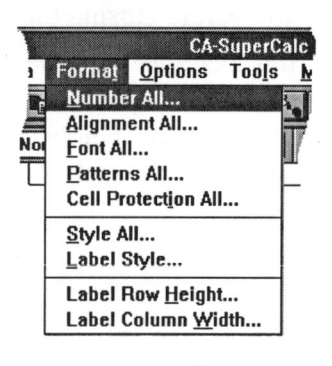

To allow the forecast values to be easily distinguished from the actual values, no matter what the view, it is worth defining a new 'forecast' style. The style used in our example simply sets the font to blue italic and leaves all other attributes unchanged. To define it use the command Format,Style. The Style dialog initially displays Normal as the Style Name with its current definition given in the Description box. Type in the new name Forecast and then click on the Define button.

*Formatting car sales* **95**

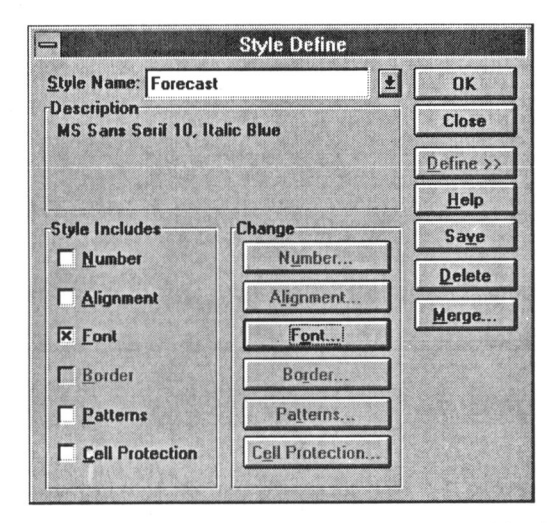

The only attribute we are interested in including in this new style is Font so uncheck the other boxes in the Style Define dialog and click on Font. Here there are two aspects to attend to. The first is to check the box besides Italic in the list headed Style. The second is to drop down the list of text colours and select blue.

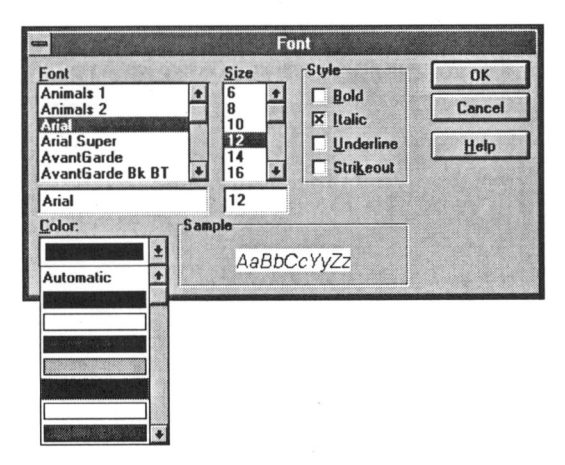

Having specified these two attributes close the Font dialog then close the Style Define by clicking on OK.

All that remains to do is to apply the new style to the item Forecast on the Budget dimension, that is to format a slice through the model. To do this pivot Budget to be one of the visible dimensions - the column dimension. Then select the Forecast column by clicking on its column header and then use the Style All command by pressing Shift while giving the Format command - then any view that you construct that shows forecast data will be displayed in blue italic.

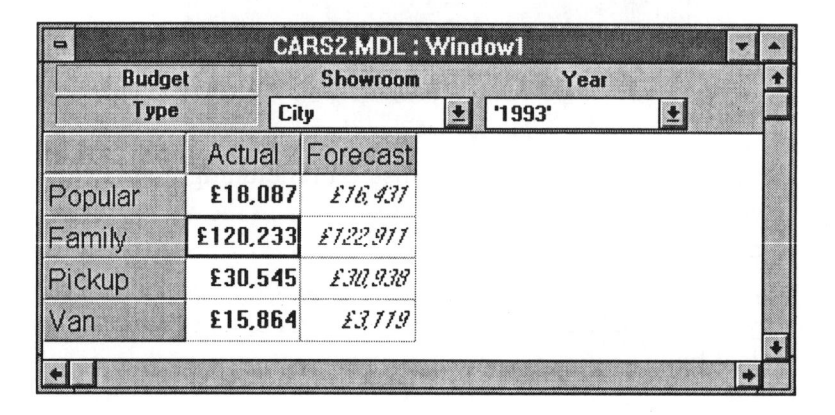

| | Actual | Forecast |
|---|---|---|
| Popular | £18,087 | *£16,431* |
| Family | £120,233 | *£122,911* |
| Pickup | £30,545 | *£30,938* |
| Van | £15,864 | *£3,119* |

Budget: Showroom / Year
Type: City / '1993'
(CARS2.MDL : Window1)

Even after this much attention you may still find views that the current format doesn't show well. In this case you should adjust row and column widths to suit. As you work with a model its format will eventually be refined to the point where all views are satisfactory.

## » Format checklist

Because of the way formatting affects a model there is a logical sequence that provides the most efficient way to work. After establishing the structure of a model you should:

> » Set the label styles. This should be done first because it determines the height needed for all label rows.

» Adjust the height of the label row to accommodate the largest point size used for the labels.

» Pivot the model so that each dimension becomes the vertical visible dimension. Set the label column width and the row heights for each one.

» Pivot the model so that each dimension becomes the horizontal visible dimension. Set the column widths for each dimension as required.

This sounds like a lot of work but if you are working with five dimensions there are only five views with each dimension playing the role of the horizontal visible dimension and five with each playing the role of the vertical visible dimension.

## Key points

» You can set a display format for any cell in the model. The display format does not alter what is stored in the cell, only how it appears.

» There are a range of attributes - format, font, colour, pattern, alignment etc. - that can be applied to any cell in the model.

» Attributes are best handled by being grouped together into named styles. Applying a named style only changes those attributes that are defined for it.

» You can apply format attributes to slices of the model using the Format All command - select Format while holding down the Shift key.

» The order that you apply formats to slices is important.

» Try to discover item names that imply a particular type of format - e.g. an item called Cost is likely to be associated with currency format data.

» You can create additional windows to view the model with different visible dimensions and fixed items. Formatting is the same in each window.

» You can set row height and column width interactively or by specifying a value in a dialog box.

» The item style can be set and you can alter the space allocated to the fixed dimension and display the dimension name.

# Chapter 7

# Page Models

There is a very special type of multidimensional model that is simple, fits a great many situations and can provide a pathway to more complex models. Page models are essentially two-dimensional in their structure but they need to be implemented as multidimensional models simply because the two-dimensional structure repeats itself like the pages in a book - hence the name "page model".

In this chapter we examine page models both as useful templates in their own right and as more practice in making use of the multidimensional facilities of SCW.

## » Pages

A common occurrence when using any traditional 2D spreadsheet is to discover that the data that has been entered recurs on a regular basis. For example, you may have recorded and analysed the sales figures for different products and different sites - only to discover that you need a new copy of the spreadsheet for each month or quarter. Equally you might set up a spreadsheet to record the progress of a member of staff undergoing training - only to discover that the same spreadsheet would be useful for each member of staff.

In each of these cases there is the need to have multiple copies of the same 2D spreadsheet. The traditional approach is to have exactly this - one instance of the spreadsheet for each situation in which it is required. If you have used SuperCalc 5 or a similar 3D spreadsheet you will already know about the alternative method of constructing a single 3D spreadsheet.

The 3D spreadsheet can be considered to be a equivalent to a "book" of 2D pages and the extension to 3D is really just a way of keeping the related spreadsheets together. Each page is usually indexed by a "page number" that provides no information as to the purpose of the page. As well as serving as a way of keeping the related data together it is also usually possible to form summary pages which total or average the data.

## » A 3D page model

Of course there is absolutely no problem in constructing a 3D page model using SCW. All you have to do is create two suitable visible dimensions to allow you to set up each page and a third, fixed, dimension to act as the index.

## A 3D page model 101

For example, if you want to record sales data for a particular item in each country it is sold for each quarter you would customise the default model as follows:

```
┌─────────────────── WORLD.MDL : Window1 ───────────────┐
│       Area           Quarter                           │
│      Volumes        │ Q1  │▼│                          │
│              │ UK │ France │ Germany │ Spain │ USA │   │
│  Number      │    │        │         │       │     │   │
│  Unit price  │    │        │         │       │     │   │
│  Total sales │    │        │         │       │     │   │
└────────────────────────────────────────────────────────┘
```

The country and sales data dimensions and items have to be set up by renaming each one but there is a short cut way to enter the quarters. All you have to do is pivot the model so that the Quarters is one of the visible dimensions. Then enter Q1 as the first item and delete the remaining items. Now when place the cursor on any cell in the Q1 column and drag you automatically create Q2, Q3 and so on. After you have finished creating new items pivot the model so that Quarter is again the fixed dimension.

The item being sold is priced in the currency of each country. To allow for additional costs and to achieve a psychologically "good" price, simple conversion of a base price using a currency exchange rate isn't sufficient. In other words, the product is priced independently in each country. This causes us no problems except for the need to actually enter the pricing data. Once the unit prices are entered the Total sales figures can be calculated using

$$=Number*Unit\ price$$

If this is converted into a global formula with scope

$$Area.Total\ sales.Q1$$

then as long as the formula is applied to its scope it calculates the entire row of Total sales.

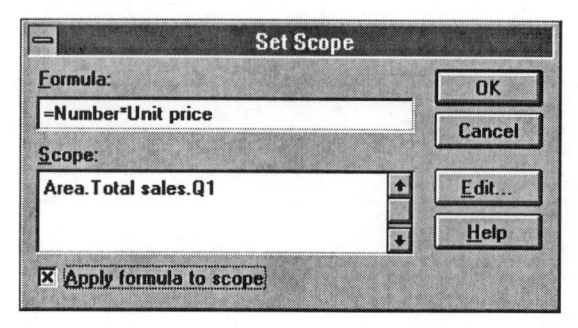

[Dialog box: Set Scope — Formula: =Number*Unit price; Scope: Area.Total sales.Q1; ☒ Apply formula to scope; buttons: OK, Cancel, Edit..., Help]

To make it absolutely clear that each currency value is in a different unit it is worth defining new numeric formats and new styles for each country. The numeric currency formats for each country are

| | |
|---|---|
| UK | >=0?£#,##0;Sign-£#,##0 |
| Germany | >=0?#,##0" Dm";Sign-#,##0" Dm" |
| Spain | >=0?#,##0" pta";Sign-#,##0" pta" |
| France | >=0?#,##0" FFr";Sign-#,##0" FFr" |
| USA | >=0?"$"#,##0;Sign-"$"#,##0 |

and these should be entered using the Format,Number command and dialog box by selecting one of the already defined currency options listed and then editing it in the Format box below the list. Notice that the sample gives an instance of the new format.

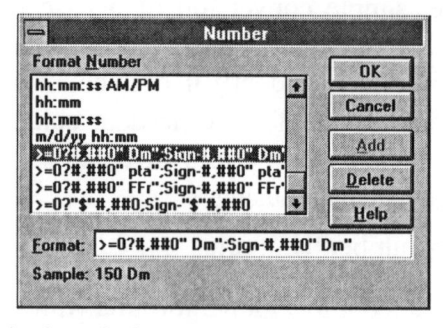

[Dialog box: Format Number — list including hh:mm:ss AM/PM, hh:mm, hh:mm:ss, m/d/yy hh:mm, >=0?#,##0" Dm";Sign-#,##0" Dm", >=0?#,##0" pta";Sign-#,##0" pta", >=0?#,##0" FFr";Sign-#,##0" FFr", >=0?"$"#,##0;Sign-"$"#,##0; Format: >=0?#,##0" Dm";Sign-#,##0" Dm"; Sample: 150 Dm; buttons: OK, Cancel, Add, Delete, Help]

Although it isn't strictly necessary, it is reasonable to define a style for each country's currency. The reason why this isn't necessary is that each style only controls one format attribute, i.e. the numeric format, but if changes to the way that country specific data should be displayed are needed a style is the easiest way to do this. For example, if you wanted to present each country's currency data with a background of a national colour - then redefining the style would achieve this automatically!

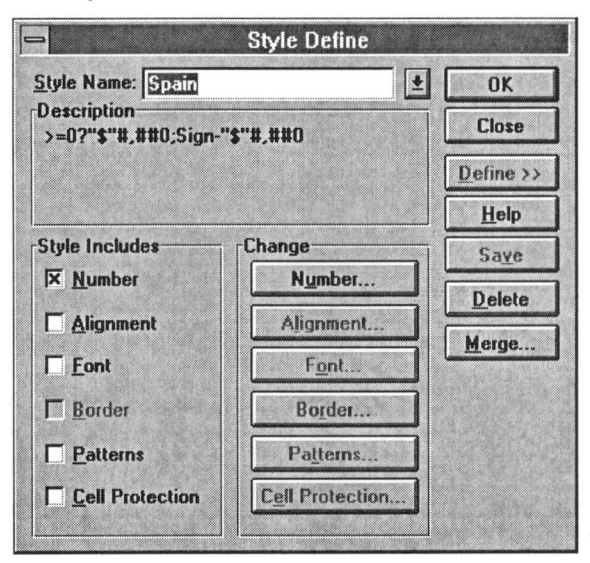

*Style Define dialog box showing Style Name: Spain, Description: >=0?"$"#,##0;Sign-"$"#,##0, with Style Includes (Number checked, Alignment, Font, Border, Patterns, Cell Protection) and Change buttons for each, plus OK, Close, Define>>, Help, Save, Delete, Merge buttons.*

After a style has been defined for each country the appropriate style can be applied to Unit price and Total sales for each country. The resulting view of the model is now complete, fully functional, and ready to receive data.

| | UK | France | Germany | Spain | USA |
|---|---|---|---|---|---|
| Number | 15 | 20 | 7 | 5 | 10 |
| Unit price | £10 | 100 FFr | 30 Dm | 2,000 pta | $20 |
| Total sales | £150 | 2,000 FFr | 210 Dm | 10,000 pta | $200 |

Area / Quarter / Volumes Q1 — WORLD2.MDL : Window1

## » Formatting pages

Notice that while this model was under construction the third dimension, i.e. Quarter, played no role at all. As far as the creation of the model is concerned all we are dealing with is a 2D spreadsheet. This approach has the advantage of simplification. It is easier to work out the details of the model in 2D than try to think of all of the multidimensional details. However, the disadvantage soon becomes apparent when we "turn the page" to start working on a new quarter's data. The new 2D spreadsheet is essentially blank and lacks any structure, apart from the dimension labels.

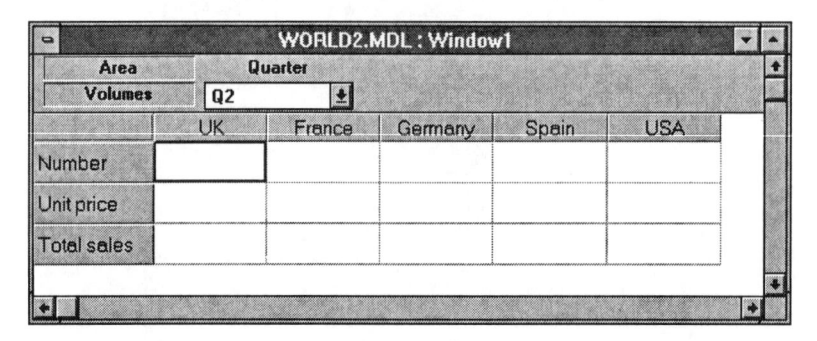

By now some of the solutions to the problem of making the second page work should be obvious. For example, to get the formula that works out Total sales to function on the second page all that is necessary is to extend its scope and apply it. If you thought first of copying the necessary formula then you are still thinking in terms of traditional 2D spreadsheets! The appropriate scope for

=Number*Unit price

is

Area.Total sales.Quarter

and the formula should be applied to its entire scope. Notice that this makes the formula active for every item on the Quarter dimension and so active on every "page".

Now we come to a slightly more subtle problem. What to do about the Unit prices? In this case copies of the unit prices are required on each "page" and the temptation is indeed to think in terms of making real copies of the values concerned. However, there is an alternative. A constant value can be treated as a global formula and so the unit prices could be applied to the appropriate scope. Which method is better? If you know in advance that the unit prices are likely to change then make copies and edit the individual values. If you are going to treat the unit prices as constants for the model then convert them into global formulae.

As a demonstration of how constant global formulae can be used, each of the unit prices entered on the first page are converted to global formulae with scopes that include the entire Quarter dimension. For example, the unit price in the UK has scope

> UK.Unit price.Quarter

Notice that if you edit the unit price for any country on any page then you have the option of entering the change as a cell level formula or as an update to the global formula.

Now we have a working 2D spreadsheet for Q2 and for that matter for Q3, Q4 and so on. The only remaining problem is that the formatting that was applied to the first page now has to be applied to each of the subsequent pages. Rather than doing this as a repetitive task it is much simpler to apply a format to a slice using the Format All option. For example, select the UK column on any page, select Format while holding down the Shift key and finally the Style All option. In the Style dialog box that appears select the UK style. After this all values associated with the item UK will show in the UK currency style. Repeating this for each of the other items on the Country dimension formats the entire model.

Unfortunately formatting all of the values associated with each country item in the same way isn't quite what is required! After you have finished this formatting task you will probably notice that the Number sold for each country is formatted in the national currency. The solution to this problem is to select the Number item and use Format All, Number All to set its slice to General. Now all of the pages are formatted correctly. Notice how the order of formatting has been used to obtain the desired result.

## » Using pivoting

Although the model has been constructed as a set of two-dimensional pages the fact that it really was multidimensional has been used to apply global formulae, global constants and formatting. A more direct benefit of using the multidimensional approach is that the model can be pivoted to provide more appropriate views. For example, what could be better for data entry than a view that has Country as the horizontal visible dimension and Quarter as the vertical visible dimension with Number as the fixed item.

| | UK | France | Germany | Spain | USA |
|---|---|---|---|---|---|
| Q1 | 15 | 20 | 7 | 5 | 10 |
| Q2 | 20 | 30 | 25 | 2 | 20 |
| Q3 | 25 | 5 | 50 | 2 | 50 |
| Q4 | 22 | 8 | 80 | 4 | 33 |

In general you may find that there are models in which the page structure is so strong that very few other views are useful. You will also have to take account of the need to alter the label row and column width and height.

## » Adding a summary page

Nearly all page models include some sort of summary page. In this example what is needed are the totals for Number and Totals Sales for each country over all quarters. By now you should be well ahead and working out what the scope of the necessary global formula is! The first thing that is needed is an additional item on the Quarter's dimension call Totals. This and subsequent operations are easier if the model is pivoted to make Quarter the vertical visible dimension.

Into one of the new cells enter the formula

=SUM(Q1:Q4)

Next use the Global button to convert this into a global formula with scope

Area.Totals.(Number,Total sales)

Notice that the range on the Volumes dimension doesn't include Unit Price. Summing unit price would not give any useful information!

| Area | Quarter | | | | |
|---|---|---|---|---|---|
| Volumes | Totals | | | | |
| | UK | France | Germany | Spain | USA |
| Number | 82 | 63 | 162 | 13 | 113 |
| Unit price | | | | | |
| Total sales | £820 | 6,300 FFr | 4,860 Dm | 26,000 pta | $2,260 |

It usually is this easy to add a summary page to a model!

## » Imported page models

One common source of page models is the import of existing SC5 3D spreadsheets. In this case the model that is constructed to hold the imported 3D spreadsheet has dimensions called Row, Column and Page and items 1, 2, 3..., A, B, C... and Page1, Page2 and so on. These dimension names and item names are chosen to make the model look as much like a 3D spreadsheet as possible but in practice a great deal of conversion work has to be performed to make the imported model actually useful. In particular labels within the body of the spreadsheet have to be converted into dimension labels, formulae have to be converted into more appropriate global forms and formats have to be rationalised. None of this work is difficult if you know about multidimensional models - but it is tedious. For more information, and an example of the conversion 3D spreadsheet for recording sales of wines, see Chapter 11 of *Mastering CA-SuperCalc for Windows*.

|     | A | B | C | D | E | F | G |
|-----|---|---|---|---|---|---|---|
| 1 | Sales of Red Wine | | | | | | |
| 2 | April 1991 | | | | | | |
| 3 | | Bordeaux | Bordeaux | Burgundy | Rioja | Rioja | Total |
| 4 | | 78 | 83 | 86 | 86 | 87 | |
| 5 | High Street | 406 | 789 | 343 | 376 | 256 | 2170 |
| 6 | Market Place | 236 | 348 | 204 | 340 | 503 | 1631 |
| 7 | Long Lane | 68 | 134 | 172 | 38 | 143 | 555 |
| 8 | Back Avenue | 55 | 76 | 160 | 52 | 26 | 369 |
| 9 | | | | | | | |
| 10 | Total | 765 | 1347 | 879 | 806 | 928 | 4725 |

(WINE1.MDL : Window1 — COL, PAGE, ROW, PAGE1)

Notice that there is nothing stopping you from creating models with dimensions called Row, Column and Page and working in an environment that looks more like an SC5 3D spreadsheet. However, if you do this you will almost certainly be missing the many important advantages of MDMs.

## » More than 3D

The international sales example is typical of a page model and the tendency is to think that all page models are 3D. This is partly due to the simplicity of the 3D model and partly because pages are usually indexed by only a single item - the page number. However, there is no reason why a page model should not be indexed by multiple dimensions.

For example, if you needed to keep records of unit trust investments for a number of different people at monthly intervals you could build a simple four-dimensional model.

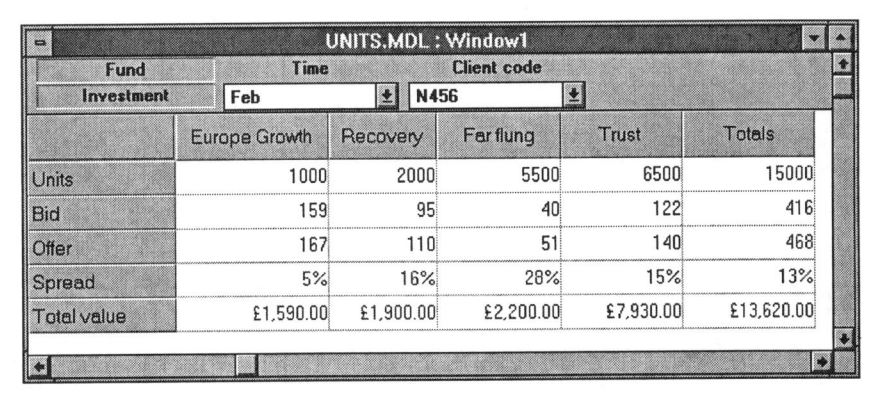

| UNITS.MDL : Window1 | | | | | |
|---|---|---|---|---|---|
| Fund | Time | | Client code | | |
| Investment | Feb | | N456 | | |
|  | Europe Growth | Recovery | Far flung | Trust | Totals |
| Units | 1000 | 2000 | 5500 | 6500 | 15000 |
| Bid | 159 | 95 | 40 | 122 | 416 |
| Offer | 167 | 110 | 51 | 140 | 468 |
| Spread | 5% | 16% | 28% | 15% | 13% |
| Total value | £1,590.00 | £1,900.00 | £2,200.00 | £7,930.00 | £13,620.00 |

Essentially this has a page structure in that all of the calculations refer to data in a 2D spreadsheet selected by the items on the two fixed dimensions.

## » Indexing dimensions

This example uses two indexing dimensions, Time and Client Code. To reach the page of information you want to view select the appropriate period and code from the fixed dimensions' drop down lists.

The ability to use the fixed dimensions as indexes allows page models to be used to store a great deal of data in a single file and be able to access manageable chunks of the information rapidly and easily. For example, if you needed to keep records of annual performance and exam marks for school pupils over their entire school careers you might set up a model with the pupils names and school years as the index dimensions.

This arrangement gives you a page per student for every year of his school career with each page showing the performance in every subject studied.

| Subject Performance | Name 'Butler, S.J' | Year Year 2 | | | | | |
|---|---|---|---|---|---|---|---|
| | French | English | Physics | Biology | Chemistry | Maths | History |
| Class work | 70 | 78 | 75 | 76 | 75 | 75 | 80 |
| Homework | 54 | 85 | 70 | 70 | 78 | 70 | 84 |
| Project | 67 | 88 | 72 | 75 | 78 | 72 | 92 |
| Mid-year Exam | 50 | 76 | 74 | 75 | 74 | 74 | 90 |
| Year-end exam | 66 | 84 | 78 | 75 | 78 | 78 | 95 |
| Weighted score | 60.6 | 81.9 | 74.5 | 74.6 | 76.5 | 74.5 | 90.3 |
| Minimum | 50 | 76 | 70 | 70 | 74 | 70 | 80 |
| Maximum | 70 | 88 | 78 | 76 | 78 | 78 | 95 |

*SCHOOL.MDL : Window1*

For the purposes of entering the data, however, a class register arrangement of the data with one subject per page is probably more appropriate. This can easily be arranged by swapping the positions of dimensions so that subject (which can be considered as a third index) is a fixed dimension with the pupil's names displayed one per row.

| SCHOOL.MDL : Window1 | | | | | | | | |
|---|---|---|---|---|---|---|---|---|
| Performance | Year | | Subject | | | | | |
| Name | Year 3 | | Biology | | | | | |
| | Class work | Homework | Project | Mid-year Exam | Year-end exam | Weighted score | Minimum | Maximum |
| Butler, S.J | 76 | 70 | 75 | 75 | 75 | 74.6 | 70 | 76 |
| Cooper, G.H | 55 | 55 | 60 | 55 | 58 | 56.9 | 55 | 60 |
| Davidson, J.A | 69 | 68 | 69 | 68 | 70 | 68.9 | 68 | 70 |
| Edwards, B.L | 70 | 75 | 75 | 75 | 78 | 75.4 | 70 | 78 |
| Frankston, K | 55 | 60 | 55 | 52 | 58 | 55.5 | 52 | 60 |
| Grant, A.B | 77 | 76 | 78 | 69 | 72 | 73.2 | 69 | 78 |
| Hopkins, F.G | 80 | 80 | 84 | 84 | 86 | 83.6 | 80 | 86 |
| Humphries, M | 66 | 66 | 70 | 69 | 68 | 68.3 | 66 | 70 |
| Knight, B | 95 | 92 | 87 | 88 | 82 | 87.1 | 82 | 95 |
| Marshall, T | 78 | 69 | 68 | 66 | 74 | 70.3 | 66 | 78 |
| Morrison, D.F | 75 | 75 | 75 | 78 | 76 | 76.2 | 75 | 78 |
| Moxon, J.A | 60 | 55 | 58 | 40 | 49 | 49.6 | 40 | 60 |
| Powell, C.J | 80 | 84 | 84 | 86 | 84 | 84.2 | 80 | 86 |
| Robertson, R.R | 77 | 76 | 78 | 69 | 68 | 72 | 68 | 78 |
| Sadler, F.S | 80 | 84 | 84 | 83 | 86 | 83.9 | 80 | 86 |
| Simpkins, N | 94 | 95 | 93 | 95 | 92 | 93.6 | 92 | 95 |
| Stavely, T.H | 79 | 77 | 76 | 78 | 69 | 74.9 | 69 | 79 |
| Thompson, A.B | | | 68 | 70 | 75 | 75 | 73.5 | 68 | 77 |
| Thompson, C.S | 55 | 58 | 55 | 60 | 55 | 56.8 | 55 | 60 |
| Watkins, D.H | 93 | 95 | 93 | 95 | 92 | 93.5 | 92 | 95 |

## » Large models

The same idea can be generalised to as many indexing dimensions as you require - up to the 12-dimensional limit of SCW of course! For example you might add the dimension Gender to this model to distinguish between the school records of boys and girls. The advantages of using models to organise large quantities of data are obvious but as a result you are likely to find yourself building large models.

It is worth noting that recalculation of large models can become tedious so it is worth setting recalculation to manual to avoid the interruptions that unwanted recalculation would otherwise cause.

# Key points

» The simplest of all models has a page structure - that is where the multidimensional aspect of the model comes from having more than one copy of the same basic page.

» Page models are useful in their own right and as the starting point for more complex MDMs.

» It is important to use the multidimensional features of SCW to extend the structure of a single page to other pages. Do not be tempted to copy formulae or constant data - use global formulae or constants.

» The simple structure of repeated pages is often broken by the need for a summary page which has formulae forming totals and average over ranges that span pages.

» Page models arise naturally when 3D SC5 spreadsheets are imported.

» Although many page models are 3D they can have more than one indexing dimension.

» Using multiple indexing dimensions can lead to the construction of large models.

# Chapter 8

# Structure, Range and Scope

You can think of the global formulae as forming the structure of a model - that is the part that calculates the results from the data stored in it. The way that ranges and scopes are specified in SCW makes it easy to work in multidimensions and this is the prime reason for not using the traditional corner to corner range of the 2D spreadsheet. However, there are other advantages to using the model style of specifying ranges that make it superior in other respects.

In this chapter we take a close look at how ranges and scopes are "self adjusting" to changes in the model, in particular how they behave when items are inserted. If you already know the concepts of absolute and relative cell references in the case of 2D spreadsheets you need to be careful not to simply apply these ideas to ranges in a model. Model cell references behave in a very different way.

## » Absolute but self adjusting

We have already seen the way that underspecification makes a formula "read correctly" at a new location. If you enter the formula

=SUM(B1:B3)

into a cell then any unspecified dimensions will be taken to be the same as the cell in which it is stored. If the formula is applied at a new location then it will still sum the range B1:B3 but using cells that have the same item values as the new cell. Looked at another way, it appears as if the formula always sums the same range of cells relative to the cell in which it is stored.

|    | A 1 | A 2 | A 3 | A 4 |
|----|-----|-----|-----|-----|
| B1 |     |     |     |     |
| B2 | A1.(B1:B3) |  | A3.(B1:B3) |  |
| B3 |     |     |     |     |
| B4 | =SUM(B1:B3) |  | =SUM(B1:B3) |  |
| B5 |     |     |     |     |

Because of underspecification the formula sums the same range relative to the cell it is stored in

If you know about 2D spreadsheets you will think that this is nothing more than a relative range reference - it isn't because the items Male and Female are very definitely absolute. If you try moving the formula into a cell that has an item value different to any of the specified dimensions then the range will not "follow" the formula in that dimension. For example, in the case of =SUM(B1:B3) the formula will sum B1:B3 no matter what the item value is on the BB dimension of the cell it is stored in.

|    | A 1 | A 2 | A 3 | A 4 |
|----|-----|-----|-----|-----|
| B1 |     |     |     |     |
| B2 | A1.(B1:B3) |   | A3.(B1:B3) |   |
| B3 |     |     |     |     |
| B4 | =SUM(B1:B3) |   |     |   |
| B5 |     |     | =SUM(B1:B3) |   |

**but if you move or apply the formula to a cell that has a different value on the BB dimension it sums the same range**

One way of summarising this is to say that a cell or range reference is relative as far as the unspecified dimensions are concerned but absolute as far as the specified dimensions are concerned. However, this terminology harks back to the 2D spreadsheet. A better way of putting it might be to say that any item that is explicitly mentioned in a reference is never altered or reinterpreted by SCW in any way.

All that really matters is that you understand the way that cell and range specifications work well enough to appreciate the effects of moving or applying a formula at any location.

Notice that the question of whether or not the range specification used in a global formula's scope is absolute or relative never arises. Why? Simply because the scope specifies where the formula can be applied and there is no sense in which anything can move to change this.

## » Relative references

By now the behaviour of an underspecified cell reference or range should be well known to you. Explicit item references are always absolute. If you say =SUM(B1:B3) the B1:B3 part of the range is always the same, no matter where the formula is stored or applied, but what if you want to sum from the cell 3 above down to the cell 1 above the current location of the formula? What you really do want is to make the B1:B3 part of the range reference relative as well as the unspecified dimensions? The answer is that you can use a true relative reference. If you write

*dim*[*n*]

were *dim* is a dimension name then this is taken to be a reference to the cell *n* items "away" from the current cell. For example, AA[1] is the next item to the right (or down) on the AA dimension, AA[0] is the same item as the current cell and AA[-1] is the item to the left (or up). You can, of course use values of *n* bigger than one to refer to items a greater distance away. Obviously if you use relative references in a range then the range is always relative to the cell that it is stored in.

|    | A 1 | A 2 | A 3 | A 4 |
|----|-----|-----|-----|-----|
| B1 |     | ← BB[-3] |   |   |
| B2 | A1.(B1:B3) |   |   | ← BB[-3] |
| B3 |     | ← BB[-1] | A3.(B2:B4) |   |
| B4 | =SUM(BB[-3]:BB[-1]) |   |   | ← BB[-1] |
| B5 |     |     | =SUM(BB[-3]:BB[-1]) |   |

### Relative references are truly relative to the cell that they are stored in.

You can mix absolute and relative references within a single range. For example, if you wanted to sum a range that included the first item on the dimension to the item just before the cell that the formula was stored in you could use

=SUM(B1:BB[-1])

No matter where you stored this formula it would add up all the values from item B1 to the cell just above where it was stored.

## » Relative pointing

If you enter a cell reference by pointing at it using the mouse then by default it is entered as an absolute reference. You can, however, change it to a relative reference using the command Formula,Reference or by pressing the F4 key. Each time you press the F4 key or use the command the reference changes from relative to absolute or absolute back to relative. If you have entered a formula which contains a number of references then the Formula,Reference command changes all of them in a single action. If you only want to change a single reference from absolute to relative or vice versa then you need to select it by dragging. In this case only the highlighted references are changed by the command.

## » Names

One of the best ways of simplifying the use of range references is to assign them names. This is more or less identical to the name facility in traditional 2D spreadsheets and shares all of the features of the name facility used in SCW sheets. To create a name you use the command Formula,Define Name which displays the Define Name dialog box.

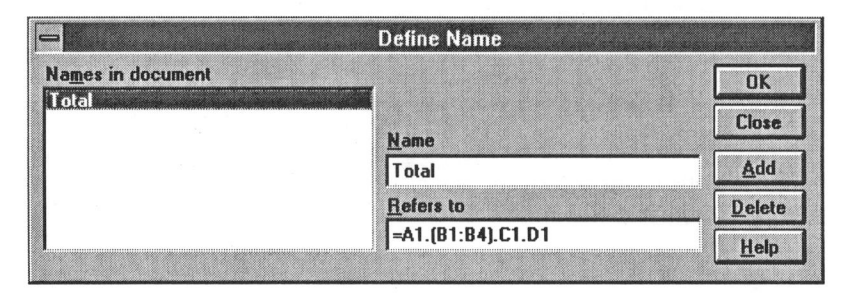

![Define Name dialog box showing Names in document: Total; Name: Total; Refers to: =A1.(B1:B4).C1.D1; with OK, Close, Add, Delete, Help buttons]

You can use this to enter the range reference and the name that you want to assign to it. By default the range you have selected before you use the command is shown in the Refers to box.

Once you have assigned a range a name it can be used in formulae in place of the range. For example, once you have defined the range name Total you can write =SUM(Total) and the formula will add up the contents of all of the cells include in the range Total. Notice that the name is absolute or relative according to whether its definition is absolute or relative and you have to take full account of underspecification in interpreting its meaning at any particular location.

Names can be used to store commonly used formulae and even constants. For example, if you define the name PI to be =3.14159 then anywhere you use the name PI the constant 3.14159 is substituted. This aspect of names is fully described in Chapter 3 of *Mastering CA-SuperCalc for Windows* but in most cases it is better to avoid using names for formulae. The reason is that global formulae provide a better way to control the application of a single formula to a range of cells within a model. Indeed there is an argument that naming ranges isn't a good idea. If you have assigned sensible names to the dimensions and their items then ranges and formulae that make use of them will also make sensible reading! In other words the use of named dimensions and named items reduces the need to name ranges.

If you define a name after entering formulae that make use of the same range you can convert all such formulae to make use of the new name using the Formula,Apply command. This displays the Apply Names dialog box.

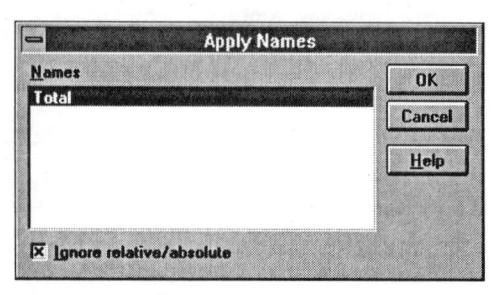

Using this you can select which name you want to apply and whether or not relative/absolute differences should be taken into account. If you select the Ignore relative/absolute box then the name will be substituted for any range that matches the range to which the name refers. If you uncheck this box then the range has to match the definition of the range name exactly - including which items are relative and which are absolute. No matter which option you choose only ranges that are currently identical to the name's definition will be replaced by the name. That is, no change to the working of the model can come about by applying names. However, what does alter is the behaviour of a formula when it is moved, copied or applied to a different cell. If the absolute and relative components of the range references have been changed by applying a name then the result that you get when the formula is used at a new location will be different.

The biggest problem with Formula,Apply names is that it is difficult to undo. The simplest solution is to use the Formula,Replace command to replace every occurrence of the name with its range definition.

This cannot, of course, restore any changes made to the absolute and relative parts of a reference.

Finally it is worth mentioning the use of the Formula,Create Names command to convert labels into range names. In a traditional 2D spreadsheet this is very useful because using text labels entered into cells is the only way to give rows and columns of data meaningful names. The command uses the labels in the top or bottom row or in the left- or right-hand column of a range to create names for the corresponding columns or rows. The range names can then be used within formulae and they correspond to the labels used within the spreadsheet.

You can still do this in a model but if you find that you need or want to use this facility then are you are probably not making proper use of the model. A model usually has little need of text labels within the body of the model. The reason is simply that the item names on each dimension serve the same purpose. If you need to label rows or columns and find yourself using the Formula,Create Names command then you need to re-examine the way that you are using SCW models.

## » Formulae - range and scope

*The material in this section is advanced and can be skipped on first reading.*

Now that we are so far into the theory of using formulae and global formulae it is worth spending a moment to consider the two uses of range references. A range reference within a formula defines which cells it uses to compute its own value. In this case the most important feature is how the range reference behaves when the formula is used in a new location. In other words, what concerns us most are the absolute and relative aspects of the range references.

For a global formula the other type of range reference that is of importance is its scope. This is an absolute range reference that defines exactly where the formula can be applied. That is, where it can calculate a result. Clearly the range references within the formula have to be interpreted from each location to which it is applied within its scope and as such the range and scope interact in important ways.

If you consider a formula's range as the collection of all of the cells that it uses to work out its result then it is obvious that range and scope do not overlap, i.e. they do not include the same cells. Why? The reason is simply that the scope specifies where the formula can be used (i.e. be applied) and so it makes little sense to allow the formula to be applied to a cell that it uses to compute its own results.

Range= (B1:B4)

|    | A 1 | A 2 | A 3 | A 4 |
|----|-----|-----|-----|-----|
| B1 |     |     |     |     |
| B2 |     |     |     |     |
| B3 |     |     |     |     |
| B4 |     |     |     |     |
| B5 | =SUM(B1:B4) |     |     |     |

Scope= (A1:A4).B5

A formula's range and scope do not overlap!

What is more, this is also true if you consider all of the ranges that the formula uses when applied to each cell in its scope. There are some rare and advanced occasions where it is advantageous to have scope and range overlapping - but not many.

The importance of the observation that range and scope do not overlap is that you can use it to detect errors of specification and to make absolutely clear you understand both concepts.

There is another, and slightly more subtle, connection between range and scope. As the scope specifies where the formula can be applied, the range will usually specify the same set of cells relative to each cell in the scope. This is a difficult idea to appreciate at first but it is simply that the formula is presumably capable of performing the same calculation from each cell in the scope and so the range of cells it uses will change to be appropriate for each cell in the scope. Notice that this doesn't imply that the range is relative to every cell in the model. For example, the formula =SUM(B1:B4) with scope (A1:A4).B5 certainly doesn't have a relative range reference. If you move =SUM(B1:B4) to B6 say then the range summed will still be B1:B4. That is, it is absolute when copied to a new cell in the BB dimension. However, if the formula is moved to any cell in its scope the summed range does change and does behave as if it were relative. Of course, the reason for this is that the relative nature of the range reference comes from its underspecification on the AA dimension.

This is no accident because it is an example of a general principle. The ranges used in global formulae are nearly always underspecified in the dimensions that have multiple items in their scope. In the case of =SUM(B1:B4) the AA dimension is underspecified because a range of AA items are included in its scope i.e. (A1:A4). Often the relationship between the scope and the underspecified dimensions is even more striking. In many cases the underspecified dimensions occur in their entirety in the scope. For example, =SUM(B1:B4) is underspecified on the AA dimension and its scope might well be defined as AA.B5.

You might be wondering what use the connection between the range and the scope is? The answer is two-fold in that it will help you understand the ideas better and provides a simple check that you have specified the range and the scope of a global formula correctly. It may also suggest to you what the maximum scope of a global formula could be and so provide you with a starting point in constructing a more restricted scope.

To summarise:

» The range that a function uses and the scope to which it can be applied divide up the model into non-overlapping ranges.

» The dimensions and dimension ranges used in a function's scope are usually not included in a function's range or ranges.

# » Inserting and deleting items

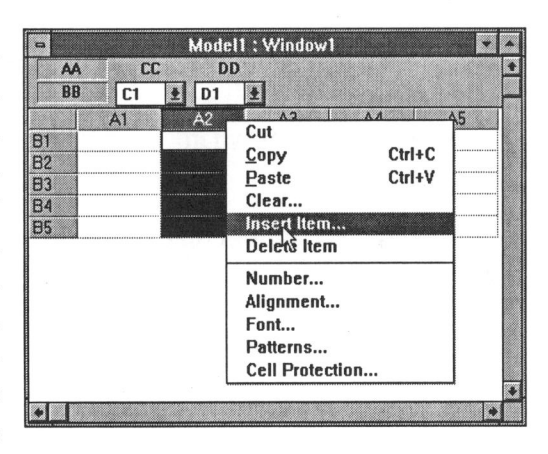

Even when a model is supposedly complete the need to insert and delete items often arises. Deleting and inserting items is easy enough. To delete an item you select it and use the command Edit,Delete Item - which is also available on the pop-up menu that appears if you click the right mouse button while an item is selected. Notice that you have to have an item selected and not just a cell in the same row or column. Also notice that you cannot delete or insert items on the fixed dimensions. In other words you have to pivot the model to make any dimension on which you want to insert or delete items one of the visible dimensions. Because of this it is always possible to think in terms of inserting or deleting a row or column of the model.

Inserting an item is just as simple. You first select an item at the position where you want to insert a new item and use the command Edit, Insert Item which is also on the pop-up menu. As far as the insert operation goes there is one minor complication in that you can choose to insert the new item before or after the selected item.

## » Surgery on models

What is more interesting is the way that ranges are adjusted to take account of item deletion and insertion. In other words how do models behave when you make structural changes?

There are two situations that have to be considered when you delete an item - what happens when the item is within a range and what happens when you delete an item that is on the edge of a range.

If you delete an item that is:

» within a range reference
there is no change to the range reference. For example, if you delete A2 then there is no change to =SUM(A1:A5).

» the start or end of an absolute range
the reference is changed to make the range smaller. For example, if you delete item A1 then =SUM(A1:A5) is changed to =SUM(A2:A5). If you delete A5 it is changed to =SUM(A1:A4) and so on. If it is impossible to make the range any smaller for example, =SUM(A1:A1) when A1 is deleted, or if the reference is a simple cell reference then a #REF error results.

» the start or the end of a relative range
there is no change to the range reference but the range of cells actually referenced clearly changes.

Inserting new items is actually a simpler situation because you cannot insert an item to become the new "edge" of the range - an item is either inserted into a range or outside a range. If you insert an item that is:

» within a range
no changes are made to the range reference but the range is naturally increased by the insertion. For example, if you insert Anew before A3 then =SUM(A1:A5) is unchanged but it now also sums the cells corresponding to the Anew item.

» outside a range
no changes are made to the range reference and the range of cells actually referenced stays the same. For example, if you insert Anew before A1 then =SUM(A1:A5) is unchanged and still sums the same cells.

## » Moving items can be harmful

The behaviour of ranges when items are inserted and deleted is very similar to the way ranges behave in standard 2D spreadsheets. However, in models you have another way of changing the structure. You can move items so as to rearrange their order on their dimension.

For example the default model usually has items A1, A2 and so on on the AA dimension but you are free to reorder these items simply by dragging them to their new locations. When you first encounter this idea of moving items around within their dimension it is natural to assume that this has no serious effect on the model. This is true if the model consists of nothing but data. However, if the model has formulae then reordering items could have very serious consequences. The reason is that modifications to take account of item reordering and not made to both absolute and relative range references.

For example, if you move B1 to be the second item on the BB dimension then the effect on the formula =SUM(B1:B4) is that it no longer sums item B2! You can see from this simple example that reordering items can have major and perhaps even devastating effects on the way that a model works.

|    | A1          |
|----|-------------|
| B2 |             |
| B1 |             |
| B3 |             |
| B4 |             |
| B5 | =SUM([B1:B4]) |

This is so serious a problem that:

» You should never reorder items after formulae have been included in a model unless you are completely clear about the resulting effect.

## » Renaming items is safe

As well as moving items you can also rename them. After the discussion of the dangers of moving you might expect this to be equally dangerous. Surprisingly it isn't at all dangerous from the point of view of the functioning of the model - but it may be from the point of view of your understanding of the model. If you rename an item any reference to that item is changed to use the new name. For example, if you rename the item B1 to Start then the formula =SUM(B1:B4) is automatically changed to =SUM(Start:B4). Of course relative references are not changed nor are they affected by renaming.

The functioning of the model is not, and cannot be, altered by a name change but your understanding can be impaired. If you have developed a model using one name for an often referenced item then changing that name could make something that has become familiar into something that looks very different. Make all name changes as soon as you can in the life of a model so that you can develop the model using a standard set of item and dimension names.

## » Duplicate item names

It happens more often than you would think that two items on the same dimension end up with the same name. Sometimes it is a simple consequence of using a short descriptive name. For example, it is tempting to call every item that serves to accumulate totals "Totals". For the same reason you will occasionally create two items on different dimensions with the same name. For example, Totals on the Education dimension and Totals on the Gender dimension in the Education model.

| Education | Low | Medium | High | Totals |
|---|---|---|---|---|
| Male | 5 | 2 | 2 | 9 |
| Female | 2 | 4 | 4 | 10 |
| Totals | 7 | 6 | 6 | 19 |

*EDU8.MDL : Window1*

It is perfectly allowable to have items of the same name on different dimensions and even on the same dimension. The question that needs answering is how do you make clear which items you are referring to in a range reference?

The answer is that you can use a notation that always specifies exactly which dimension and which item you are referring to. In the default model the dimensions AA, BB are numbered 1, 2 and so on. On each dimension the items are numbered 1, 2 and so on. These dimension and item index values do not change if you rename the dimensions or items but they do if you move an item.

To refer to a particular item on a particular dimension you simply have to give the dimension's number or index and the item's index on that dimension in the format

[*dim,item*]

where *dim* is the dimension index and *item* is the item index. This notation can only be used to indicate which of a number of identically named items is being referenced. In this case you have to write the item name first and then its dimension and item index.

For example, in the case of the modified Education model Total[1,4] refers to the total on the dimension that used to be the AA dimension - Education in this case. In the same way if there were two items called Total on the same dimension then you would distinguish between them by giving the appropriate item index. In practice cell references and range references are often entered indirectly by pointing. In this case the appropriate index values will be added if they are necessary.

Notice that when you insert new items the default naming used often creates items that have the same names as items that already exist.

## » Updating the scope

So far we have only considered the effects of changes on the ranges that are used within a formula. We still need to answer similar questions regarding the scope of a global formula. There is no need to consider questions regarding the relative or absolute character of a scope because there is no sense in which a global formula can move. Indeed the scope defines where the formula may be applied within the model and so if anything it is, and needs to be, absolute.

When you delete items a scope behaves much like a standard range reference. That is, if you delete items that are on the "edge" of a scope then the scope specification is reduced accordingly. For example, if a global formula has scope given by (A3:A6).B5.C1.D1 then deleting item A3 changes it to (A4:A6).B5.C1.D1.

If you delete an entire dimension then all reference to it is removed from the scope of all global formulae. However, if you add a new dimension it is not automatically added to the scopes of existing global formulae. Both of these actions are reasonable and what you would expect.

You can also rename items without affecting the scope of a global formula. If you change the name of item A3 to "Totals" then the scope (A3:A6).B5.C1.D1 would be automatically changed to (Totals:A6).B5.C1.D1.

A slightly more complicated situation arises when you insert new items into a scope. In this case the definition of the scope isn't altered but obviously it will be enlarged by the new items falling within its item ranges. For example, if you insert a new item called Totals just before A4 then the scope definition (A3:A6).B5.C1.D1 isn't altered but clearly the range A3:A6 now includes the additional item Totals. Even though the new item is within the scope of the global formula there is still the question of whether or not it should be applied? There is also the possibility that there will be more than one global formula with a scope that now includes the the new item - which formula, if any, should be applied?

To solve these problems the Insert Item dialog box includes a section called " Global Inheritance". This sounds very grand but essentially all it means is "should a global formula be applied to its extended range" and "if there is a choice of global formulae which one should be applied". However, these questions are phrased in a slightly different way within the dialog box. Which global formula to apply is solved by selecting the existing item to inherit from using the From box. However, it only applies the formula selected if the Inherit global formulas box is checked.

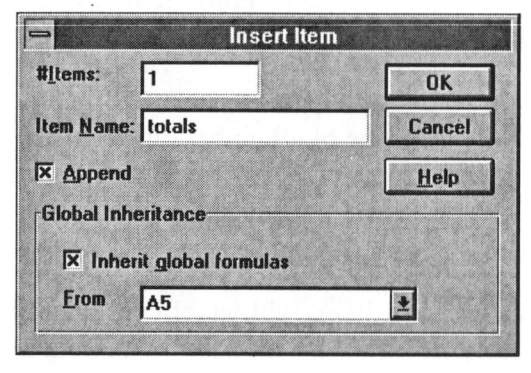

```
┌─────────────── Insert Item ───────────────┐
│ #Items:    [1]              [  OK    ]    │
│ Item Name: [totals]         [ Cancel ]    │
│ [X] Append                  [  Help  ]    │
│ ┌─Global Inheritance──────────────────┐   │
│ │  [X] Inherit global formulas        │   │
│ │  From  [A5              ▼]          │   │
│ └─────────────────────────────────────┘   │
└───────────────────────────────────────────┘
```

This sounds simple enough but it is easy to miss how powerful this inheritance actually is. The item that is selected to provide the global formulae i.e. the one that the new item inherits from, acts like a sort of formulae template for the new item. Each new cell has the global formula that has been applied to the corresponding cell in the "inherit from" item.

This description is a bit abstract so think for a moment about the new item as forming a new column - after all you can only insert new items on the visible dimensions. If you select another item for the new column to inherit global formulae from then each cell in the new column will have the same global formulae applied as the existing column. It is in this sense that the nominated item acts as a template for the new item.

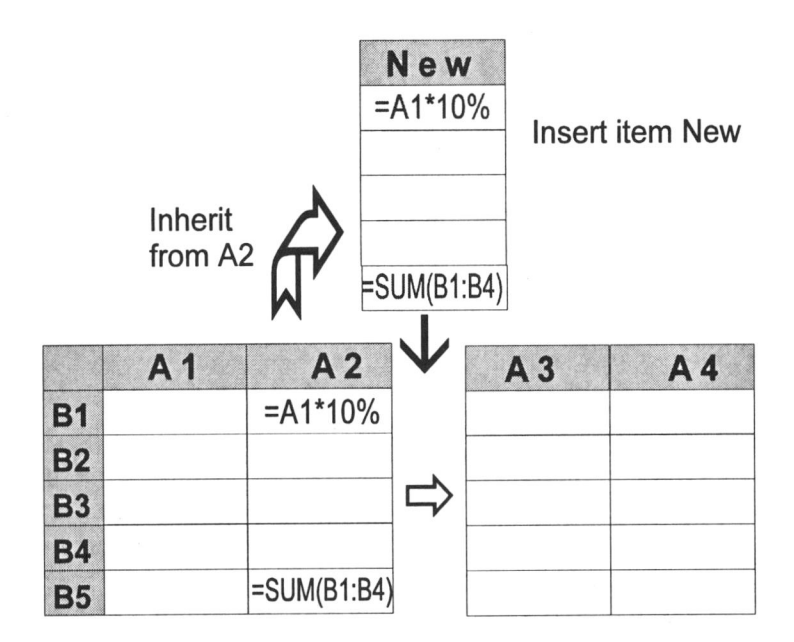

Notice that while this global inheritance is easy to see in terms of the newly inserted column, the formulae are also inherited on the fixed dimensions. That is, if you are working with a 3D model and insert a new "column" with global inheritance, you are in fact inserting a new "slice" into the model. The entire slice will inherit the applied global formulae in the nominated existing slice.

If you don't allow new items to globally inherit a set of global formulae then you can always apply each formula manually to the new cells. However, in a well designed model your aim should always be to use global inheritance to populate a new area of the model with appropriate formulae.

**132** *Structure, Range and Scope*          *Chapter 8*

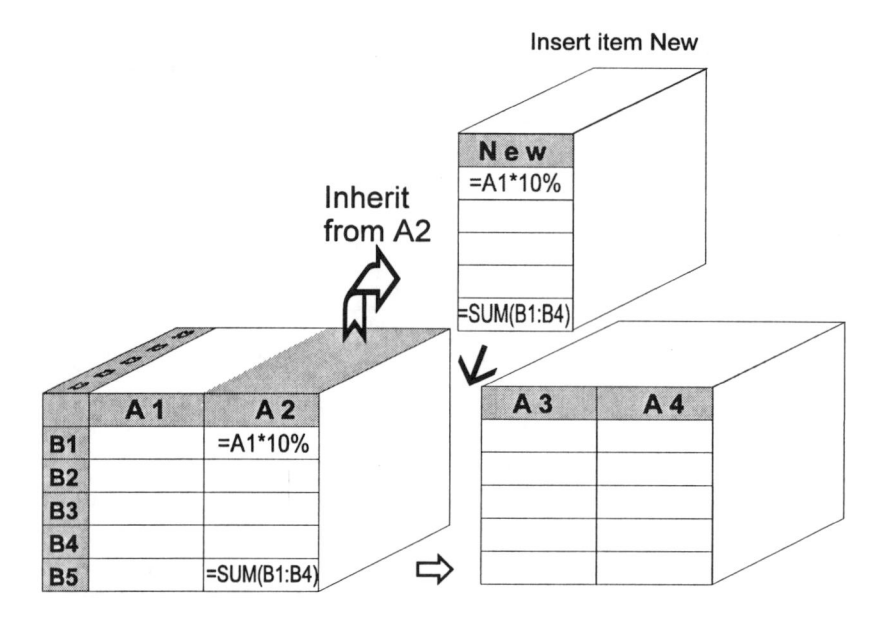

*The new "slice" inherits formulae from the complete A2 "slice"*

## » Moving items and scope

Finally, a word of warning. If you move items after a global formula has been defined then the scope behaves much like a standard range. That is, the scope definition will not be altered but it might gain a new meaning because of the shift in items. All the cells to which the formula was applied will carry on displaying the formula and its results - although they may well now be outside the formula's scope. If you look at the scope definition of a formula that has been moved out of scope then you will find that it has been updated to include the cell. However, if you look at the scope of one of the instances that is still in scope you will find it unchanged. What is more, if you try to apply a global formula to a cell that is out of scope you will find that, according to the Apply Formula dialog box, there are no global formulae in scope - even though one is clearly already in use!

As you can tell the situation with respect to moving items is very confusing. In short - don't do it!

## » Structure and scope

One of the biggest sources of error in traditional spreadsheet use is the insertion of a new row or column. The problem is caused by the failure to copy the necessary formulae into the new row or column but this is just a reflection of the deeper fact that row or column insertion doesn't take any account of the existing structure of the spreadsheet.

From the discussion of the way that formula range, scope and global inheritance works you can see that a well constructed model doesn't, or at least should not, suffer from these problems. A model should be naturally extensible in the sense that inserting new items should extend the way that the model works rather than causing serious problems.

The guidelines for constructing such easy to extend models are:

» Choose dimension and item names appropriately and carefully. Dimension names should be descriptive and item names should form a natural series. However, you need to be careful when using simple numbering schemes because inserting a new item between item1 and item2 results in a naming problem!

» Always use global formulae with the largest scopes possible and make sure that the ranges to which they are applied are the same as their scope.

» Always use global inheritance when you insert a new item. If you don't make sure that you are clear about creating a non-standard slice in the model.

## » World sales

As a simple example of extending a model, consider the world sales data model introduced in the previous chapter. In this case the total sales volume is recorded in each national currency but it is also desirable to have the totals shown in the currency used by the home company. To convert the values to Sterling a range of conversion factors are necessary - one for each currency. If currency rates did not fluctuate than there might be a case for using global constants, or even a named constant. However, they do fluctuate and so a new item is needed to introduce a row of currency rates for each quarter.

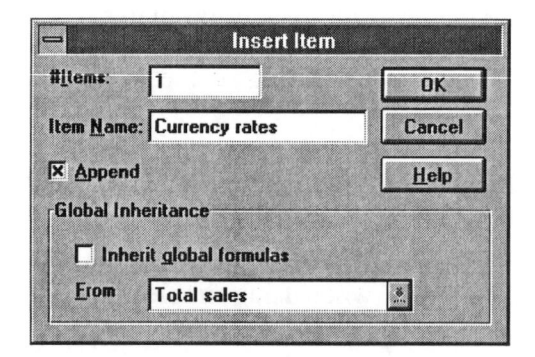

In this case the row needs to be inserted below Total sales and it does not need to inherit the global formulae from this row. As it happens, even if the Inherit global formulas box was checked the new row would be out of the scope of the global formulae in Total sales.

Once the new row is created all that is necessary is to enter the appropriate currency rates. As these are going to change each month there is no need to copy them to the other pages or to establish them as global constants.

*World sales* **135**

| | UK | France | Germany | Spain | USA |
|---|---|---|---|---|---|
| Number | 15 | 20 | 7 | 5 | 10 |
| Unit price | £10 | 100 FFr | 30 Dm | 2,000 pta | $20 |
| Total sales | £150 | 2,000 FFr | 210 Dm | 10,000 pta | $200 |
| Currency rates | 1 | 8.57 | 2.5 | 189 | 1.5 |

The next step is to insert another item to work out the sterling total sales figure. This item can be inserted above Currency rates and again it does not inherit any global formulae.

The global formula that it needs is

=Total sales/Currency rates

with scope

Area.'Total sales (£)'.Quarter

Now we have the sterling totals for each quarter and the grand total page.

| | UK | France | Germany | Spain | USA |
|---|---|---|---|---|---|
| Number | 15 | 20 | 7 | 5 | 10 |
| Unit price | £10 | 100 FFr | 30 Dm | 2,000 pta | $20 |
| Total sales | £150 | 2,000 FFr | 210 Dm | 10,000 pta | $200 |
| Total sales (£) | £150 | 233 FFr | 84 Dm | 53 pta | $133 |
| Currency rates | 1 | 8.57 | 2.5 | 189 | 1.5 |

However, if you examine the model you will discover two problems. The first is relatively trivial in that the sterling values are all shown formatted according to country. This isn't unreasonable if you recall that each country item was formatted as a slice. The solution is to select Total sales (£) and use the Format,Style All command to format it to UK style.

The second problem is a little more subtle. If you look at the Totals page you will find sterling values for the Total sales figures but these are obtained from Total sales using the currency rates on the same page. This is obviously incorrect as each quarter's currency rates should be used to form the total. The solution is to use a SUM function to total the sterling sales figures on each page and not just extend the scope of the function that converts the national sales figures in each quarter.

This is an example of where the power of an MDM can lead you to the wrong conclusion! The correct solution is to extend the scope of the function that forms the other totals by summing over the range Q1:Q4.

The global formula

=SUM(Q1:Q4)

should be edited to have scope

Totals.(Number,Total sales,'Total sales (£)').Area

and

=Total sales/Currency rates

should be edited to have scope

(Q1:Q4).'Total sales (£)'.Area

Don't be tempted to leave this scope unchanged because otherwise it will override the correct SUM formula the next time you apply it to its scope.

In general it is much easier to extend a model than an equivalent sheet but you need to be careful and check that new cells haven't changed the meaning of the model sufficient to invalidate your earlier assumptions. When additions fit into the structure of the model then the model is self extending. When the additions change the structure in some way you have to modify the model. Contrast this with the behaviour of a sheet which never self extends and always needs editing to take account of additions!

# Key points

» Ranges are absolute with respect to specified dimensions but relative with respect to underspecified dimensions.

» Specified ranges can be made relative using the notation *dim[offset]* where *dim* is the dimension name and *offset* the number of items away from the current cell.

» You can change an absolute reference into a relative reference or vice versa using Formula,Reference or by pressing the F4 key.

» Ranges can be assigned to names which can be used in their place. Range names are less important in models than in 2D spreadsheets but their use can still simplify formulae.

» The range and scope of a formula divide up the model into non-overlapping areas. Cells that are within the range, and so used by the formula, cannot be in its scope where the formulae can be applied without creating a circular reference.

» Unspecified dimensions in the range of a global formula correspond to dimensions used in the scope.

» Ranges are adjusted when items are deleted. They are not adjusted when items are inserted.

» When a new item is inserted it can inherit the global formulae from another slice of the model.

» Moving items is confusing and damaging to both formula ranges and scopes.

# Chapter 9

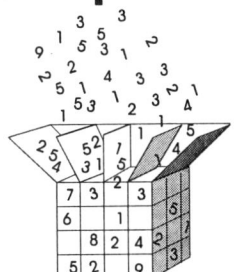

# Crosstab Models

In this chapter we examine the way that multidimensional models can be used to analyse and summarise existing data. In many cases this data will initially be in the form of a traditional database and part of the problem will be the actual conversion into a multidimensional model. However, after the model has been constructed from the data you still have to add formulae to summarise it in an attempt to make sense of it.

At the simplest level these formulae will calculate sums and averages; at the most advanced level perhaps a full statistical test is required. Of course, in the real world a model is unlikely to be just a pure attempt at data analysis - it may contain formulae to work out values associated with the data such as variable costs or sales projections - but, for the sake of simplicity, these aspects of modelling are dealt with in subsequent chapters.

# » Discrete data

The basic idea of building an MDM from a database has already been introduced in earlier chapters and so the basic ideas should be familiar. Essentially what we are doing is constructing a cross-tabulation, or crosstab, of the data. The data can be considered to be made up of a sets of values, each consisting of measurements made on the same entity. For example, you might have a data relating to the performance and pay of a work force:

| Name | Gender | Age | Group | Salary | Bonus | Absent days |
|---|---|---|---|---|---|---|
| Smith | M | 25 | A | 22 | 4 | 4 |
| Jackson | F | 33 | B | 24 | 3 | 9 |
| Jones | M | 21 | B | 20 | 2 | 15 |
| Taylor | F | 34 | A | 25 | 5 | 2 |
| Roberts | M | 46 | C | 26 | 2 | 5 |
| Anderson | M | 38 | C | 24 | 1 | 8 |

Each row of the table consists of values relating to the same entity - in this case a person. The columns correspond to a particular measurement made on each of the entities. What you call the rows and columns of such a table depends very much on how you are thinking about it. For example, if you think of the table as a database then each row is a record and each column is a field. In statistical terms each row is a vector and each column is a variable. It doesn't really matter what words you use as long as you are clear about the way values relate to measurements made on entities.

If you examine this table you will notice that there are two distinct type of measurements. A variable or field such as Gender is discrete in the sense that only a small number of values are possible, i.e. M or F in this case. Variables such as Salary, Age, Bonus or Absent days would normally be regarded as continuous variables because they can have values that vary over a wide and continuous range. This distinction is important when converting a database into an MDM.

In practice the distinction between discrete and continuous variables can be very vague. For example, if you are measuring a quantity such as temperature, length, weight etc., then it is obvious that any value within a reasonable range may be obtained in practice. A variable such as "bonus" is more problematic because although it can vary continuously in theory it might be that the allocation of bonus payments is such that only values of £500, £1000 and £1500 can arise in practice. So is bonus a discrete or a continuous variable? The answer is that it is up to you! If the number of possible values that you can obtain for a variable is sufficiently small then you may regard it as discrete or continuous as suits your purpose.

## » Making categories

If a variable has too many possible values then you always have the choice of reducing it to a discrete variable by grouping values into a number of ranges. For example, if bonus payments were any value in the range £0 to £5000 you could convert this to a discrete variable using the following ranges

| Bonus | Code |
|---|---|
| less than or equal to 500 | 1 |
| more than 500 to 1000 | 2 |
| more than 1000 to 2000 | 3 |
| more than 2000 to 3000 | 4 |
| more than 3000 to 4000 | 5 |
| more than 4000 | 6 |

Notice that in this case not all of the ranges are the same size and the coding isn't particularly informative as to the actual bonus received. Neither of these features make the conversion to a smaller number of categories invalid but you need to keep in mind that using ranges of different size may alter the results of any analysis that you will perform. This is just a special case of the more general fact that whenever you reduce the number of categories measured by a variable then you are throwing some information away. For example, if going from a bonus of £500 to one of £1000 marks some change in the way the staff are working then this will be masked by using a categorisation that assigns all bonuses in the range £0 to £1000 to the same category. The principle is that as you reduce the number of categories you lose more and more fine detail. If you increase the number of categories in some part of the range at the expense of another then you have a chance of seeing finer detail in this favoured range.

## » Discrete variables = dimensions

The reason that you need to be clear about the distinction between discrete and continuous variable is that discrete variables are converted into dimensions when a database is converted into a model. The reason is that the discrete variables can be used to categorise or divide up the other measurements into groups. For example, the Gender variable categorises the data into two groups corresponding to the values M and F and so this can be converted into a Gender dimension with items M and F. The continuous variables in the database correspond to the values recorded in each cell of the MDM.

That is

> » discrete variables can be converted into dimensions with items that correspond to the values.

For example, if you use Gender and Group as dimensions to construct a model then the values on these two fields determine which cell values of Age, say, are stored in.

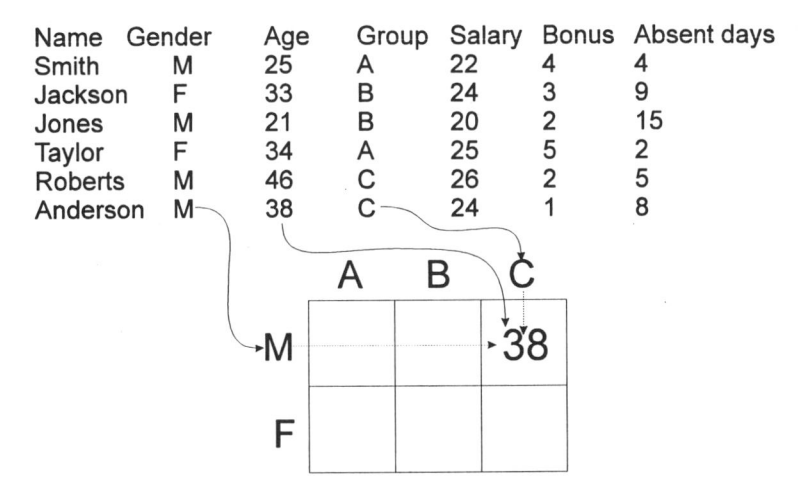

| Name | Gender | Age | Group | Salary | Bonus | Absent days |
|---|---|---|---|---|---|---|
| Smith | M | 25 | A | 22 | 4 | 4 |
| Jackson | F | 33 | B | 24 | 3 | 9 |
| Jones | M | 21 | B | 20 | 2 | 15 |
| Taylor | F | 34 | A | 25 | 5 | 2 |
| Roberts | M | 46 | C | 26 | 2 | 5 |
| Anderson | M | 38 | C | 24 | 1 | 8 |

|   | A | B | C |
|---|---|---|---|
| M |   |   | 38 |
| F |   |   |   |

## » The Variables dimension

When you convert a database into an MDM you can select which of the categorical variables are to be used as dimensions and which are to be used as the values recorded in the cells of the model. If there are multiple continuous variables then you could build one model per variable but it is simpler to introduce a new dimension called Variables and create an item for each of the variables. For example, you could create an additional dimension called Variables with items Salary, Bonus, Age and Absence days.

That is:

» multiple variables can be included in a single model as items on a Variables dimension.

## » Sources of databases

All talk about converting databases into MDMs raises the question of where the database to be converted actually comes from. In some cases the data will be entered directly into a multidimensional template constructed using theoretical knowledge of the data. In other cases the data will have already been entered in the form of a table into a sheet. In yet others it will take the form of a selection of records and fields from a full, external, database. Entering data directly into a model isn't particularly difficult but converting a data table stored in a sheet or an external database is something new and needs examining further.

## » The DBF format

The only database file format that SCW can import is the dBase III DBF format - but this is usually sufficient. The reason is that nearly all database packages can export data in DBF format and so can provide data that can be used by SCW to create either a sheet or a model. The DBF format is very simple and consequently nearly always works but of course it has its limitations. Data fields stored in database programs are usually assigned a specific data type. SCW will only read in text, numeric, date and logical (i.e. true/false) values. If your database allows you to define more complex types of data then they will either have to be converted to one of the standard types or they will be ignored by SCW. In most cases the conversion is performed automatically and you might never realise that it is occurring.

Notice that in most cases you will not simply export the entire database in DBF format. This would generally result in far too much data to make model construction easy. In nearly all cases you will have to run a query to select just the records and fields that are needed within the model and export the result of this as a DBF file. In practice you may even need to do a little more than a simple query because of the need to consolidate repeated measurements, as discussed later.

## » Importing a DBF file into a sheet

If you have a database table available in DBF format then importing it into a sheet it very simple. Use the command File,Open and select dBase III in the List Files of Type box. This will result in you being shown a list of DBF files in the current directory. If you select one you are next presented with a choice of importing it into a sheet or a model. If you select sheet then a new sheet is created with the database data entered into its rows and columns in the usual table format. A dBase file contains enough information for SCW to discover the original field names and these are stored in row one as column headings.

For example, if you import the dBase III file Staff1.dbf which contains the staff data listed earlier the result is a sheet containing a table of data complete with column headings.

| | A | B | C | D | E | F | G |
|---|---|---|---|---|---|---|---|
| 1 | Name | Gender | Age | Group | Salary | Bonus | Absent_day |
| 2 | Smith | M | 25 | A | 22 | 4 | 4 |
| 3 | Jackson | F | 33 | B | 24 | 3 | 9 |
| 4 | Jones | M | 21 | B | 20 | 2 | 15 |
| 5 | Taylor | F | 34 | A | 25 | 5 | 2 |
| 6 | Roberts | M | 46 | C | 26 | 2 | 5 |
| 7 | Anderson | M | 38 | C | 24 | 1 | 8 |
| 8 | | | | | | | |

If you already know about the use of the Data command within sheets then you will notice that the field names at the top of the column make it possible to use the imported data as a data table. This is an important and useful observation.

## » Sheets to models

You can convert a data table stored in a sheet into a DBF file very easily. As well as providing a link between sheets and any database you may be using, exporting to a DBF file also provides a link between sheets and models. If you first export the data to DBF format you can then import it into a model.

sheet -> DBF file -> model

If you try to export the data in a sheet using the command Save As and selecting dBase III as the file type then, unless you are lucky, you will find that it doesn't work. The reason is that you need to first define a database table in the sheet. A database table has a standard format with the first row consisting of field names and subsequent rows consisting of data. The field names in the table are converted into field names within the DBF file.

To define a data table all you need to do is select the area that the table occupies - including the row that contains the field names - and use the command Data,Set Database. Alternatively you can simply use the Formula,Define Name command to create a range name called Database. The Data,Set Database command is simply a shortcut way of creating this range name. When you use the File,Save As command the data table determined by the current definition of the name Database is saved to disk.

## » Importing DBF files to a model

Importing a DBF file to a model is a little more difficult but only because you have to decide the status of each of the fields in the database. For each field you have to decide if it is to play the role of a dimension, i.e. its values should be items that categorise the data, or the role of a variable, i.e. its field name should be an item on a dimension and its values should be stored in the cells of the model. SCW makes an initial attempt at classifying the fields according to whether they are text or numeric. It is a reasonable assumption that text fields should be converted into dimensions and numeric fields into variables - but you can change this default assignment.

To import a DBF file into a model you simply use the File,Open command, select dBase III as the file type and Model in the Import To dialog box that appears. Next you will see the dBase III Import dialog box.

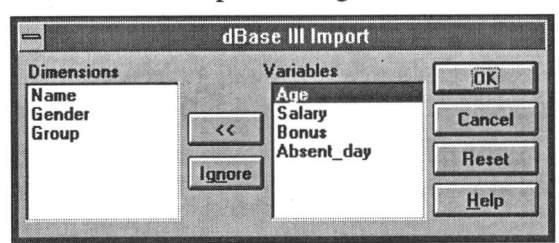

```
          dBase III Import
Dimensions      Variables
Name            Age           [  OK  ]
Gender          Salary
Group    [ << ] Bonus         [ Cancel ]
                Absent_day
         [Ignore]             [ Reset ]

                              [ Help ]
```

This dialog box lists all of the field names that the database contains and divides them up into two lists - those that will be converted into dimensions and those that will be converted into variables. You can change this classification by selecting field names and using the arrow button which moves the fields from their current group to the alternative group. You can eliminate any fields that you don't want to import using the Ignore button. If you make a mistake and want the list of field names restored then simply click on the Reset button. When you have finished assigning fields to dimensions and variables you simply click on OK and the new model is created.

|            | STAFF1.MDL : Window1 |        |       |            |
|------------|----------------------|--------|-------|------------|
| VARIABLES  | Gender               | Group  |       |            |
| Name       | M                    | A      |       |            |
|            | Age                  | Salary | Bonus | Absent_day |
| Smith      | 25                   | 22     | 4     | 4          |
| Jackson    |                      |        |       |            |
| Jones      |                      |        |       |            |
| Taylor     |                      |        |       |            |
| Roberts    |                      |        |       |            |

## » The Staff model

As an example of converting a DBF file into a model, consider the data stored in Staff.dbf listed earlier. In this case the default assignment of fields is as shown in the previous section. If you accept this default the resulting model has four dimensions - Gender, Group and Name which correspond to the original fields of the same names and Variables which includes Age, Salary, Bonus and Absent_days as its items.

The resulting model is perfectly reasonable as a conversion of the "flat" data table but it if you examine it you will find that it has very few cells with data.

The reason for this is that including Name as a dimension results in a model that can only have one data entry per item on that dimension. For example, there can only be one set of data entries for Smith, i.e. Gender equal to M and Group equal to A. All the cells corresponding to Smith and other items on the Gender and Group dimensions will be empty. For example, Smith.F.A is empty because Smith is not female.

This occurrence of cells which are empty for reasons of logic rather than just because you didn't obtain the data is common. You can see that the reason for it is simply that giving the item on the Name dimension is sufficient to identify the entity that the data corresponds to without the need for items on the other dimensions. Indeed giving the person's name determines the items on the other dimensions. However, you can't simply ignore the Name dimension because the reverse is not true - that is giving the value of Gender and Group does not determine the person that the data corresponds to. We will return to this topic later.

## » Exporting DBF from a model

You can also export the data in a model as a DBF file. To do so you have to indicate which of the dimensions should be treated as a variable. To do this you either have to rename the dimension Variables or pivot the model so that its items label the columns. In either case the items on the variables dimension are converted into fields. The other dimensions are converted into field names and their items into values.

## » Repeated measures

In the simplest possible crosstab model each cell will correspond to exactly one set of values. That is, for every combination of items, one from each dimension, there is one and only one value to be stored in the cell. This seems so obvious and simple that it is difficult at first to imagine that there can be any other possibility but in fact this situation is rare when you convert a database to a model. The reason is that it corresponds to the condition in the database that every possible combination of values of the dimension fields occurs just once.

For example, consider the staff database again but this time converted to a model ignoring the Name field.

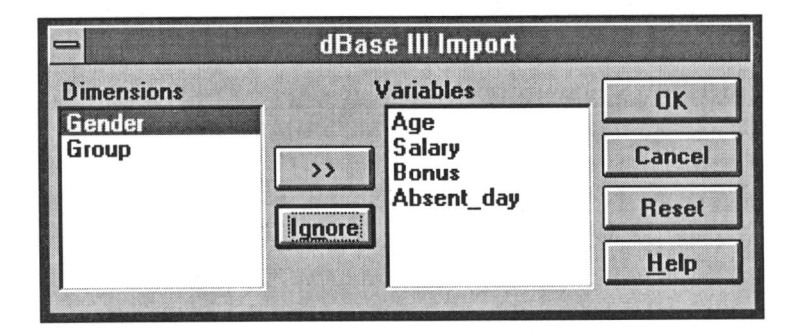

## 150  Crosstab Models    Chapter 9

In this case the two dimensions Gender and Group are being used to categorise each record in the database. This works fine apart from the fact that the last two records:

| Name | Gender | Age | Group | Salary | Bonus | Absent days |
|---|---|---|---|---|---|---|
| Roberts | M | 46 | C | 26 | 2 | 5 |
| Anderson | M | 38 | C | 24 | 1 | 8 |

share the same values of of Gender and Group and this means that there are two sets of data that could be used to fill the cell M.C.Age; two that could be used to fill M.C.Salary and so on.

| Name | Gender | Age | Group | Salary | Bonus | Absent days |
|---|---|---|---|---|---|---|
| Smith | M | 25 | A | 22 | 4 | 4 |
| Jackson | F | 33 | B | 24 | 3 | 9 |
| Jones | M | 21 | B | 20 | 2 | 15 |
| Taylor | F | 34 | A | 25 | 5 | 2 |
| Roberts | M | 46 | C | 26 | 2 | 5 |
| Anderson | M | 38 | C | 24 | 1 | 8 |

|   | A | B | C |
|---|---|---|---|
| M |   |   | 38 or 46? |
| F |   |   |   |

If you try to import the data table what SCW does is to store the values of the variables into the appropriate cell of the model for each and every record in the database. If there is already a value stored in the model then the later value overwrites it. In other words, the last record read that is appropriate for that cell is the value stored in the model. In the case of the staff database only the data relating to Anderson will be found in the model. Notice that this problem didn't arise when the Name field was included as a dimension because this made every record in the database unique.

To summarise:

» Records with the same values in the dimension fields will be stored in the same cell of the model but only the last value to be stored is retained.

» Only when every record in the database has a unique set of dimension field values is all of the data stored in the model.

# » Aggregation

If you are lucky the database selection that you want to convert into a model may contain only unique records with respect to the dimension fields but what should you do if this is not the case? The answer is that you have to aggregate or summarise the measurements in some way. For example, you could take the average, total, maximum, minimum etc. of the variables that correspond to a particular cell or you could simply count the number of occurrences of records that correspond to a particular cell.

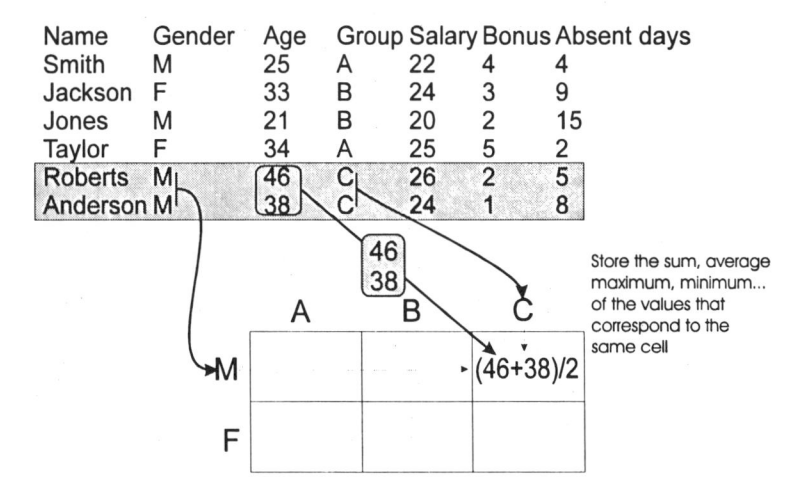

| Name | Gender | Age | Group | Salary | Bonus | Absent days |
|---|---|---|---|---|---|---|
| Smith | M | 25 | A | 22 | 4 | 4 |
| Jackson | F | 33 | B | 24 | 3 | 9 |
| Jones | M | 21 | B | 20 | 2 | 15 |
| Taylor | F | 34 | A | 25 | 5 | 2 |
| Roberts | M | 46 | C | 26 | 2 | 5 |
| Anderson | M | 38 | C | 24 | 1 | 8 |

Store the sum, average maximum, minimum... of the values that correspond to the same cell

(46+38)/2

For example, in the case of the staff database it would be reasonable to average Age, Salary, Bonus and Absent days. The resulting model would then give you a picture of how Gender and Group interacted with average Age, Salary etc..

As SCW performs no aggregation when reading in a database but simply takes the last set of values this raises the question of how to perform the aggregation needed? There are three possible routes:

» You can import the database into a sheet and make use of a combination of database functions and a data table to aggregate the data. This only works for one and two dimensional models but the method can be extended using a user defined function - see later.

» You can make use of the database package that the data is currently stored in to aggregate the data.

» You can create a model that include an extra dimension that makes every record unique and perform the aggregation within the model.

If the database is small enough to make it reasonable to store it in a sheet, or if a sheet is the original source of the data, then aggregating it within the sheet is a reasonable method.

Similarly if the number of unique cases isn't too large to make constructing a model using it as a dimension unreasonable then this approach works but it has a number of drawbacks compared to consolidating the data within a sheet. What you have to do is insert an additional item and use it and a global formula to calculate the sum or average or perform whatever aggregation method you want to use. The disadvantage of this approach is that it can be difficult to see how to aggregate a model and you cannot delete the redundant items without converting the global formula to values - something that cannot be done globally.

For example, if you import the staff database file complete with personnel names then you can perform an aggregation simply by adding an extra item to the Names dimension, called Average say. Into one of the cells in this new row you would enter the global formula

=AVERAGE((Smith:Anderson))

with scope

VARIABLES.Average.Gender.Group

In this case the effects of aggregation only become apparent when you examine the data for Gender equal to M and Group equal to C.

| | Age | Salary | Bonus | Absent_day |
|---|---|---|---|---|
| Smith | | | | |
| Jackson | | | | |
| Jones | | | | |
| Taylor | | | | |
| Roberts | 46 | 26 | 2 | 5 |
| Anderson | 38 | 24 | 1 | 8 |
| Average | 42 | 25 | 1.5 | 6.5 |

STAFF2.MDL : Window1 — M, 'C'

As you can see the aggregation has been performed correctly but converting the AVERAGE formulae to a value, using Copy and Paste Special, and then deleting the redundant Name items is a tedious task.

Because of these difficulties performing the aggregation within a database package is likely to be simplest method of handling large quantities of data. In other words it is better to import pre-aggregated data into SCW.

## » Aggregation using a sheet

As long as the data is small enough to be stored and manipulated easily within a sheet, it is possible to aggregate the data directly. For example, the Education data introduced in Chapter 2 was initially presented as a data table stored in a sheet. In this example it was reasonable to aggregate the data table by manual counting - but what if it had been substantially bigger?

| | A | B | C |
|---|---|---|---|
| 1 | Record | Education | Gender |
| 2 | 1 | High | F |
| 3 | 2 | Low | M |
| 4 | 3 | Medium | F |
| 5 | 4 | Medium | M |
| 6 | 5 | Low | M |
| 7 | 6 | Low | M |
| 8 | 7 | Medium | F |
| 9 | 8 | High | F |
| 10 | 9 | Low | F |
| 11 | 10 | Medium | F |
| 12 | 11 | Low | M |
| 13 | 12 | Medium | M |
| 14 | 13 | Low | F |
| 15 | 14 | High | M |
| 16 | 15 | High | F |
| 17 | 16 | High | F |
| 18 | 17 | Medium | F |
| 19 | 18 | High | M |
| 20 | 19 | Low | M |

It is possible to reduce this table to a table of counts using nothing but the standard facilities in SCW. Essentially what you would do is create a data table to tabulate the DCOUNT database function for all values of Gender and Education. However, this doesn't produce a table of counts that is in the correct form to convert into a model and it only works when there are no more than two categorical dimensions. To create a method that works no matter how many dimensions are involved and which produces a table in the correct format we need to create a user-defined function.

The aggregate function defined below will scan through a database and calculate almost any aggregation function you could need. More precisely it will compute any of the available database functions. Exactly how this user-defined function works is quite interesting but you don't have to understand its workings to make use of it. All you do have to do is enter it exactly as listed (or load it from the I/O Press companion disk) into the macro file GLOBAL.MDM which is stored in the same directory as the SCW program files, usually C:\SCW.

```
function aggregate(SCol,ECol,ThisRow,Fun,Field)
R=NumToStr(ThisRow)
Range=SCol+R+":"+Ecol+R
C=CmdEvaluateText("=SHEETADDRESS(
          ROW(Criteria)+1,COLUMN(Criteria),1,1)")
CmdEditDuplicate(Range,C)
Form="="+Fun+"(Database,"
Form=Form+Chr$(34)+Field+Chr$(34)+",Criteria)"
x=CmdEvaluate(Form)
return x
end function
```

Notice that the line beginning C=CmdEvaluate... should not be split before ROW(Criteria)+...when you type in the user defined function.

Once you have loaded or entered the user-defined function into GLOBAL.MDM and saved it you can make use of it from any sheet. To understand how to use it you need to know a little more about the format of the table you are trying to create.

The aggregated table is stored in another part of the sheet and its first columns consist of the fields that are to form the standard dimensions of the model. Each set of combinations of the dimensions should only occur once. In other words, each row of this part of the table should be unique and this gives us the clue about how to construct it automatically.

All you have to do is to define the original table as a database table and set up an extraction area which lists only the fields that you are going to use as dimensions in the model. Then you set up a blank criteria area and use the command Data,Extract and select the unique check box. This may sound complicated but in practice it is very easy. For example, in the case of the education data the steps are:

1) Select A1:C20 and use the command Data,Set Database to define the database areas.

2) Make a copy of the field names that are going to form the dimensions in the model, i.e. Education and Gender at A25:B25. The location can be any convenient free area of the sheet.

3) Select the newly entered field names and enough rows below to hold the extracted data and use the command Data,Set Extract to define the extraction area.

4) Set up the criteria area by making another copy of the field names in A25:B25 at F25:G25. Again you can use any convenient area of the sheet. Use the command Data,Set Criteria to define the criteria area.

5) Finally use the command Data,Extract and check the Unique records only box.

The result should be a listing of all of the combinations of the dimension fields that occur in the original table but excluding any repeats.

The columns to the right of this new table are where the aggregation functions will be

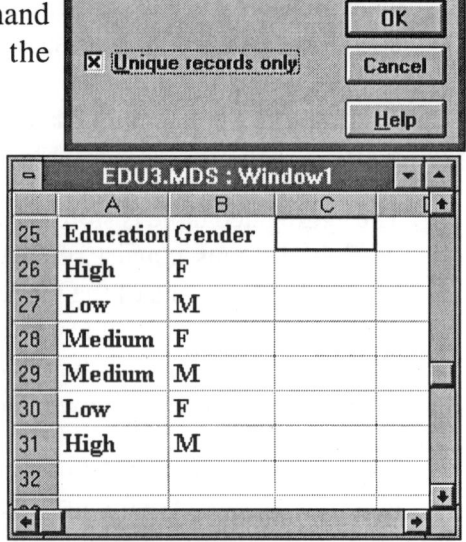

## Aggregation using a sheet 157

calculated. In this case the only option is to count the number of cases that correspond to the values to the left.

This, of course, is where the aggregate function comes into play. The function should be called as

aggregate("S","E",ROW(),"fun","field")

Where S and E are the column letters of the first and last column holding the dimension data, in this case columns A and B. The function ROW() has to be included to supply the current row number to the user defined function - you don't have to worry about this but always make sure that you include it. You can replace "fun" by the name of any of the database functions that you would like to use to aggregate the values. Finally "field" should be replaced by the name of the field that the database function is to be calculated on.

In the case of the education database all you have to do is enter the formula

=aggregate("A","B",ROW(),"DCOUNTA","Gender")

into C26 and then copy it down the column C26:C31. In this case the aggregation function is DCOUNTA which simply counts all the non-blank entries in the Gender field of each combination of values in columns A and B.

| | A | B | C |
|---|---|---|---|
| 25 | Education | Gender | Count |
| 26 | High | F | 4 |
| 27 | Low | M | 5 |
| 28 | Medium | F | 4 |
| 29 | Medium | M | 2 |
| 30 | Low | F | 2 |
| 31 | High | M | 2 |
| 32 | | | |

EDU3.MDS : Window1

The only thing that you have to be careful of is that this function makes use of the Criteria range even though it isn't explicitly one of the parameters. This is because it works by transferring each of the values into the criteria range and then calculating the corresponding database function. It is also a good idea to set calculation to manual because of the time it takes to calculate a full set of aggregate functions.

You can use the aggregate function to calculate any of the database functions just as easily. As a more complex example, consider the problem of working out averages of an attainment score added to the education data. If this is added in column D using field name Score then the only major change is the need to redefine the database as A1:D20. The new aggregate formula is

=aggregate("A","B",ROW(),"DAVERAGE","Score")

and this should be entered into cell D26 and copied into D26:D31. When you next recalculate the sheet both the counts and the averages are updated.

| | A | B | C | D |
|---|---|---|---|---|
| 25 | Education | Gender | Count | Average |
| 26 | High | F | 4 | 64.25 |
| 27 | Low | M | 5 | 44.4 |
| 28 | Medium | F | 4 | 66 |
| 29 | Medium | M | 2 | 88 |
| 30 | Low | F | 2 | 44 |
| 31 | High | M | 2 | 59.5 |
| 32 | | | | |

Of course the final step is to export the aggregated table as a DBF file. To do this you have to redefine the database table to be the new aggregation table, A26:D31 in this case, and then save sheet in DBF format. Once the aggregated data is exported it can be re-imported to create a model. In this example the dimensions are Gender and Education and the variables are Count and Average.

| Gender | VARIABLES | |
|---|---|---|
| Education | Count | |
| | F | M |
| High | 4 | 2 |
| Low | 2 | 5 |
| Medium | 4 | 2 |

## » Fully crossed and nested models

Earlier in this chapter we saw that when individuals were identified by a unique name and this was included in a model then the result was a lot of empty cells. This situation is very common. Whenever you have a model that includes a dimension that uniquely identifies each measurement entity then there will be empty cells. The reason is of course that there will be only one set of values for each item on that dimension.

For example, in the model given by with four dimensions

$$\text{Name.Gender.Group.Variables}$$

the range

$$\text{Smith.Gender.Group.Age}$$

can only contain one value because Smith identifies the person uniquely and only the cell Smith.M.A.Age has a value stored in it - simply because there is no "Smith" and could be no "Smith" corresponding to Smith.F.A.Age or any other combination of Gender.Group.

In this case we say that Name is "nested" within the other dimensions of the model because not all possible combinations of items are logically possible. This situation should be contrasted with a fully crossed dimension where each and every combination of items is logically valid. In this case any empty cells have to be regarded as missing data.

Although there are analyses that are appropriate to nested models, analysis of variance (ANOVA) for example, in most cases it is better to remove the nested dimension from the model and aggregate the measurements to produce a fully crossed model. In this sense nesting and repeated measurements are similar.

## » Analysing crosstab models

So far we have concentrated on the construction of a crosstab model. There is also the question of what to do with it once it has been constructed? Of course you are free to analyse the data in any way that you see fit or appropriate but usually this amounts to two general approaches - computing marginals and deviations.

## » Marginals

It is obvious that you can form row and column sums, counts or averages of values. Although these are referred to as "row" and "column" sums it is obvious this idea of summing over all of the items in a category while keeping the others fixed generalises to more than two dimensions. To save having to use two-dimensional language it is more appropriate to call such sums "marginals" because they are generally stored in extra cells added to the "edge" of the model.

For example, if you have a model with dimensions AA, BB, CC and DD then the simple marginals are formed by summing over one dimension while holding the others fixed. That is SUM(AA.B1.C1.D1) is a marginal which sums all of the values stored along dimension AA with BB fixed at B1 and so on. Obviously in practice you would store such a formula in a cell at the edge, e.g. A5.B1.C1.D1 in the default model and by the rules of underspecification, and making sure not to include A5 in the sum, it could be written as SUM(A1:A4). Similarly all such marginals could then be calculated by setting the scope to A5.BB.CC.DD. You could also calculate the marginals that sum the other dimensions BB, CC and DD, again storing the results in cells corresponding to items B5, C5 and D5. The easiest way of achieving this is to pivot the model so that the dimension that you are summing over is one of the visible dimensions.

If you do set up a model that calculates the marginals on each dimension then any view of the model that does not include A5, B5, C5 or D5 as a fixed dimension looks like a very simple and familiar row and column sum layout.

```
                    MARGIN.MDL : Window1
        AA      DD      CC
        BB     [D1]    [C1]
                A1      A2      A3      A4      A5
        B1                                       0
        B2                                       0
        B3                                       0
        B4                                       0
        B5       0       0       0       0       0
```

If, however, you select A5, B5, C5 or D5 as the fixed item in any of the fixed dimensions then you might not be so sure of what you are looking at. Instead of the single row and column of sums you will see a complete 2D slice of sums.

```
                    MARGIN.MDL : Window1
        AA      DD      CC
        BB     [D5]    [C1]
                A1      A2      A3      A4      A5
        B1       0       0       0       0       0
        B2       0       0       0       0       0
        B3       0       0       0       0       0
        B4       0       0       0       0       0
        B5       0       0       0       0       0
```

The formulae in the the middle of the table are just the marginals that sum values over a single dimension but viewed all at the same time. For example, the sum formula in A1.B1.C1.D5 totals all of the values in D1.D4 with items A1.B1.C1 fixed and so on. The interesting formulae are the ones around the edge of the view. These sum marginals calculated elsewhere in the model. For example, the formulae in A1.B5.C1.D5 still sums the range D1:D4 but in this case the values in D1:D4 are themselves sums. As all of the cells corresponding to item B5 sum B1:B4 the result in A1.B5.C1.D5 is a total of all of the B1:B4 sums over D1:D4. In other words, it is summed over the range A1.B1:B4.C1.D1:D4 - that is, a marginal summed over two dimensions. Confused? I'm not surprised. The problem is that it is very difficult to follow what is going on when you start working with multidimensional marginals in this way. You can see more clearly what is happening it we change each of the item names that store the sums i.e. A5, B5, C5 and D5 to ASUMS, BSUMS, CSUMS and DSUMS. Now when you look at the same view of the model you can see that all of the values that we are looking at correspond to sums over D1:D4.

| AA | DD | | CC | | |
|---|---|---|---|---|---|
| BB | DSUMS | | C1 | | |
| | A1 | A2 | A3 | A4 | ASUMS |
| B1 | 0 | 0 | 0 | 0 | 0 |
| B2 | 0 | 0 | 0 | 0 | 0 |
| B3 | 0 | 0 | 0 | 0 | 0 |
| B4 | 0 | 0 | 0 | 0 | 0 |
| BSUMS | 0 | 0 | 0 | 0 | 0 |

In addition the values in the bottom row are also summed over B1:B4, the values in the right-hand column are also summed over A1:A4 and finally the value in the bottom right-hand corner is summed over A1:A4.B1:B4.C1.D1:D4. In other words, it is a triple marginal summed over three dimensions.

In the same way if you arrange the fixed dimensions to show sums for C5 and D5 what you are again looking at are sums of sums.

| | | MARGIN.MDL : Window1 | | | |
|---|---|---|---|---|---|
| AA | | DD | CC | | |
| BB | | DSUMS | CSUMS | | |
| | A1 | A2 | A3 | A4 | ASUMS |
| B1 | 0 | 0 | 0 | 0 | 0 |
| B2 | 0 | 0 | 0 | 0 | 0 |
| B3 | 0 | 0 | 0 | 0 | 0 |
| B4 | 0 | 0 | 0 | 0 | 0 |
| BSUMS | 0 | 0 | 0 | 0 | 0 |

The difference is that now every sum in the body of the table is a double sum - over D1:D4 and over C1:C4. The sums around the edges are triple sums and the sum in the bottom right-hand corner is a quadruple sum over A1:A4.B1:B4.C1:C4.D1:D4. That is, it is the grand total of all of the sums.

You may find this idea difficult at first but after a little practice and experience it soon becomes second nature. It helps to give the items used for the sums sensible names so that when they occur in combination it is easy to understand what you are looking at. The biggest problem in computing such marginals is making sure that you have the scopes correctly specified for all of the global formulae.

## » Marginals - an example

At the end of Chapter 7 an example of a unit trust portfolio was introduced. The model used four dimensions - Fund, Time, Client and Investment. Although it is obvious that calculating totals for each fund for each client and for each time period is an obvious thing to do, other marginals are also of interest such as sums over time, over fund and over client. Starting from the original model the first step is to add totals for the six monthly period.

| | Europe Growth | Recovery | Far flung | Trust | Totals |
|---|---|---|---|---|---|
| Units | 1000 | 2000 | 5500 | 6500 | 15000 |
| Bid | 159 | 95 | 40 | 122 | 416 |
| Offer | 167 | 110 | 51 | 140 | 468 |
| Spread | 5% | 16% | 28% | 15% | 13% |
| Total value | £1,590.00 | £1,900.00 | £2,200.00 | £7,930.00 | £13,620.00 |

(Fund: Investment; Time: Feb; Client code: N456)

To do this it is simpler to pivot the model so that time is the vertical dimension. This allows you to add a new time item by dragging any cell on the bottom row. Call this new item Half year totals or something similar. Next enter the formula

=SUM((Jan:June))

into a cell in the new row (you can use the Auto Sum button if you want to). Convert this formula into a global formula and set its scope equal to

Fund.Half year totals.(Total value,Units).Client code

Notice that on the Investment dimension we only want to sum Total value and Units over time.

| | Europe Growth | Recovery | Far flung | Trust |
|---|---|---|---|---|
| Jan | 0 | 0 | 0 | 0 |
| Feb | 1000 | 2000 | 5500 | 6500 |
| Mar | 1211 | 3000 | 400 | 4000 |
| Apr | 2000 | 4000 | 4000 | 5000 |
| May | 3000 | 0 | 4000 | 5000 |
| June | 0 | 0 | 8000 | 5000 |
| Half year totals | 7211 | 9000 | 21900 | 25500 |

(Fund: Investment; Time; Units; Client code: N456)

## Marginals - an example

To form marginals over fund, pivot so that Fund is the vertical dimension and repeat the procedure. That is drag any of the cells in the bottom row to create a new item named All Funds total and enter the global formula

=SUM((Europe Growth:Trust ))

with scope

(Units,Total value).All Funds total.Time.Client code

Again notice that we only want to sum Units and Total value.

| | Units | Bid | Offer | Spread | Total value |
|---|---|---|---|---|---|
| Europe Growth | 1000 | 159 | 167 | 5% | £1,590.00 |
| Recovery | 2000 | 95 | 110 | 16% | £1,900.00 |
| Far flung | 5500 | 40 | 50 | 25% | £2,200.00 |
| Trust | 6500 | 122 | 140 | 15% | £7,930.00 |
| All Funds total | 15000 | | | #DIV/0! | £13,620.00 |

(Investment: Fund = Feb; Time; Client code = N456; File: UNITS2.MDL : Window1)

The only worrying feature of this model is the appearance of #DIV/0! in the Spread column. The reason for this is that the global formula calculating the spread originally had the scope

Spread.Fund.Time.Client code

and this means that the formula applies to the new item on the Fund dimension and to the new item on the Time dimension. The solution is to change the scope to

Spread.(Europe Growth:Trust ).(Jan:June).Client code

This sort of mistake is common but very easy to fix.

Finally the whole process is repeated again to calculate client marginals. Pivot the module to make Client the vertical dimension and add the item All client total. Enter the formula

=SUM((Europe Growth:Trust ))

and make it global with scope

(Units,Total value).Client code.Time.All Funds total

You also have to change the scope of the global formula that calculates spread to avoid error messages. The new scope is

Spread.(Europe Growth:Trust).(Jan:June).(N104:N456)

Now all of the marginals are available for use. From the discussion in the previous section you should have no difficulty in interpreting the model view that has All Funds total and All client total as the two fixed items.

| Investment | Fund | | Client code | | |
|---|---|---|---|---|---|
| Time | All Funds total | | All client total | | |
| | Units | Bid | Offer | Spread | Total value |
| Jan | 0 | | | | £0.00 |
| Feb | 15000 | | | | £13,620.00 |
| Mar | 8611 | | | | £8,931.40 |
| Apr | 15000 | | | | £13,400.00 |
| May | 12000 | | | | £10,200.00 |
| June | 13000 | | | | £9,400.00 |
| Half year totals | 63611 | | | | £55,551.40 |

The value in the bottom right-hand corner is the total value of all funds held for all clients summed over the six month period. Notice that in this case the sum over all clients and all funds makes sense but to sum this gives you a figure that isn't useful. The point is that while you can always calculate marginals they do not always make sense. In some cases averaging or taking the maximum is more appropriate or even a mixture. For example, you could sum over funds and client to get total holdings and then average over time to get average monthly total holdings. The principles are the same no matter what functions you are using.

## » Deviations

In most cases once the data is stored in a model it is sufficient to look at it and try to make sense of it. However, unless you have an expectation of a particular result it can be difficult to interpret a model. For example, if you examine the staff data, used to construct a crosstab model earlier in this chapter, inspecting the number of days absent variable, you might like to ask if there is any relationship between gender, group and number of days off. Perhaps the sort of idea that is in your mind is the males in the lower performing groups have more days off and this is a reason for their under performance.

Examining the model which shows the total count of the number of days absent classified according to Gender and Group doesn't give you any clear idea of what is going on.

```
STAFF3.MDL : Window1
Gender      VARIABLES
Group       Absent_day
              M        F       Gender totals
A             4        2            6
B            15        9           24
C             6                     6
Group totals 25       11           36
```

What is needed is some prediction of the total number of absent days you would expect in each cell if you assumed that Gender and Group have an effect. Fortunately this isn't difficult. If you examine the table you can see that there are a total of 6 absence days in group A. You can also see that there are a total of 25 male absence days. The question is what number of male group A absence days would you expect if Gender and Group have no influence?

The total number of absence days is 36 and this divides down into 25 Male and 11 Female absence days and into 6 Group A, 24 Group B and 6 Group C absence days. So, given any number of absence days, D, the number of Male absences should be D*25/36. By the same reasoning, the fraction of this number that should come from Group A is 6/36. So the number of Male absences from Group A should be

$$D*(25/36)*(6/36)$$

So what number would you expect to see in the cell Male.Group A? In this case D is the total number of absence days i.e. 36 and so the answer is

$$\frac{36*25*6}{36*36}$$

or cancelling the 36s on the top and bottom

$$\frac{25*6}{36}$$

If you think about this argument you will see that it applies to each cell in the model and so the number that we would expect to see in cell item1.item2 is

$$\frac{\text{item1 marginal} * \text{item2 marginal}}{\text{grand total}}$$

For example, the number of female absences you would expect in group C is given by 11, the female marginal, times 6, the group C marginal divided by 36, the total i.e. 1.8. Now given that the actual number is 0 there is a discrepancy that suggests that females that are members of group C behave differently to other females. In fact, drawing a conclusion of this sort is almost certainly unjustified until you look at the results for the entire table.

Notice that the calculation of the value you would expect to get depends on the assumption that the value in any cell should be proportional to the marginals. This is often but not always the case and you need to think very carefully about whether or not this sort of analysis is appropriate. If it isn't then you need to find alternative ways of calculating what you expect to see - but the general principle of comparing what you observe with what you expect still holds.

## » A predicted table

If you have a table of values and you would like to calculate the expected values then you can easily extend the model to make this possible. In most cases it is simple to add an extra dimension - Model type and create two items Actual and Predicted. The cells corresponding to the Actual item hold the data and the cells corresponding to the Predicted item hold the expected values. To compute the expected values you also need the marginals for the entire model but we have already seen how to create these.

```
STAFF4.MDL : Window1
          Gender      VARIABLES       Model type
          Group     Absent_day       Predicted
                         M         F      Gender totals
A                    4.1666667  1.8333333              6
B                   16.666667   7.3333333             24
C                    4.1666667  1.8333333              6
Group totals              25          11              36
```

To calculate the predicted values all you have to do is enter

=Group totals.Actual*Gender totals.Actual/
        Gender totals.Group totals.Actual

into one of the cells in the predicted part of the model and convert it to a global formula with scope

(M:F).(A:C).VARIABLES.Predicted

Notice that you cannot enter the prediction formula by pointing because it refers to cells outside a simple 2D range.

Once you have the predicted figures it is helpful to calculate the difference between the predicted and observed values. To do this simply add another item to the Model Type dimension, Deviation say, then enter the formula

=Predicted-Actual

into a cell and convert it into a global formula with scope

(M:F).(A:C).VARIABLES.Deviation

This computes the deviations for all of the cell values.

| Gender | VARIABLES | | Model type | |
|---|---|---|---|---|
| Group | Absent_day | | Deviation | |
| | M | F | Gender totals |
| A | 0.1666667 | -0.166667 | 2.22045E-16 |
| B | 1.6666667 | -1.666667 | 8.88178E-16 |
| C | -1.833333 | 1.8333333 | 2.22045E-16 |
| Group totals | 1.776E-15 | -4.44E-16 | 1.33227E-15 |

## » Statistics

At this point you might like to know how big a deviation needs to be before it can be taken as evidence of an effect. The answer is that it all depends on the size of the deviation and on the inherent variability of the data. For example, a deviation of 10 is nothing surprising if the values are in the 100s but it is much more evidence of an effect if the values are in the same range. In other words you should really look at percentage rather than absolute deviation.

The second question is more difficult. Statistics deals with the problem of how to evaluate evidence that is subject to random variations. For example in the case of the staff data the number of absent days is likely to vary for each period to which the data relates. What we have is a single sample of data. It is possible that the number of absences in any given group is higher or lower than the long term average in this particular sample purely because of chance alone.

To find out how much the expected table and the actual table differ you can calculate a single number that measures how far apart they are:

$$\text{Chi squared} = \Sigma \frac{(\text{observed} - \text{expected})^2}{\text{expected}}$$

where $\Sigma$, the Sigma, means sum all of the terms like the one that follows. In other words, to work out Chi squared you simply subtract the corresponding observed and expected figures, square the difference, divide by the expected and add up all such values. The bigger the value of Chi squared the bigger the difference between the observed and the expected tables. You might be wondering why you can't simply add up all the differences between the observed and the expected to get an overall measure of discrepancy? The answer is that some of the differences are positive and some negative and these would cancel out. By squaring the difference we eliminate the negatives (a minus times a minus is a plus) and by dividing by the expected value we work with a percentage difference.

## Crosstab Models

It isn't difficult to calculate Chi squared. All you have to do is change the global formula in the calculated differences to read

$$=(Predicted-Actual)^{\wedge}2/Predicted$$

with scope

(M:F).(A:C).VARIABLES.Deviation

| Gender / Group | VARIABLES Absent_day | | Model type Deviation |
|---|---|---|---|
| | M | F | Gender totals |
| A | 0.0066667 | 0.0151515 | 0.021818182 |
| B | 0.1666667 | 0.3787879 | 0.545454545 |
| C | 0.8066667 | 1.8333333 | 2.64 |
| Group totals | 0.98 | 2.2272727 | 3.20727273 |

The values that you see in the body of the table are the components of Chi squared that have to be added together to give the overall value. As the model automatically calculates the margins the value of Chi squared is already available in the bottom right-hand corner - i.e. 3.2.

You can calculate Chi squared whenever you want to compare a predicted set of values and an actual set of values. A big value of Chi squared indicates that there is a real difference between the two tables. Of course the next question is what is a big value?

The answer to this is where statistics enters the picture. If you know the type of variability in the data - specifically whether the values are multinomially or normally distributed - then the value of Chi squared is associated with known probabilities. These probabilities are called the "significance level" and tell us how probable it is to see a discrepancy of a certain magnitude given that in fact there really is no difference. For example, if you look up the significance of Chi squared and discover that it is .045 then this can be interpreted as saying that the value of Chi squared that you have obtained will happen 4.5 times in 100 even if there is no real difference between the predicted values and the observed data. That is 4.5 times in 100 random fluctuations alone would produce as big a discrepancy.

Obviously at this point we are diverging from SCW and going deep into the basic ideas of statistics and to explain them in detail would take us well away from modelling but this is at least an outline of how it all works. One final point is that on average you can expect a value of Chi squared about the same size as one less than the number of values you have compared. That is one less than the number of components of Chi squared that you have added together. This is usually called the "degrees of freedom". So for example, in the staff example there are four cells in the table and so four components of Chi squared which gives 3 degrees of freedom. Given that the value of Chi squared is only 3.2 you can see that this discrepancy isn't very large.

Finally notice that while comparing the actual with predicted values in a multidimensional model is useful, it may not indicate more basic information contained in models of lower dimension. For example, if you examine the marginals for Gender or Group you can very quickly see that the distribution of days off isn't what you would expect from a simple "no-effect" model. That is, there are many more male absences than female and many more group B absences. Of course to interpret these results you would have to look at the number of males and females and the size of each group.

The important point is that in any particular analysis you have to understand the data, the model and formulate exact questions that you would like the answers to. There are no automatic methods.

## » Missing data

The curse of dimensionality has already been mentioned in earlier chapters but it is particularly relevant to crosstab models. Put simply the problem is that as your model gains dimensions it gains even more cells! For example, a two-dimensional model with three items on each dimension has only nine cells. Add a dimension with three items and it has 27, another and it has 81 and a four-dimensional model with only three items on each dimension has 243 cells. Even a very reasonable sounding model such as a five-dimensional model with five items on each dimension quickly becomes unmanageable with 3125 cells.

As a result missing data in crosstabulation models is a fact of life. In some cases there is very little you can do about it other than to accept it as missing and leave the cells blank. However, there are a range of strategies that can be used to estimate missing values. For example, if you have enough values you can use the mean, or average, of them as a substitute for the missing values. The disadvantage of this approach is that it tends to reduce the variability in the data and may obscure relationships with other variables.

A much better, but more advanced idea, is to try to predict the missing value using a regression on other variables - see Chapter 11.

Intermediate between these two extremes is to use the pattern of distribution of one variable to fill in the missing values. SCW has a special tool Allocate to enable you to do this

## » Allocate

The Tools,Allocate command will use the data that you have for one variable to create values for a variable for which you only have a total. The basic idea is that the total will be allocated in the same proportion as the known data. For example, if the known data is

$$10,20,30,40$$

which has a total of 100 and the missing values are known to total 200 then the Allocate command would divide this up in the same proportions to give

$$20,40,60,80$$

|    | A1 | A2 | A3 | A4 | Totals |
|----|----|----|----|----|--------|
| B1 |    |    |    |    |        |
| B2 | 10 | 20 | 30 | 40 | 100    |
| B3 |    |    |    |    | 200    |
| B4 |    |    |    |    |        |
| B5 |    |    |    |    |        |

You can see the total has been split up in the same proportions as the known data. The formula that is needed to do this is simply:

$$\frac{\text{total to be allocated} * \text{known value}}{\text{known total}}$$

Although this is a very simple formula SCW provides a function to work it out for you

ALLOC(known value,total to be allocated, known total)

The reason for the introduction of this function is that it is used by the Tools,Allocate command to automatically estimate missing values. You can, if you want to, enter the ALLOC commands yourself or even enter the equivalent formulae.

Using the Tools,Allocate command is very easy but a simple example will help to make everything plain. Starting from the model shown opposite we need to estimate the missing values that should be in row B3 using the known total of 200 and the known values of some other variable in row B2 and their total.

To do this first select the cell containing the total to be allocated - i.e. the one containing 200 - and then select the Tools,Allocate command. This displays the Allocate dialog box. The various elements of this dialog box can be confusing at first so it is worth following this simple example carefully.

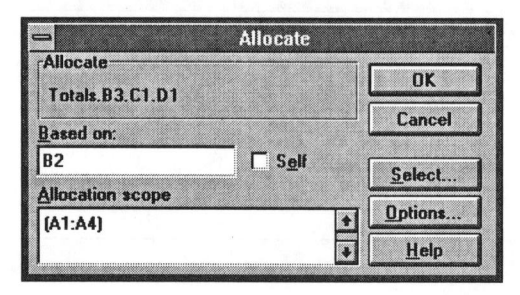

```
┌─────────────────── Allocate ───────────────────┐
│ ┌Allocate──────────────────────┐   ┌────────┐  │
│ │ Totals.B3.C1.D1              │   │   OK   │  │
│ └──────────────────────────────┘   ├────────┤  │
│  Based on:                         │ Cancel │  │
│ ┌──────────────────┐  ┌─ Self      ├────────┤  │
│ │ B2               │  │            │ Select…│  │
│ └──────────────────┘               ├────────┤  │
│  Allocation scope                  │Options…│  │
│ ┌──────────────────┐ ▲             ├────────┤  │
│ │ (A1:A4)          │ ▼             │  Help  │  │
│ └──────────────────┘               └────────┘  │
└────────────────────────────────────────────────┘
```

The Allocate section lists the cell reference of the total that you are going to allocate on the basis of the known data i.e. the cell containing the 200. The Based on text box holds the cell reference of the known total and the Allocation Scope is the range that will hold the ALLOC functions that estimate the missing values. The known values are assumed to be in the same row as the known total and the same column as the missing value it is used to estimate. The same ideas work with the roles of rows and columns swapped over.

If you examine the ALLOC functions that have been inserted then you will find that they are all the same

=ALLOC(B2,Totals,Totals.B2)

and that underspecification has been used to make each work in its respective location. Notice that once the ALLOC functions have been created there is nothing to stop you from editing them.

The Tools,Allocate command works in the same way in a sheet but, of course, all of the range references are 2D and relative and absolute references are used to make the ALLOC formula correct at each location.

If you are using Tools,Allocate in a model then you can also specify ranges using the Select button with displays the Create Reference dialog box.

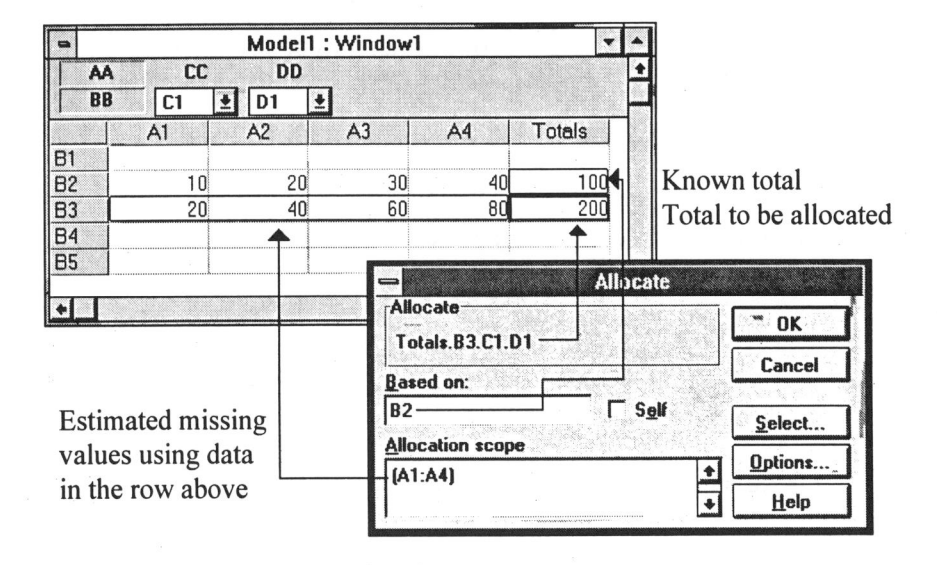

## » Advanced allocation

Once you know how easy Allocate actually is the few options that it offers also seem easy. The default behaviour of the Tools, Allocate command is to treat blank cells in the known data as being zeros. This results in an ALLOC function being created for each blank calculating a zero for the estimate of the missing value.

If you want to ignore blanks because they are not true zeros or because you simply want to avoid creating lots of ALLOC functions you can use the Options button and the Allocate Options dialog box to select Skip blanks.

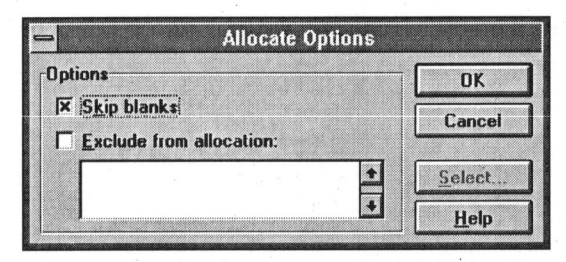

A more general problem is omitting rows or columns that do not, and should not, contain data or those where not all data values are missing. For example, you may use a column to separate sections of the data or you may have some known values mixed in. Notice that you cannot exclude values by making the allocation scope a discontinuous range because the Tools,Allocate command insists that this is continuous.

The reason for this is that the excluded range has to be treated in a slightly more sophisticated way that just being left out. In particular, any values in the excluded range corresponding to the variable with missing values should be subtracted from the total being allocated. The reason is that this proportion of the total has already been allocated by virtue of being known data!

A similar argument suggests that the known data that would have been used to estimate the excluded data should also be subtracted from the known total. SCW achieves both of these actions by entering a modified form of the ALLOC function that uses SUM functions to total the data in the excluded ranges.

For example, let's repeat the previous allocation but with A2:A3 excluded. In this instance the ALLOC formula inserted is

$$=\text{ALLOC}(B2,\text{Totals}-\text{SUM}((A2:A3)),$$
$$\text{Totals}.B2-\text{SUM}((A2:A3).B2))$$

This clearly demonstrates the way that the appropriate sum of the excluded range is subtracted from the totals. The resulting model looks as if the excluded range has just been ignored but if you enter the values 40 and 60 in A2.B3 and A3.B3 respectively you will see that the entire allocation works out as before - which is exactly how it should be as the two observed values entered are identical to their estimates as missing values!

|    | A1 | A2 | A3 | A4  | Totals |
|----|----|----|----|-----|--------|
| B1 |    |    |    |     |        |
| B2 | 10 | 20 | 30 | 40  | 100    |
| B3 | 40 |    |    | 160 | 200    |
| B4 |    |    |    |     |        |
| B5 |    |    |    |     |        |

ALLOC2.MDL : Window1 — AA / BB / CC [C1] / DD [D1]

## » Self allocation

The Tools, Allocate command has one last trick ready to help you. It can be used to allocate a new total over an existing set of data and in the same proportions as the original values.

For example, suppose we have assigned departmental budgets so that department A gets 10, B gets 20, C 30 and D 40. If suddenly the total budget is enlarged from 100 to 200 we might want to reallocate the total cash in the same proportions.

To do this select the cell containing the total and use the Tools,Allocate command. In the Allocate dialog box select the Self option and the text box next to it changes its caption to New Value. Enter into this the new total that you want to allocate and select the Allocation scope in the usual way. When you click on OK the value that you entered is distributed to the cells in the allocation scope in the same proportions as the existing data. As long as the total at the end of the row is calculated using a SUM function it will automatically change to show the new value.

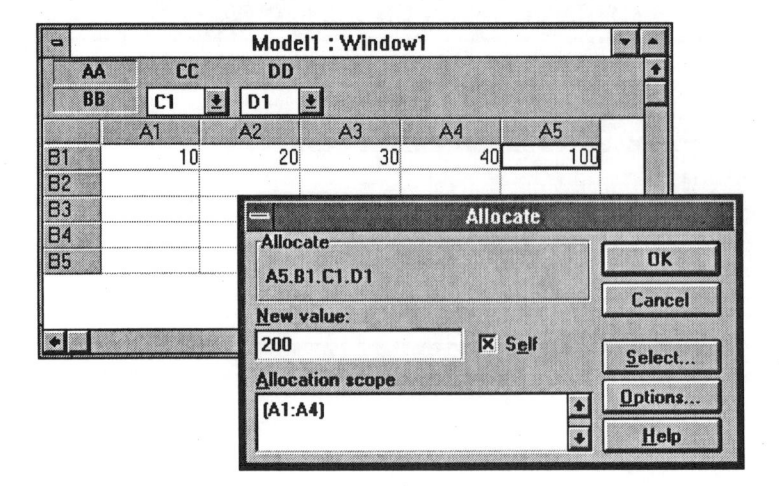

Self allocation works not by overwriting the old values with the new but by entering formulae that use the old values in combination with an ALLOC function. In the example shown above the formula entered into the cell originally containing the value 10 was

=10+ALLOC(10,200-100,100)

You can see that what the Tools,Allocate command has done is to construct a formula that allocates the extra, i.e. 200-100, added to the total in the same proportion as the original value. This allows you to recover the original values by editing out the ALLOC function.

# Key points

» A crosstab model categorises values. The items on each dimension are the categories.

» A database can be converted into a crosstab model by treating some of the fields as categorical dimensions and others as variables.

» You can convert a dBase III format database into a model and vice versa. This also provides a way of converting sheets into models and models into sheets.

» If you have multiple values for each category then you have to aggregate the data by taking an average value, the maximum, the minimum etc. so that only one summary value remains in each category.

» Categorical dimensions in a crosstab model are either fully crossed i.e. a value is possible in every cell of the model, or nested, i.e. only one cell for each item on the dimension will contain a value. Nested dimensions often suggest that the model needs to be aggregated to eliminate them.

» The analysis of crosstab models usually involves computing marginal sums or averages. These are also used in comparing the actual values to expected values. The Chi squared test can be used to judge if a model deviates significantly from what you would expect.

» Missing values are usually a serious problem in any crosstab model. You can estimate missing values using the average of the known values or by using the Allocate tool to create data in the same proportions as another variable.

# Chapter 10

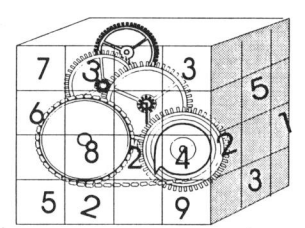

## Functional Models

In the previous chapter the emphasis was on getting data into a model, analysing it and estimating missing values. Such data oriented MDMs are very common but so are models in which virtually no data is entered. What is important in this class of model are the functions which calculate values that depend on items in any, and perhaps all, of the dimensions.

You can think of these "functional" models as being just elaborate multidimensional tables but this underestimates how much power being able to pivot the model provides. By pivoting to a new view you can begin to understand the relationships built into the model. If you also add a chart of the data, your understanding can be helped by selecting different combinations of fixed items and seeing how the chart alters. Of course, as with the discussion of data driven models in the previous chapter, it has to be added that many models are a mixture of the two types - containing both data and functional tabulations.

## » A simple investment

The best way to understand some of the difficulties of functional modelling is to try to construct a simple model. Suppose that you have a sum of money to invest on a long term basis and you want to explore how much it will be worth at particular rates of interest of over particular time periods. SCW provides a financial function which allows you to work this out directly. The function

COMPBAL(*rate,term,deposit*)

will work out the value of *deposit* which earns *rate*% interest per annum for *term* years. For example, if you invest £1000 at 5% for 10 years its final worth is COMPBAL(5%,10,1000) or £1628.89 to the nearest penny.

To investigate the way that the investment grows and its final value we need to tabulate the COMPBAL function for a range of rates and terms. To do this a reasonable first step is to create a model with dimensions called Rate and Term. You could then enter a suitable range of percentages and years as items on these two dimensions.

| Term / Rate | 5 | 10 | 15 | 20 | 25 |
|---|---|---|---|---|---|
| 2% | | | | | |
| 5% | | | | | |
| 8% | | | | | |
| 10% | | | | | |
| 12% | | | | | |

To create the tabulation the what we need is some way of referring to an item name within a formula. This is what the LABEL function allows us to do.

## » The LABEL function

The LABEL function can only be used in a model because it returns the item name corresponding to a particular dimension in a cell reference. For example, in the default model

LABEL("CC",A1.B1.C1.D1)

evaluates to C1. In general

LABEL("*dimension name*", *ref*)

gives the item in the cell reference corresponding to the named dimension. You may not at the moment think that this is a very useful function because after all if you can enter the cell reference you already know the name of the item you are after! However, the cell reference or the dimension name can be specified by functions which change their value. For example, if you enter the formula

=LABEL(A1.B3,A1.B1.C1.D1)

then the item returned will depend on the dimension name that you enter into A1.B3.

The version of the LABEL function that is most useful, however, is obtained by omitting the cell reference altogether. In this case the item name that is returned is the one corresponding to the cell that the function is stored in. For example, if you enter

=LABEL("BB")

into any cell the result is that cell's item on the BB dimension.

The LABEL function is just one of a number of special functions which allow you to access dimension and item names. These are described later.

## » Using items in functions

Returning now to the tabulation of the simple investment it is clear that we can use the LABEL function to supply the values of Rate and Term in the COMPBAL function. The LABEL("Rate") function will return the interest rate item for the current cell and the LABEL("Term") function will return the number of years the investment is to run. Putting these two together with the COMPBAL function gives

=COMPBAL(LABEL("Rate"),LABEL("Term"),50000)

which can be entered into any cell and then made into a global formula with scope

Term.Rate

that is, the entire model. If you do this you will discover that most of the model displays the correct results but the column corresponding to a 5 year investment shows the error #VALUE!

| Term \ Rate | 5 | 10 | 15 | 20 | 25 |
|---|---|---|---|---|---|
| 2% | #VALUE! | £60,949.72 | £67,293.42 | £74,297.37 | £82,030.30 |
| 5% | #VALUE! | £81,444.73 | £103,946.41 | £132,664.89 | £169,317.75 |
| 8% | #VALUE! | £107,946.25 | £158,608.46 | £233,047.86 | £342,423.76 |
| 10% | #VALUE! | £129,687.12 | £208,862.41 | £336,375.00 | £541,735.30 |
| 12% | #VALUE! | £155,292.41 | £273,678.29 | £482,314.65 | £850,003.22 |

The reason for this is that the item name returned by LABEL is a text value. As long as this text value makes sense as part of arithmetic then SCW will automatically convert it into a numeric value for you. For example, the Rate items are returned as text "5%" and so on but these are converted to numeric values when used in arithmetic or in the COMPBAL function. However, something seems to go wrong with single digit item names. The solution to the problem is either to change the item name to 05 or to use the VALUE function to explicitly convert the "5" to a numeric 5. That is the function should be

=COMPBAL(LABEL("Rate"),
    VALUE(LABEL("Term")),50000)

and with this change the final version of the model works perfectly.

| Term \ Rate | 5 | 10 | 15 | 20 | 25 |
|---|---|---|---|---|---|
| 2% | £55,204.04 | £60,949.72 | £67,293.42 | £74,297.37 | £82,030.30 |
| 5% | £63,814.08 | £81,444.73 | £103,946.41 | £132,664.89 | £169,317.75 |
| 8% | £73,466.40 | £107,946.25 | £158,608.46 | £233,047.86 | £342,423.76 |
| 10% | £80,525.50 | £129,687.12 | £208,862.41 | £336,375.00 | £541,735.30 |
| 12% | £88,117.08 | £155,292.41 | £273,678.29 | £482,314.65 | £850,003.22 |

## » Dealing with text labels

The LABEL function works very well as a way of obtaining the current label so that it can be used within a formula but only if the label is numeric. For example, suppose you had used labels such as "10 years" on the Term dimension of the previous example. In this case the item name returned by LABEL would not be usable within a formula because it is text not numeric. In some cases you can arrange to extract the numeric component of the item name using string or text functions. For example, in the case of item names such as "10 years" the problem can be solved using the LEFT text function. LEFT(*text,n*) returns the leftmost *n* characters of *text* and so LEFT("10 years",2) returns the text value "10" which is suitable for conversion into a value.

Putting this together with COMPBAL gives

=COMPBAL(LABEL("Rate"),
    VALUE(LEFT(LABEL("Term"),2)),50000)

You can use similar tricks, mainly based on the text functions FIND, LEFT, RIGHT and MID, to extract the numeric part of most item names. However, this doesn't help if the item name doesn't contain an embedded numeric value. In this case you need to look a little deeper into the way that SCW works with models.

## » Index values

As already mentioned in connection with the problem of repeated item names, SCW doesn't use item names nor dimension names internally. Each dimension is assigned an index number as it is created and each item is similarly assigned an index value. If you delete a dimension or item then the index numbers are reassigned. That is, in a five-dimensional model the dimensions are always indexed 1,2,3,4 and 5. Similarly if there are four items on a dimension they are always indexed 1,2,3 and 4.

To enable you to access the dimension and item index values SCW provides a number of specialised functions. There are two that allow you to convert from dimension and item names to index values:

DIMENSION("*dimension name*")
ITEMINDEX("*dimension name*", *ref*)

The first returns the dimension index given its name and the second the item index given the dimension and a cell reference. As with the LABEL command, if you leave out the cell reference then the item index of the cell in which the function is stored is returned.

There are also two functions that convert index values back into names:

DIMENSIONNAME(*index*)
ITEMNAME(*dimension index,item index*)

The first returns the dimension name corresponding to *index* and the second the item name corresponding to *item index* and *dimension index.*

A related function is:

DIMENSIONS()

which simply returns the number of dimensions in the current model. This is most often used within macros as part of a loop that examines or processes each dimension in turn.

## » Index expressions

You can see that by using the formula

=ITEMINDEX("*dimension name*")

you can convert any item name into a value. For example, if you have a model with a Years dimension and items 1992, 1993, 1994 etc. then you can use ITEMINDEX to convert the dates into year 1, 2 and so on. That is

=ITEMINDEX("Years")

gives 1 when stored in a cell that has 1992 as its item, 2 when the item is 1993 and so on. You can easily see that this value could be used in a calculation that involved the duration of a project, say.

You can always convert an item to a value in this way but in some cases this value may not be quite what you need to take part in the calculation that you are planning.

For example, if you use

=COMPBAL(LABEL("Rate"),
    ITEMINDEX("Term"),50000)

in the previous investment model you will find that the formula works out but it doesn't give the correct results. The reason is that the ITEMINDEX("Term") part of the formula gives values of 1,2,3, 4 and 5 and we need 5, 10, 15, 20 and 25. In this case the solution is to simply multiply the index by 5. That is,

=COMPBAL(LABEL("Rate"),
    5*ITEMINDEX("Term"),50000)

gives the correct result.

Almost any regular set of values can be generated from the item index in this way. But irregular values usually cannot. For example, try to find a transformation of 1,2,3,4 and 5 that produces the rates used in the model i.e. 2%, 5%, 8%, 10% and 12% and you will fail. There are a number of ways of dealing with irregular values but in most it is simpler to try to use the values as item names. In the case of the Rate dimension there are few enough values to make use of the CHOOSE function. This can be used to pick a value from a list.

CHOOSE(*n,list*)

will return the *n*th value from *list*. For example,

CHOOSE(3,6,8,7,100,2,4)

returns the third value from the list i.e. 7. Using this you can see that

CHOOSE(ITEMINDEX("Rate"),2%,5%,8%,10%,12%)

will select the correct interest rate according to the current Rate item. This is relatively simple but put into the complete COMPBAL formula it looks very intimidating.

=COMPBAL(CHOOSE(ITEMINDEX("Rate")
,2%,5%,8%,10%,12%),
5*ITEMINDEX("Term"),50000)

Of course if the list of values was even longer the formula would look even more intimidating and more importantly would be difficult to enter and edit.

## » External lookup tables

If you do need to select from a large number of irregular values on the basis of an item's index value then the best solution is to use a lookup table. (Lookup tables are described in some detail in Chapter 8 of *Mastering CA-SuperCalc for Windows*.) The LOOKUP function can be used in a similar fashion to CHOOSE to select a value from a list. In this case, though, the list has to be stored in the cells of a model or a sheet. In practice it is usually logically easier to create a separate sheet to hold the lookup table rather than introduce a lookup dimension into on otherwise neat and tidy model! There is no problem in using a sheet in this way because you can refer to a range of cells in a sheet from another sheet or a model simply by quoting the sheet's name. So if the lookup table is stored in Sheet1.MDS in A1:B10 you can refer to this in a model formula using the range reference

'Sheet1.MDS'!'A1:B10'

Notice that even though this is being used within a formula within a model you still have to play by the rules of sheet range references. See Chapter 12 for more details of using models and sheets together.

The lookup table consists of two columns or rows of data. The first must contain the values that you are looking up and they must be sorted into ascending order. As the values that we are looking up are just the item index values, the first column or row of the table will consist of 1,2,3, and so on. The second column or row contains the values to be returned by the LOOKUP function

$$\text{LOOKUP}(result\ range, lookup\ range, value)$$

where *value* is looked up in the *lookup range* and the corresponding value in the *result range* is returned.

Using this information it is relatively easy to create a lookup sheet and formula to give the range of interest rates used in the previous model. Create a new sheet and enter 1 to 5 in A1:A5 and the rates 2%, 5%,8%,10% and 12% in B1:B5. Save the table under a convenient name, DEMO.MDS in this example.

| | A | B |
|---|---|---|
| 1 | 1 | 2% |
| 2 | 2 | 5% |
| 3 | 3 | 8% |
| 4 | 4 | 10% |
| 5 | 5 | 12% |
| 6 | | |

You can now use this lookup table from within the original investment model but as a demonstration it is better to start a new model and enter the formula

=LOOKUP('DEMO.MDS'!$B$1:$B$5',
  'DEMO.MDS'!$A$1:$A$5',ITEMINDEX("BB"))

This simply returns the rate corresponding to the current item on the BB dimension. It looks complicated but only because of the need to include the sheet name in the range reference. If you leave this out then the formula looks more approachable

=LOOKUP('$B$1:$B$5','$A$1:$A$5',
  ITEMINDEX("BB"))

which you can see just looks up the current item's index in A1:A5 and returns the value in B1:B5. In practice it is usually simpler to enter range references in external sheets using pointing. Just start to enter the model formula in the usual way and when you reach the point where a sheet reference is required simply select the sheet and point to the area using the mouse. Working with multiple sheets and models is also made easier if you define a suitable workspace which will save and load them all as a single set, see Chapter 12.

The lookup is performed each time the model is recalculated and this can be a problem. If you convert the lookup formula into a global formula with scope

>    AA.BB.CC.DD

then you will discover that it takes some time to update the formula if you make a change to the sheet. This isn't unreasonable as the entire model has 625 lookups to perform! The solution is to set recalculation mode to manual - use the command Options,Calculations and check the "Manual" box in the dialog box that appears. Once calculation mode is set to manual you can press F9 or click on the Recalc button to update the model as necessary.

## » A 3D example

The previous example of an investment model doesn't really give you the flavour of the way a multidimensional functional model can show you the relationships between the values and the parameters. Instead of tabulating the final worth of a single deposit investment of a fixed sum let's look at the related problem of investing a regular sum. In this case there is usually a choice of how much to save per month and how long the plan will last. The exact interest rate over the term of the investment is usually out of your control and so it is important to see what the result of a range of rates is on the savings plan. (The same set of arguments, and indeed the same model, can be used to work out the value of an annuity where a lump sum is deposited and regular payments are received.)

The model is easy enough to construct using the FV or Future Value function.

$$=FV(rate, term, pay)$$

calculates the final worth of an investment of £*pay* each period for a total of *term* periods at *rate*%. The only complication here is that the term and the interest rate have to be expressed in terms of the same basic period. For example, if you deposit £10 per month for 12 months then the interest rate has to be a monthly rate. If the interest rate is quoted as an annual rate then dividing by 12 gives the monthly rate. That is the future value is given by

$$FV(rate/12, 12, 10)$$

Constructing the model is now simply a matter of setting up Interest, Payment and Term dimensions complete with suitable item names that cover the ranges that you would like to explore. In this example, Payment ranges from £10 to £50 in £10 steps, Interest is 4%, 4.5%, 5%, 5.5%, 6%, 8% and 10% and Term covers from 1 to 15 years. The quoted interest rates are assumed to be annual rates and the payments are monthly so the formula needed is

=FV(LABEL("Interest")/12,
    VALUE(LABEL("Term"))*12,-LABEL("Payment"))

which can be entered into any cell and then converted to a global formula with scope

Interest.Term.Payment

Once the model is complete you can use it to investigate the consequences of your investment decisions and the effect of

*Charts and models* **195**

| | 4% | 4.5% | 5% | 5.5% | 6% | 8% | 10% |
|---|---|---|---|---|---|---|---|
| 1 | £122.22 | £122.51 | £122.79 | £123.07 | £123.36 | £124.50 | £125.66 |
| 2 | £249.43 | £250.64 | £251.86 | £253.09 | £254.32 | £259.33 | £264.47 |
| 3 | £381.82 | £384.66 | £387.53 | £390.43 | £393.36 | £405.36 | £417.82 |
| 4 | £519.60 | £524.84 | £530.15 | £535.53 | £540.98 | £563.50 | £587.22 |
| 5 | £662.99 | £671.46 | £680.06 | £688.81 | £697.70 | £734.77 | £774.37 |
| 6 | £812.23 | £824.81 | £837.64 | £850.73 | £864.09 | £920.25 | £981.11 |
| 7 | £967.54 | £985.21 | £1,003.29 | £1,021.79 | £1,040.74 | £1,121.13 | £1,209.50 |
| 8 | £1,129.19 | £1,152.97 | £1,177.41 | £1,202.50 | £1,228.29 | £1,338.69 | £1,461.81 |
| 9 | £1,297.41 | £1,328.45 | £1,360.43 | £1,393.41 | £1,427.40 | £1,574.30 | £1,740.54 |
| 10 | £1,472.50 | £1,511.98 | £1,552.82 | £1,595.08 | £1,638.79 | £1,829.46 | £2,048.45 |
| 11 | £1,654.71 | £1,703.95 | £1,755.06 | £1,808.12 | £1,863.23 | £2,105.80 | £2,388.60 |
| 12 | £1,844.35 | £1,904.73 | £1,967.64 | £2,033.19 | £2,101.50 | £2,405.08 | £2,764.38 |
| 13 | £2,041.72 | £2,114.74 | £2,191.09 | £2,270.95 | £2,354.47 | £2,729.20 | £3,179.50 |
| 14 | £2,247.13 | £2,334.40 | £2,425.98 | £2,522.12 | £2,623.05 | £3,080.23 | £3,638.09 |
| 15 | £2,460.90 | £2,564.15 | £2,672.89 | £2,787.46 | £2,908.19 | £3,460.38 | £4,144.70 |

interest rate changes. If you want to see how a monthly payment will grow at different interest rates then make Payment the fixed dimension. To see how an assumed interest rate affects the monthly investment needed pivot so that Interest is the fixed dimension.

## » Charts and models

Charts are described in detail in *Mastering CA-SuperCalc for Windows*. In this section we look at the features that only make sense, or are particularly useful, in connection with models. You create a chart by selecting the range containing the data, then clicking on the chart button allows you to drag to define the area in the model's window that you would like the chart to occupy. Notice that, unlike in a sheet, the chart can be positioned so that it occupies an area of the model window that doesn't obscure any cells.

Perhaps the most important thing to realise about charts and models is that a chart works with data from a 2D slice of the model interpreted as rows of data values and columns of variables. In other words, the data for each variable to be plotted on the chart has to be arranged as a single column of values. This restriction to a 2D slice of rows and columns has two consequences:

» The chart is only visible when the model is pivoted so that the visible dimensions correspond to the original rows and columns that were used to define the chart.

» If you pivot the model so that the original row dimension is now the column dimension and vice versa then the chart will also be redefined to use the new columns as variables and the new rows as data.

However, as long as you have pivoted the model so that the chart is displayed, the data plotted on the chart will be taken from the current view, no matter what the values of the fixed dimensions are. In other words,

» When you define a chart you are in fact defining a family of charts - one for each combination of the fixed dimensions.

The easiest way to make these three ideas clear is via a simple example.

## » Charting the investment data

Returning to the model of regular saving, a chart showing how the total value of the fund grows over time would be helpful. To do this you have to pivot the model so that Interest and Term are the visible dimensions with Term as the vertical or row dimension. Selecting all of the data in this view, clicking on the chart button and dragging a rectangle on the model results in the default bar chart being drawn. To customise this double click on the chart and when the Chart menu appears click on the Chart type button. From this you can select a line chart which allows you to see the way that the value of the investment increases over time for a range of interest rates.

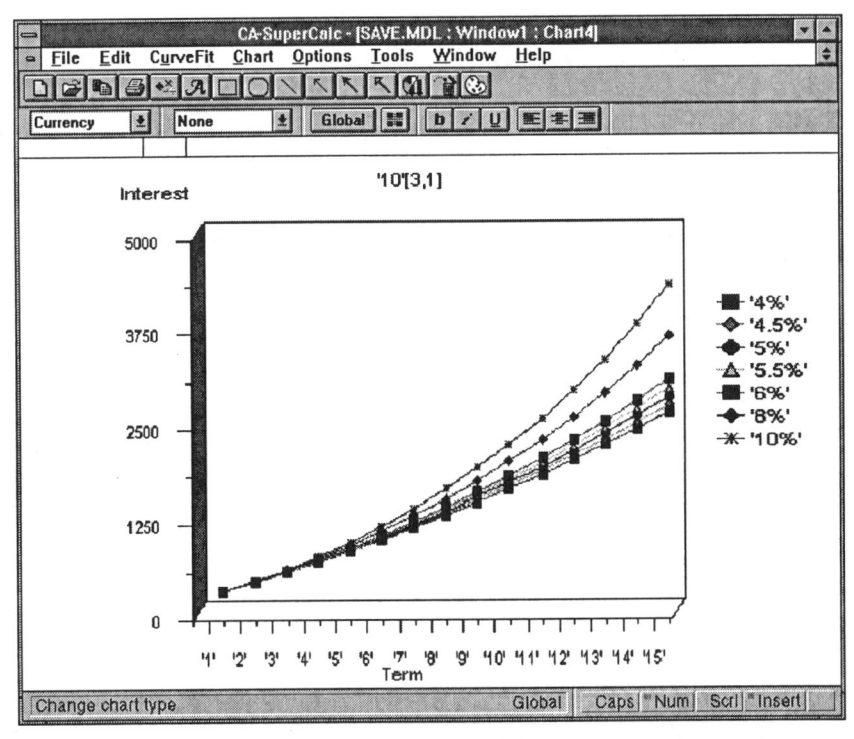

Notice that the columns of the model have been used as separate Y variables which have been plotted against the Row Number as the X variable. That is, each column has been used as a separate variable.

If you return to the model you will now discover that by selecting different items on the fixed dimension you can see the same chart for regular savings of £10 per month, £20 per month and so on.. This ability to see charts for different values of the fixed dimensions is a very powerful method of exploring the model and it works no matter how many fixed dimensions the model has.

Pivoting the model so that either Term or Interest are the fixed dimension makes the chart vanish - as is perfectly reasonable. However, pivoting so that Term becomes the horizontal, i.e. column rather than row, dimension produces a result that you might not have expected. In this case you will have 15 lines on the line chart - one for each term from 1 year to 15 years with the data plotted for each line corresponding to the five interest rates.

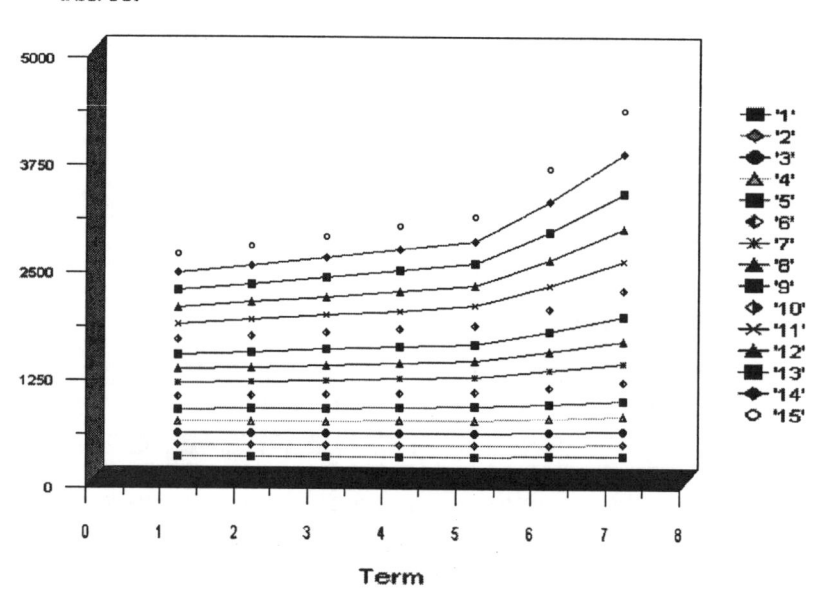

What makes this chart confusing is that the default labels that have been applied to the axes have not been changed and so it still claims to be a plot against Term and not against Rate. In most cases you should avoid viewing a chart pivoted so that the rows and columns have been swapped in this way - but occasionally it can be useful.

## » Plotting row labels

One final feature of SCW's charting facilities that only makes sense when applied to models is the option to plot row labels as opposed to row numbers. In a sheet, and in a model, it is sometimes useful to use row numbers as the X variable but in a model you might want to make use of the item labels as data to include on the chart. You can do this by selecting Row Label in the dialog box that appears after you have selected a chart type.

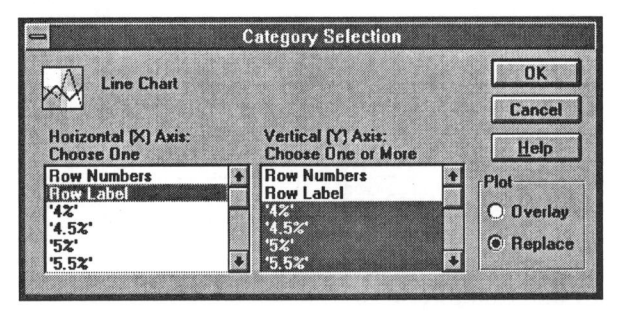

You can think of Row Numbers as corresponding to item index values and Row Labels as the item names themselves. Notice that Row Labels are always treated as text items and so they are always plotted using equal intervals, irrespective of their numeric value. For example, if you select Row Labels and the items names are 1%, 5%, 20% and 50% then these will be plotted on the X axis with the same distance between them - even though the distance from 1% to 5% should be smaller than from 5% to 20% or from 20% to 50%.

## » Terms

Terms are a special type of global formula that can be applied to the entire model or to a restricted scope. A term is different from an ordinary global formula in that it isn't stored in any particular cell and it doesn't modify what is actually stored in any cell. You can use a term to scale the results of a model or apply a transformation to the results. For example, in the savings model you could decide to display the results in dollars rather than in pounds and this could be achieved by defining a term which applied a conversion factor.

To define a term you use the command Formula,Terms which displays the Terms dialog box.

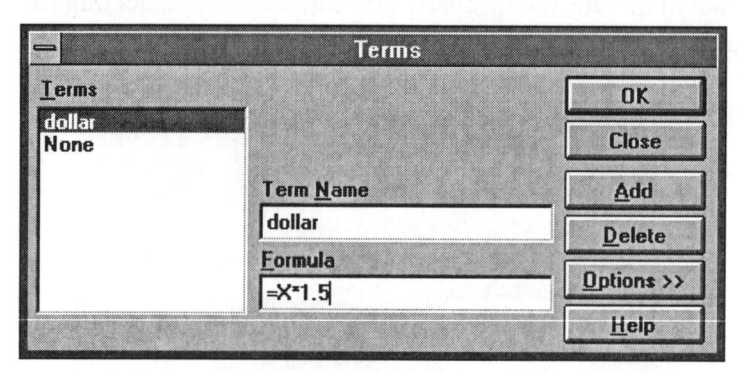

[Terms dialog box showing:
- Terms list: dollar, None
- Term Name: dollar
- Formula: =X*1.5
- Buttons: OK, Close, Add, Delete, Options >>, Help]

You can use this to add, edit or delete terms. Each term has a name which is listed in the Terms text box. The formula that corresponds to the term is entered or displayed in the Formula box. You can enter any valid SCW formula into the Formula box the only difference is that in a term the symbol X stands for the data stored in the cell that the term is being applied to.

So, for example, to convert pounds to dollars you simply use the formula

$$=X*1.5$$

assuming that there are 1.5 dollars to the pound. When you apply this term all of the values in the model are displayed multiplied by 1.5. Notice that none of the formulae or data already stored in the model are changed by applying a term.

You can select which term is applied to a model either by using the Formula,Terms command and selecting the name of the term that you want to apply or by using the Terms drop down list in the model bar. To display the model without a term modifying the values select "None".

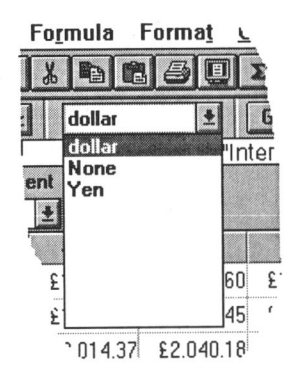

In addition to applying a simple term you can also associate each term with its own format. To do this you have to click on the Options button which results in the larger version of the Terms dialog box being displayed.

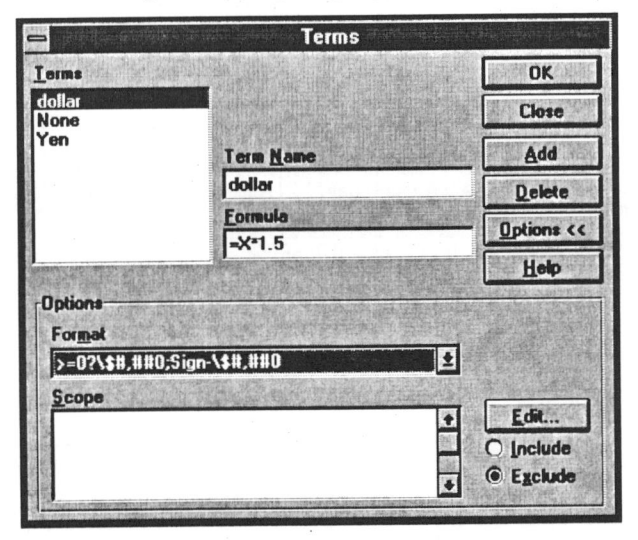

You can select any format, including any that you may have defined earlier, in the Format list. When you apply the term then the format will also be applied to the data.

The Options button also reveals the Scope entry box. You can use this to specify the scope to which the term is to be applied. As long as you understand the idea of the scope of a global function then this facility will need no further explanation. There is one difference, however, in that you can use the scope to specify either the cells that are to be included or the cells that are to be excluded from the application of the term. Use whichever one you find easier to define and which seems to fit the logic of the situation. Notice that you can only apply one term at a time.

That's almost all there is to terms but, as with general formulae, the power of a term depends on how imaginative you are in using the standard facilities. For example, you can make use of cell references in a term and this means that you can create terms that express values as percentages of marginal totals say. For example, in the staff data example introduced in the previous chapter you could define a term which divides all of the values by the grand total stored in Gender totals.Group totals.

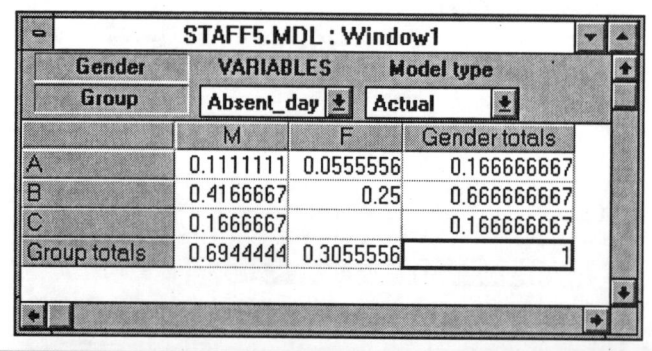

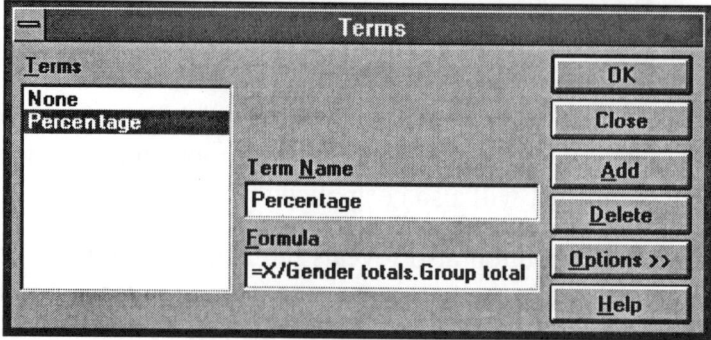

| | | STAFF5.MDL : Window1 | | |
|---|---|---|---|---|
| | Gender | VARIABLES | Model type | |
| | Group | Absent_day | Actual | |
| | | M | F | Gender totals |
| A | | 0.1111111 | 0.0555556 | 0.166666667 |
| B | | 0.4166667 | 0.25 | 0.666666667 |
| C | | 0.1666667 | | 0.166666667 |
| Group totals | | 0.6944444 | 0.3055556 | 1 |

Terms

Terms:
None
Percentage

Term Name: Percentage

Formula: =X/Gender totals.Group total

[OK] [Close] [Add] [Delete] [Options >>] [Help]

Notice that you can make use of underspecification to make a term relative. For example if you define a term in the staff model as

=X/(Gender totals)

then the marginal from each row would be used on that row to calculate the proportion. In other words, the term behaves as if it was stored in each cell in turn as it is being calculated.

## » Entering values using terms

At their simplest, terms can be used to modify how the values in the model display. However, as long as you keep the term formula relatively simple, a term can also be used to modify values as they are input. For example, if you create a term called Scale defined as =X/1000 then all of the values in the model will show 1000 times smaller than they are. Now if you enter a value into a cell the value that you enter will appear to be unchanged - even though the term is supposed to be reducing everything displayed by a factor of 1000.

What has happened is that the term has been used to modify the input value so that it is 1000 times larger - hence when the term is applied there is no change! What SCW actually enters when a term is in force is a formula that undoes the effect of the term. For example if the term is X/1000 and you enter a value of 50 say SCW will actually enter =(50)*1000. Put simply it looks as if you are entering values on a scale that fits with the currently applied term. In most cases this is exactly what you want to happen - if you are working with a term that changes pounds to dollars then you want to enter data in dollars but have it converted to pounds when the term is removed.

The only condition on all of this is that the term has to be simple enough for SCW to be able to work out what its reverse is. This means that you cannot use any of SCW's functions and you can only use X once in the term. However, you can use cell references and this means you can enter values in terms of the percentage of some other value if you want to.

## » Analysing a mailshot

As a more realistic example of using a functional model, consider the problem of working out the economics of a direct mail campaign. The product being offered can be made in various batch sizes - 1000 off, 2000 and so on. There is an initial cost in producing the entire batch which is independent of the number actually sold. In this example it is assumed that the production cost is a fixed unit cost times the batch size. It would be perfectly possible to build in a variable unit cost using a lookup table, see Chapter 12. When sold to the customer the product brings in an income of £10 per item but there are also mailing costs of £1.5 per item. To allow the analysis to explore the effect of the product mailing cost this item is kept separate. The advertising expenditure consists of the cost to print the flyer and its mailing cost. Each of these is a simple unit cost times the size of the advertising campaign. You can see that we have a number of variables

        Production cost
        Sales income
        Product postage
        Flyer cost
        Flyer postage

and their sum gives us the total profit on the campaign. We also have two parameters, Batch size and Campaign size, which obviously need to be dimensions along which the functions are tabulated. In other words, we need a simple 3D model.

A suitable structure for the model can be seen below although of course you are free to choose your own names for the dimensions, variables and the item ranges.

```
            MAILSHOT.MDL : Window1
  Batch size      No of flyers
  Variables       '10000'
                  1000   2000   3000   4000   5000
Production cost
Flyer print cost
Flyer mail cost
Sales income
Product mail cost
Profit
```

Now all we need to do is enter some formulae. The Production cost is given by

=-LABEL("Batch size")*1.5

The Flyer print cost is

=-LABEL("No of flyers")*0.02

The Flyer mail cost is

=-LABEL("No of flyers")*0.2

A more complicated formula is the one needed for Sales income. The reason is that you have to assume that a particular proportion of the flyers generate sales - 4% say. This means that the number of items that you sell is given by

LABEL("No of flyers")*4%

but if this number is larger than the batch size you cannot meet the order. In other words, you have to compare the total sales with the batch size and make sure you don't sell more than you have produced. The resulting formula is

=IF((LABEL("No of flyers")*4%)>
    VALUE(LABEL("Batch size")),
        LABEL("Batch size")*10,
            LABEL("No of flyers")*4%*10)

In the same way the formula for Product mail cost is

=-IF(LABEL("No of flyers")*3%>
    VALUE(LABEL("Batch size")),
        LABEL("Batch size")*1.5,
            LABEL("No of flyers")*4%*1.5)

Notice that the second LABEL function needs to be used with VALUE because it is not involved in any arithmetic and so SCW will not automatically convert it to a number.

Finally the formula to total all of the costs is

    =SUM((Production cost:Product mail cost))

All of these formulae have to be entered into convenient cells and then converted to global formulae with scope

        Batch size.Profit.No of flyers

MAILSHOT.MDL : Window1

| Batch size | No of flyers | | | | |
|---|---|---|---|---|---|
| Variables | '10000' | | | | |
|  | 1000 | 2000 | 3000 | 4000 | 5000 |
| Production cost | -£1,500.00 | -£3,000.00 | -£4,500.00 | -£6,000.00 | -£7,500.00 |
| Flyer print cost | -£200.00 | -£200.00 | -£200.00 | -£200.00 | -£200.00 |
| Flyer mail cost | -£2,000.00 | -£2,000.00 | -£2,000.00 | -£2,000.00 | -£2,000.00 |
| Sales income | £4,000.00 | £4,000.00 | £4,000.00 | £4,000.00 | £4,000.00 |
| Product mail cost | -£600.00 | -£600.00 | -£600.00 | -£600.00 | -£600.00 |
| Profit | -£300.00 | -£1,800.00 | -£3,300.00 | -£4,800.00 | -£6,300.00 |

## Analysing a mailshot

From the finished model you can quickly see that there is no point in making the product at all with a mailing of only 10,000 flyers. If you examine the model for other mailshot sizes you will find that you do eventually make a profit but a much simpler way of examining the relationship between number of flyers and profit is to pivot the model so that Variables becomes the fixed dimension. In this view you can immediately see the middle band that shows an overall profit.

| Batch size / No of flyers | Variables / Profit | | | | |
|---|---|---|---|---|---|
| | 1000 | 2000 | 3000 | 4000 | 5000 |
| 10000 | -£300.00 | -£1,800.00 | -£3,300.00 | -£4,800.00 | -£6,300.00 |
| 20000 | £900.00 | -£600.00 | -£2,100.00 | -£3,600.00 | -£5,100.00 |
| 50000 | -£4,000.00 | £3,000.00 | £1,500.00 | £0.00 | -£1,500.00 |
| 75000 | -£9,500.00 | -£2,500.00 | £4,500.00 | £3,000.00 | £1,500.00 |
| 100000 | -£15,000.00 | -£8,000.00 | -£1,000.00 | £6,000.00 | £4,500.00 |

This particular view also suggests constructing a chart of profit against number of flyers for each batch size. This also allows you to inspect the pattern of cost for each of the variables in turn.

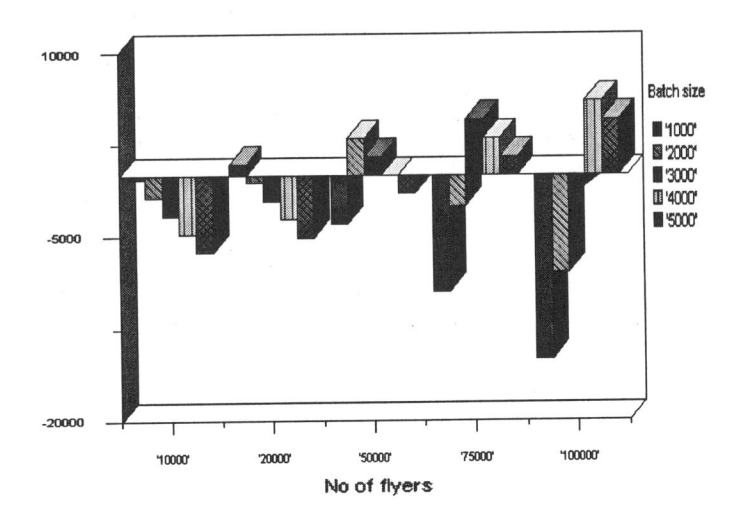

After using the model for a few minutes it becomes apparent that a dimension has been left out. As well as batch size and number of flyers, it would be interesting to view the way profit varied with the effectiveness of the mailshot. In other words, we need to add a fourth dimension - Hit rate,say - and tabulate all of the functions for a range of values. This is easily done. Add another dimension called Hit rate with eight items and make sure that it inherits the global formulae. Next change the items names to 1% to 8% and edit the formula for Sales income to read

=IF((LABEL("No of flyers")*LABEL("Hit rate"))>
    VALUE(LABEL("Batch size")),
      LABEL("Batch size")*10,
        LABEL("No of flyers")*LABEL("Hit rate")*10)

and edit the formula for product mailing cost to

=-IF(LABEL("No of flyers")*LABEL("Hit rate")>
    VALUE(LABEL("Batch size")),
      LABEL("Batch size")*1.5,
        LABEL("No of flyers")*LABEL("Hit rate")*1.5)

If you look at these formulae you will see that the only difference is the use of LABEL("Hit rate") in place of the 4% hit rate used in the originals.

| Hit rate / No of flyers | 1% | 2% | 3% | 4% | 5% | 6% | 7% | 8% |
|---|---|---|---|---|---|---|---|---|
| 10000 | -£5,850.00 | -£5,000.00 | -£4,150.00 | -£3,300.00 | -£2,450.00 | -£1,600.00 | -£750.00 | £100.00 |
| 20000 | -£7,200.00 | -£5,500.00 | -£3,800.00 | -£2,100.00 | -£400.00 | £1,300.00 | £3,000.00 | £4,700.00 |
| 50000 | -£11,250.00 | -£7,000.00 | -£2,750.00 | £1,500.00 | £5,750.00 | £10,000.00 | £10,000.00 | £10,000.00 |
| 75000 | -£14,625.00 | -£8,250.00 | -£1,875.00 | £4,500.00 | £4,500.00 | £4,500.00 | £4,500.00 | £4,500.00 |
| 100000 | -£18,000.00 | -£9,500.00 | -£1,000.00 | -£1,000.00 | -£1,000.00 | -£1,000.00 | -£1,000.00 | -£1,000.00 |

Variables: Profit; Batch size: '3000'

*Analysing a mailshot* **209**

The final model allows you to explore the effect of quality of advertising and marketing on profit. You can also look at the original chart of profit against number of flyers for each batch size but now you can also set the percentage hit rate. Other charts are also useful. For example, charting profit against number of flyers for each hit rate at fixed batch sizes is also interesting.

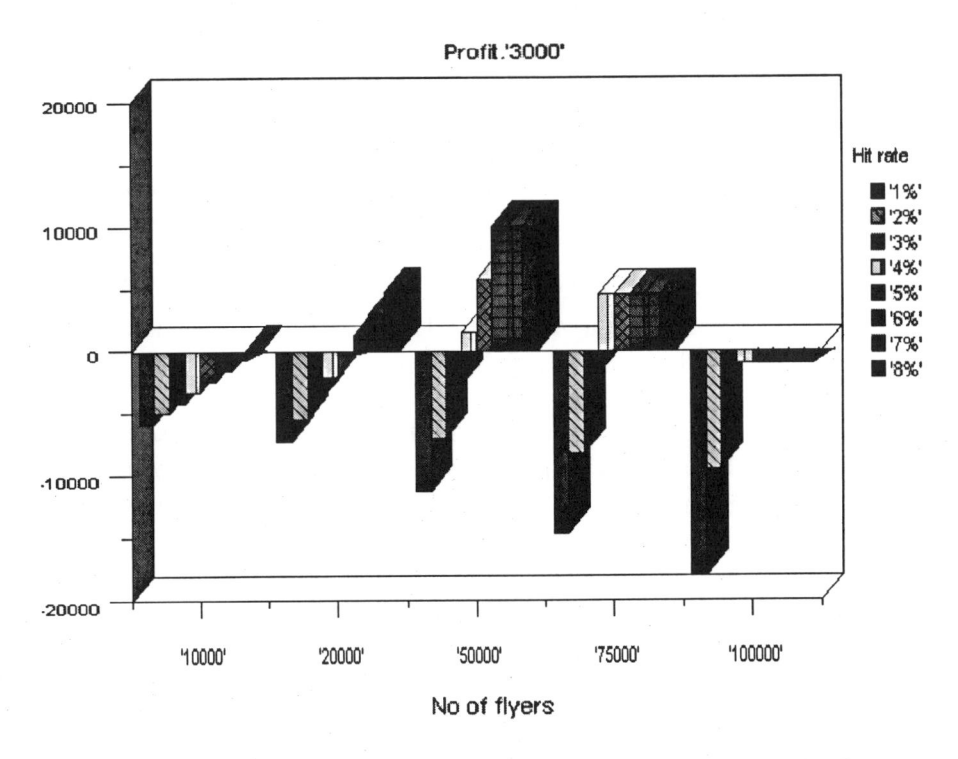

Profit.'3000'

No of flyers

Hit rate
- '1%'
- '2%'
- '3%'
- '4%'
- '5%'
- '6%'
- '7%'
- '8%'

You can continue to elaborate this model and obviously the accuracy of its results depend crucially on the validity of its assumptions. In particular, there is likely to be an economy of scale in most of the costs that is not included in this model but could be with just a little extra effort, see Chapter 12.

## Key points

» Functional models can be used to tabulate multidimensional quantities.

» Formulae within the functional model often make use of the current item value. The function LABEL("dimensionname") can be used to discover the current item label and the VALUE function can be used to convert this into a numeric value.

» Item names can be converted to regular numeric values using the ITEMINDEX function.

» To convert item index values into an irregular series of values you need to use the CHOOSE function or the LOOKUP function in combination with a sheet.

» Charts can be constructed using the values in the model in just the same way as in sheets. The only difference is that the data is taken from a specified 2D range and the chart will be drawn using the current fixed items. That is, charts are "indexed" by the fixed items.

» Terms are a special type of global formula which can be applied to the whole model or a selected range without altering the contents of the cells. You can associate a particular format with a term.

» Terms can also be used to enter values in the natural scale implied by the term.

# Chapter 11

# Estimation and Prediction

A fundamental purpose of modelling is to make estimates or predictions of unknown values. This subject is a branch of statistics and as such takes us into some potentially complex ideas. However, the basic principles of estimation and prediction are essentially common sense - provided you can see exactly what is going on! Closely related to the idea of estimation and prediction is the idea of a relationship between variables.

Although nearly all of the estimation and prediction facilities described in this chapter apply to models as well as sheets it is simpler to describe their use, and give examples, using sheets.

## » Curves and relationships

The whole topic of estimation and prediction can be reduced to the problem of finding relationships between variables. If you know the relationship between variables then you can use the variables you know to predict or estimate the unknown variables. The question is, what do we mean by a relationship between variables? This is best answered graphically. If you take two variables, X and Y, and make measurements that give you the value of Y for a particular value of X then to see if there is any relationship between the two the best course of action is to draw a graph. If there is a relationship between the variables you will see the plotted points form a curve of some shape or other. The relationship between X and Y is summarised by this curve because using it you can estimate the value of Y corresponding to any given value of X.

For example, if you measure and plot the annual profit made by a company and the size of its workforce you might get a curve that looked something like:

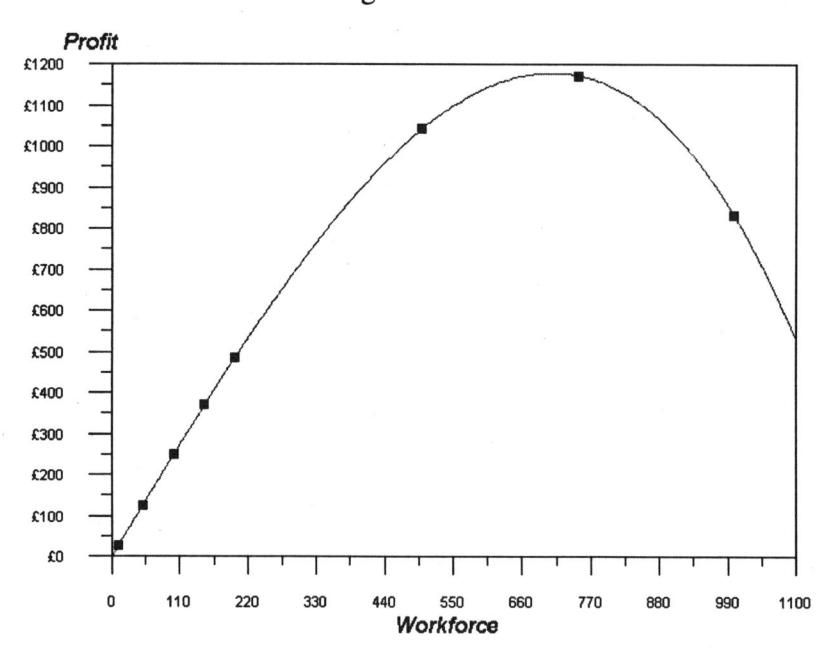

I have to admit that the data in this plot is entirely fictional but you can see that it fits in with the preconception that profit increases with size of company but then decreases once the company is very large! The curve can be used to predict the profit a company would make given the size of its workforce. All you have to do is locate the workforce value on the X-axis, follow the vertical line up until it meets the curve and then read off horizontally the related profit figure.

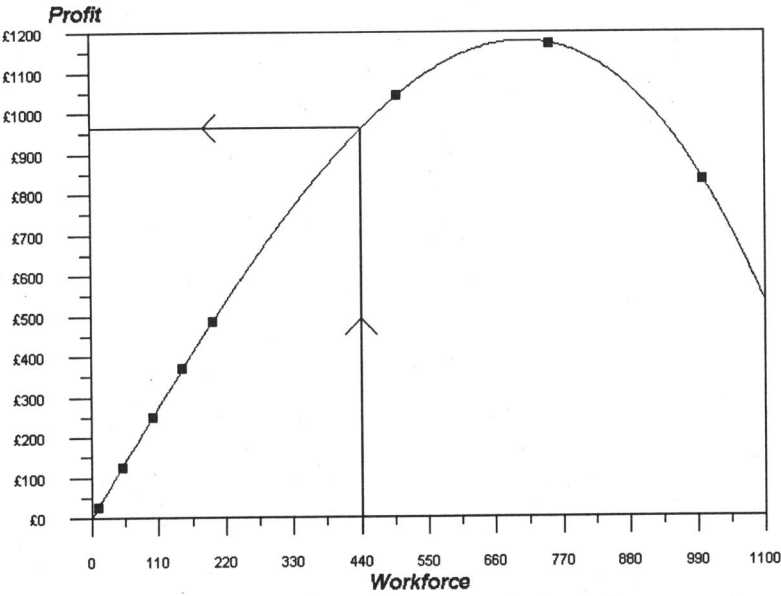

In this relationship Workforce is referred to as the "independent variable" because it is the one that you use to look up the value of Profit which is called the "dependent variable".

## » Simple curves

Clearly discovering a relationship between two variables is potentially very useful but the relationship has to be usable. In the example of Workforce and Profit only a few actual data points in the relationship are known and it is assumed that what happens between the known points can be represented by a smooth curve. If this is not the case then you will need to gather many more points. The more complex the relationship the more points are needed to create an accurate curve which can be used to predict new values. The most practical types of relationship correspond to simple curves and the simplest of all curves is the straight line. The reason why a straight line is so simple is that it only needs two observed points to determine the line for all values. Notice that while two points determine a single line there are an infinity of possible curves that pass through them.

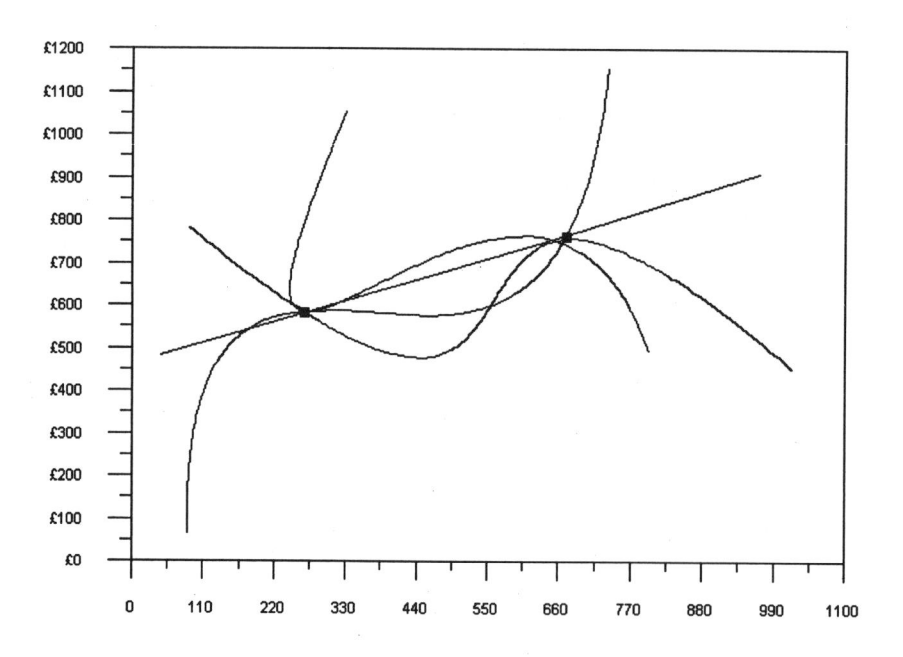

If a relationship doesn't happen to fit the form of a straight line then we have to look to more curves that are just a little more complicated - polynomials and exponential curves - and these are discussed later.

## » Inexact relationships

So far the relationships that we have been looking at have been assumed to be exact. That is, the points on the chart fall exactly on the curve. In practice this is a rare occurrence for a wide range of reasons. The most common reason is that the influence of random factors will alter the true value away from the curve. In other words, instead of measuring a value Y which lies exactly on the curve we measure a value Y+error which is displaced above or below the curve.

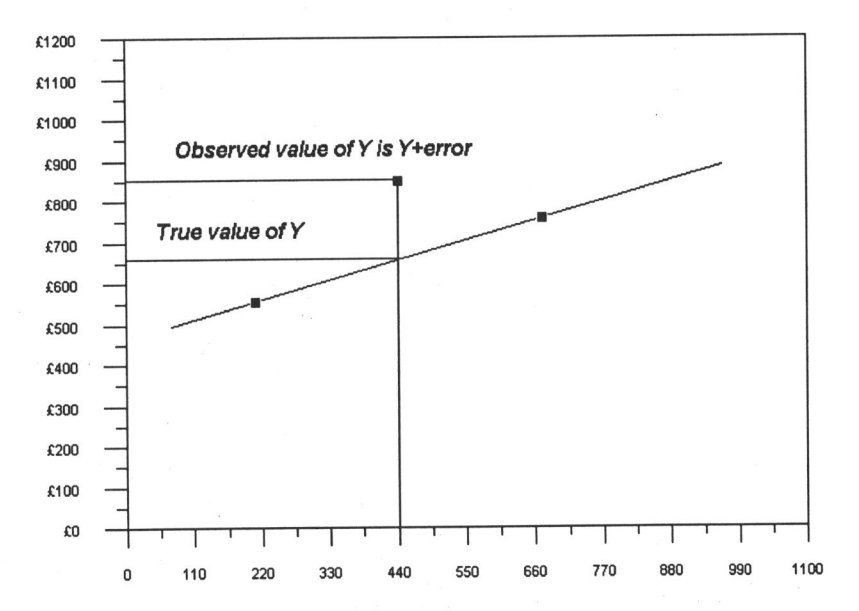

This isn't a difficult idea and given that you have the true curve your best estimate of Y is still the value that it predicts. In any particular case this will be a little high or a little low but on average it is closer to the value than any other estimate.

A more difficult problem is how you find the curve given that you only have imperfect data? For example, if the true relationship between X and Y is a straight line and you can make perfect measurements then all of the points will lie on the line and all you have to do is join them up. If the data is imperfect then all of the points will be displaced from the true line and there is no simple way to work out where it should be.

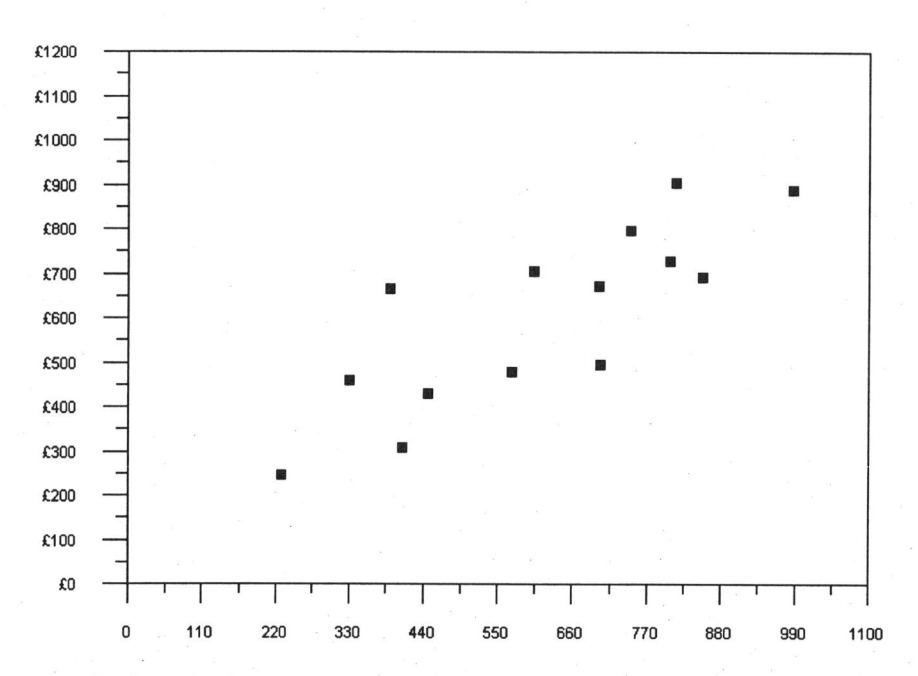

In fact the best we can say is that the points look as if they cluster around a line. This is the key to estimating where the line is. What we do is try to place a line on the chart that "best fits" the observed points. Of course this raises the question of what we mean by "best fits" and the answer is that it is up to you to decide what it should mean. The simplest method is to take a clear plastic ruler and move it around until you judge that the line best fits the data. This is simple but it has the disadvantage of being subjective. That is, two different people are likely to find two different lines.

A more objective measure is to find a line the minimises the average deviation of the points from it. The only problem with this approach is that deviations can be positive and negative and so they cancel each out. The traditional solution to this problem is to average the squared deviations from the proposed line, remember the square of a negative value is positive. The line is then adjusted until it is in a position that produces the smallest total squared deviation. This is the familiar "least squares" or "regression method" of fitting a line to data.

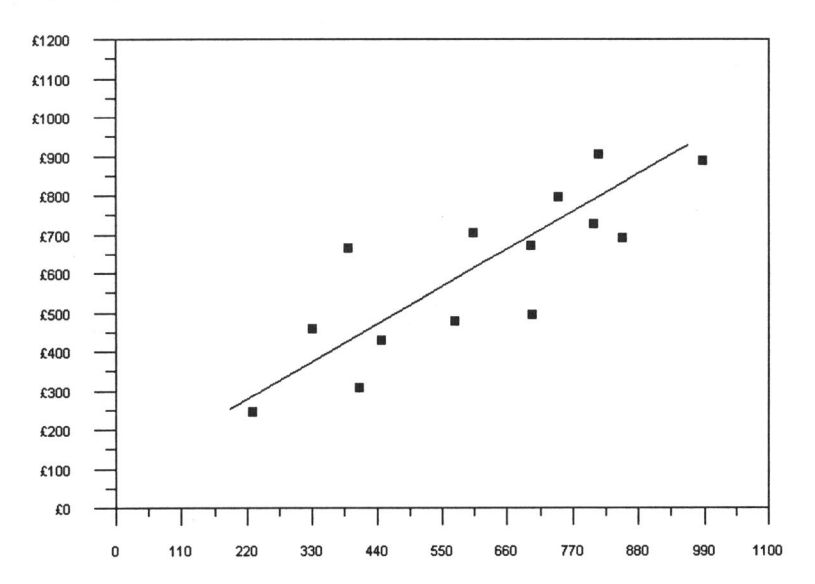

## » Practical estimation

You can use a chart to estimate a value of Y given a value of X but it isn't very convenient. What you really would like is a formula that converts X into Y. For simple curves this is entirely possible, and indeed relatively easy. For example, any relationship that can be summarised by a straight line is associated with a formula of the type

$$Y=S*X+C$$

where S and C are values that depend upon the line. For example, if S was 10 and C was 30 the formula giving the value of Y would be

$$Y=10*X+30$$

For any line there is a value of S and a value of C that allows you to predict Y given X. The value S corresponds to the slope of the line, i.e. how steep the relationship is, and C corresponds to the position of the line on chart, i.e. where it intersects the Y-axis.

## » Curve Builder

So far the discussion has been theoretical but it is often the case that you know the value of a variable and would like to use it to estimate another. SCW provides a very powerful tool, Curve Builder, to help you with this very situation. However, unless you understand the basic ideas of using a curve to estimate unknown variables it isn't likely to make very much sense. The most important thing to realise is that there are two stages in estimating an unknown variable - obtaining the curve and using it. Curve Builder provides a number of options to help you specify or discover the curve and then uses it to estimate the unknown quantity.

Before you give the Tools,Curve Builder command you have to select the cell that will contain the value you are trying to estimate. The Curve Builder dialog box then appears and gives you a range of choices concerning the type of curve and how it will be specified.

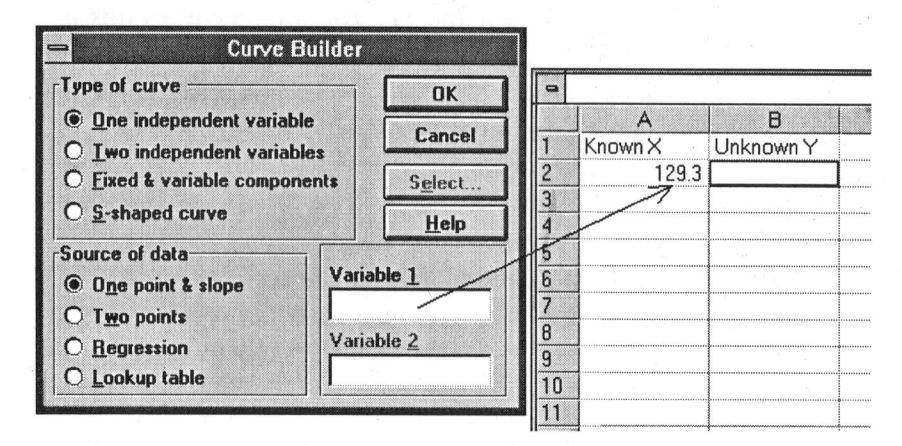

After you have selected the type of curve you also need to specify the cell which contains the X value that will be used to predict the Y value. Notice that at this stage we ignore the problem of specifying the curve exactly - all that enters our consideration is the X value, the general form of the curve and the cell that the result, i.e. Y, will be stored in.

If you click on OK the next dialog box that you see is concerned with the exact specification of the curve that is going to be used to estimate Y from X. Obviously the format of this dialog box is going to depend on the type of curve you have selected and how you are going to specify it. There are four general curve types and four ways of specifying them. Not all methods of specification apply to all curve types.

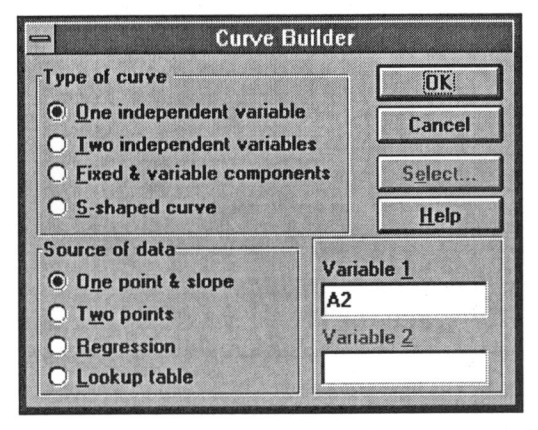

For the moment it is simpler to restrict our attention to the "One independent variable" type of curve as this corresponds to using a line to predict a Y value given a single X value. For this type of curve all four methods of specifying the curve are valid. The first three make sense if you think of the curve as a simple line. To specify the line you can:

» give one point on the line and its slope

» give two points that the line passes through

» supply a set of known X and known Y values and let SCW calculate a line using regression.

For example, if you select the One independent variable and the One point & slope options then the dialog box asks you to supply an X and Y value for the known point on the line and a percentage slope. It uses these values to work out the equation of the line and then applies this to the known X value supplied in the first dialog box.

*Slope*

*Known X value*

*Known Y value*

**One independent variable - one point & slope**

Data
A2
20

Slope (%)
10

cost
30

Express cost
● As cost
○ As a ratio

Make axes
○ Both log
○ Log on cost
● Both linear

OK
Cancel
Select...
Help

There are other options in the dialog box that affect the type of curve used to estimate the Y value. The Express cost section merely allows you to estimate Y either as a simple value or as a proportion of the known X value. Notice that SCW often refers to the Y variable as "Cost" because this is a commonly estimated variable. If you choose the option As a ratio SCW assumes that the curve that you are working with estimates the value of Y as a proportion of the known X variable. So to estimate the actual value of Y it multiplies by the known X value. That is, the curve is assumed to estimate Y/X.

The Make axes section of the dialog box allows you to select between three types of curve - Both log, Log on cost and Both linear. These descriptions correspond to three different characteristic curve shapes. The only shape that we have discussed so far is the straight line - the Both linear option. The two log options are described in more detail later in this chapter.

## » Estimation formulae

If you select the Cost and Linear options then an estimate of the unknown Y value will be placed in the cell that you selected before

|   | A | B |
|---|---|---|
| 1 | Known X | Unknown Y |
| 2 | 129.3 | -117.555 |

using the Tools,Curve Builder command. If you examine the contents of the cell containing the estimate then you will discover that rather than a value it contains a formula.

Curve Builder doesn't use an internal mechanism to estimate the unknown value. Instead it uses the information that you provide it with via its dialog boxes to construct a formula using the standard statistical functions. If you want to you can use these statistical functions directly and by-pass Curve Builder. For example, the estimate of the unknown Y described earlier is given by

=TREND((30,30*10%),(20,2*20),A2)

TREND is a general purpose function that will both work out the details of the line and estimate the value of Y given a value of X. Details of the statistical functions, including some that Curve Builder doesn't use, are given later in this chapter.

The main consequence of Curve Builder's use of statistical functions is that once you have an estimate you can change the value of X and see a new estimate of Y.

## » Specifying the curve

Now that we have a general overview of the way that Curve Builder works we need to take a closer look at the different ways it allows us to specify the exact form of the curve.

### » Point and slope

In this case you have to supply a known X and Y value and a percentage slope. You can either enter these as constant values into the dialog box or as cell references. SCW uses the information to work out a second point that lies on the line. (If X and Y are known points on a line of slope S then so is 2*X, S*X+Y.) In this sense the point and slope specification is no different to the two-point specification.

### » Two points

Specifying a line by giving two points that lie on it is conceptually the simplest option. You can either enter a pair of known X and Y values as constants or use cell references.

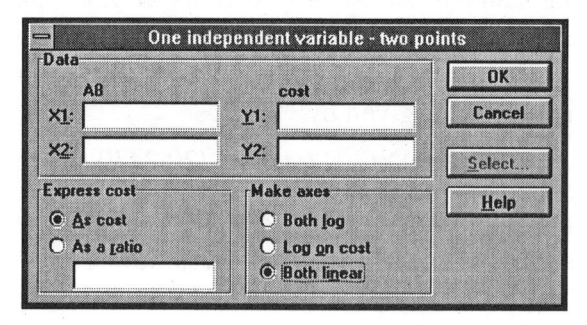

### » Regression

As already described, regression is a method of finding a line that best fits the data. In this case you have to specify a range that contains the known X values and the known Y values. Each range has to be a list of values and there have to be the same number of values in each. SCW uses the data to

## Bug Box - One point & slope

There is a bug in the way that SCW version 1 makes use of the One point & slope specification of a line. Given the point $X_1,Y_1$ and the slope S it attempts to calculate a second point on the line. This is given by $2*X_1, S*X_1+Y_1$, but unfortunately SCW calculates this as $2*X_1, S*Y_1$, which is of course not on the line. As a result the estimate of y is incorrect. The solution is to edit the formula inserted by the Curve Builder command so that the second Y value is given by $S*X_1+Y_1$. There are similar problems when used with LogLinear curves but it is correct for LogLog curves - see later.

calculate a best fitting line and then uses this to calculate the best estimate of Y. Notice that the first text box is used for the known X range and the second for the known Y range.

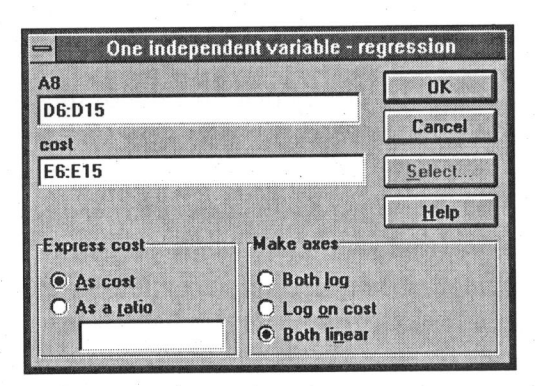

Each of these methods uses the TREND function to estimate the line. TREND calculates a best fitting line to the data it is supplied with. If it is only supplied with two data points then it calculates an exact line through the two points. Hence when used with one point and slope or with the two point option TREND calculates an exact line and when used with the regression option it calculates a best fitting line.

## » LogLinear and LogLog curves

There are two variations on the basic straight line that you can use as a relationship between two variables. These curves are obtained from the straight line by simple changes in the way the X and Y values are measured. For example, if you have a Y value which doubles each time X is increased by the same amount then you most certainly do not have a straight line relationship. For example, if you plot the data

| X | Y |
|---|---|
| 1 | 2 |
| 2 | 4 |
| 3 | 8 |
| 4 | 16 |
| 5 | 32 |

then the curve that you see is indeed a curve. Notice that the data simply corresponds to a doubling of the Y value each time the X value increases by one.

It looks as if there is no way that the relationship between X and Y can be a linear one - but it is very easy to recast the relationship so that it is a perfect line. All you have to do is plot the log of Y against X and you will immediately see a perfect straight line relationship. Such a relationship is often referred to as a LogLinear relationship and SCW allows you to automatically use a LogLinear curve to estimate a Y value.

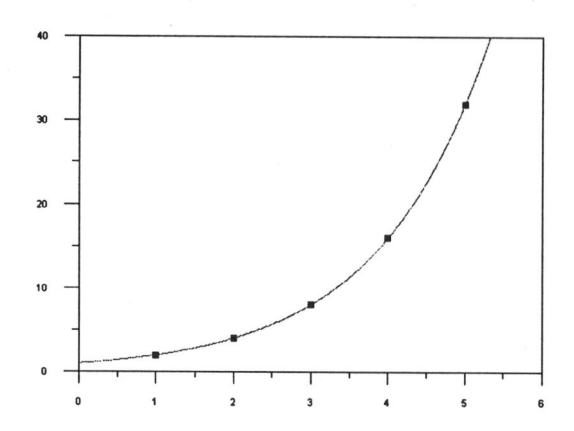

## LogLinear and LogLog curves

Doubling Y for each increase in X is just a special case of Y changing by some fixed percentage each time X is increased by the same amount. For example, the action of compound interest on a deposit increases it by a fixed percentage each time period. This and all such similar relationships are LogLinear.

As you might have guessed if there is a LogLinear curve then there is likely to be a LogLog curve! In this case the relationship between X and Y is such that Y increases by a fixed percentage each time you multiply X by a constant. For example, if you double the workforce you might find that productivity increases by 95% (i.e. less than the 100% a linear relationship would suggest). In the case of the following data the Y value increases by 50% each time X doubles -

| X | Y |
|---|---|
| 1 | 1 |
| 2 | 1.5 |
| 4 | 2.25 |
| 8 | 3.375 |
| 16 | 5.0625 |

If you draw a chart of this data you can see the characteristic shape of the LogLog curve. As you might expect plotting the Log of X against the Log of Y produces a straight line.

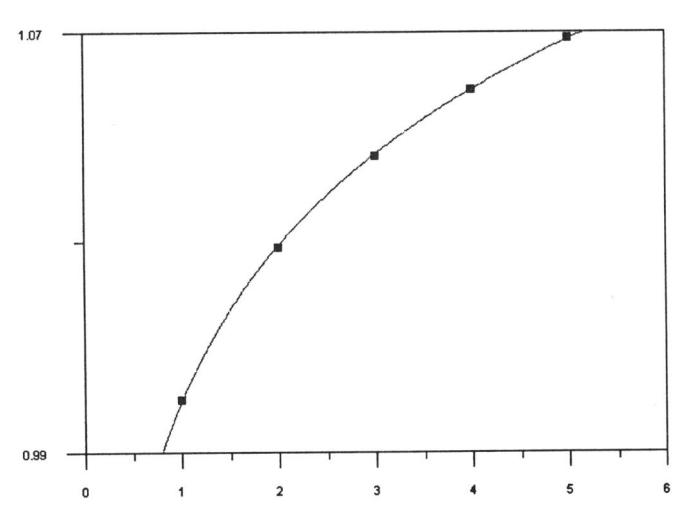

## » Log curves using Curve Builder

You can use LogLinear and LogLog curves to estimate new Y values via Curve Builder. If you proceed as if you were going to use a simple line to estimate the Y value and then select either Both log or Log on cost in the second dialog box then a LogLog or LogLinear curve will be used respectively.

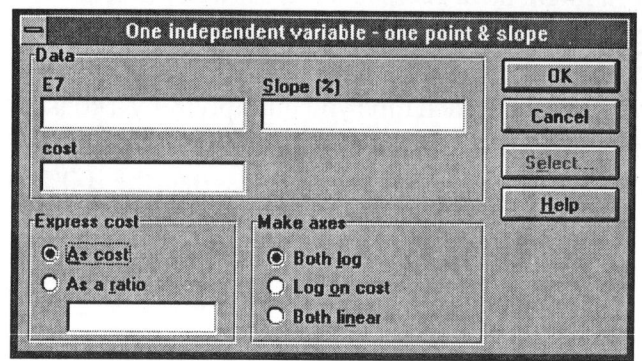

You can use any of the familiar methods of specifying the curve - one point and slope, two points or regression - when working with LogLog or LogLinear curves. Notice, however, that the point and slope method is a little strange in that the slope you specify is the percentage change in Y when you double the X value for the LogLog curve and the percentage change when you increase X by 1 in the LogLinear model.

---

### Bug Box - LogLinear curve

The bug in the One point & slope specification described earlier in connection with linear estimation also applies to the LogLinear curve. Again, the second point is obtained by doubling the supplied X value which should change the Y value by a factor of S% in the case of the LogLog curve and by S%^X for the LogLinear curve. In both cases SCW takes S% of the original Y value. In other words, it uses 2*X and Y*S% as the second point which is correct for the LogLog curve but the LogLinear curve should use 2*X, Y*S%^X.

## Log curves using Curve Builder

As an example of using Curve Builder with LogLinear and LogLog curves, consider the two sets of data shown below. Column B contains LogLinear data and column C contains LogLog data. The task is to estimate the value of Y for X equal to 7 in each case. The first step is to select cell B8 and use the command Tools,Curve Builder. In the dialog box that appears enter A8 as the X variable for which you want to predict the associated Y value, i.e. Variable 1 and select Regression as the method of specifying the curve.

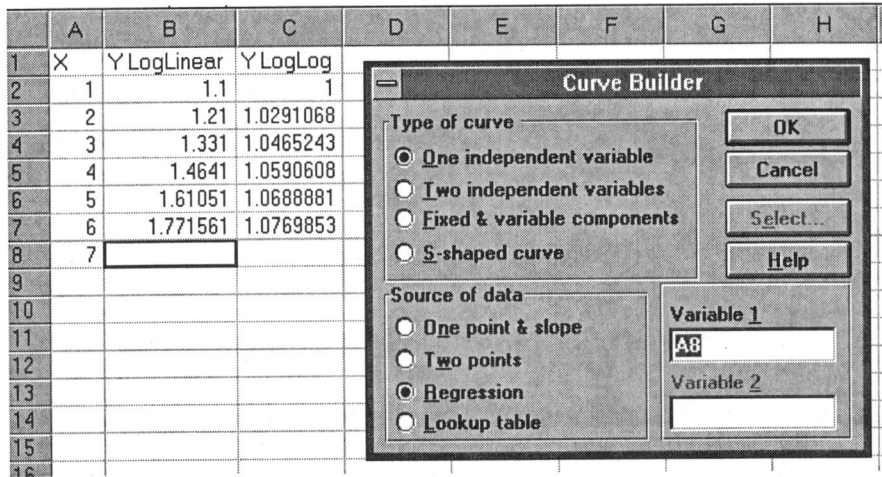

|   | A | B | C |
|---|---|---|---|
| 1 | X | Y LogLinear | Y LogLog |
| 2 | 1 | 1.1 | 1 |
| 3 | 2 | 1.21 | 1.0291068 |
| 4 | 3 | 1.331 | 1.0465243 |
| 5 | 4 | 1.4641 | 1.0590608 |
| 6 | 5 | 1.61051 | 1.0688881 |
| 7 | 6 | 1.771561 | 1.0769853 |
| 8 | 7 | | |

Next we have to fill in the dialog box to specify where the data used to estimate the curve is and the exact type of curve. The X data values are in A2:A7 and the known Y data values are in B2:B7. All that remains is to select As cost and Log on cost to specify a LogLinear curve and Curve Builder will insert the formula =GROWTH(B2:B7,A2:A7,A8) into B8. The GROWTH function calculates a LogLinear curve in exactly the same way as the TREND function does for a line, see later.

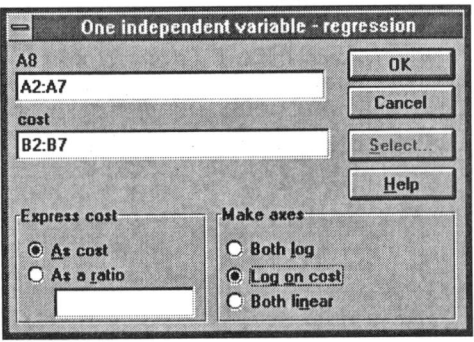

If you repeat the procedure for C8 using A8 as the known X value, A2:A7 and C2:C7 for the known X and Y values used in the regression and the Both log option then Curve Builder will insert the formula =COST(C2:C7,A2:A7,A8) as the estimate of Y using a LogLog curve.

## » A lookup table curve

As long as the relationship between X and Y is smooth you can usually get by using a curve - line, LogLinear or LogLog - that approximates the relationship. However, some relationships are exact but not smooth enough to be captured by a simple curve.

For example, you may know the volume of daily ice-cream sales in July for a range of recorded temperatures but when you look at a chart it doesn't look like a straight line relationship nor a LogLinear or LogLog one. In this case you probably have enough information to use the data itself to estimate the consumption. All you need is a lookup table giving pairs of known temperature and consumption figures and then look up the current temperature to discover the estimate of the consumption. You could create the necessary lookup table manually but there are advantages to using Curve Builder to do the job for you.

If the temperature, i.e. the X variable, is stored in column A, the Volume, i.e. the Y variable, is stored in column B, and the new temperature that you want to look up is stored in A8, you can use Curve Builder to insert a suitable lookup formula into B8. First you should select B8 and then use the Tools, Curve Builder command. Select Lookup table as the source of data. You should then enter A8 as the X value that you want to look up in the table to give the corresponding Y value.

## A lookup table curve

|   | A | B | C | D | E | F | G |
|---|---|---|---|---|---|---|---|
| 1 | Temp | Volume | | | | | |
| 2 | 15 | 5 | | | | | |
| 3 | 16 | 15 | | | | | |
| 4 | 18 | 20 | | | | | |
| 5 | 20 | 25 | | | | | |
| 6 | 22 | 28 | | | | | |
| 7 | | | | | | | |
| 8 | 21 | | | | | | |

Curve Builder dialog:
- Type of curve:
  - ● One independent variable
  - ○ Two independent variables
  - ○ Fixed & variable components
  - ○ S-shaped curve
- Source of data:
  - ○ One point & slope
  - ○ Two points
  - ○ Regression
  - ● Lookup table
- Variable 1: A8
- Variable 2:
- Buttons: OK, Cancel, Select..., Help

At this point you can click on OK and move to the next dialog box. This looks similar to the one that appears for estimating the curve using regression.

In the first text box you have to specify the list of known X values, i.e. A2:A6 and in the second text box the list of known Y values, i.e. B2:B6. Notice that unlike the regression option the data isn't used to estimate a line but to construct a lookup table. Finally, if you select No smoothing and click on OK the formula

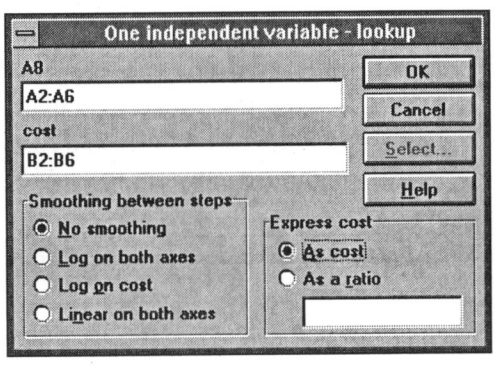

=LOOKUP(B2:B6,A2:A6,A8)

is inserted in B8 and the result of this lookup is 25.

The formula that is inserted is exactly what you would expect - a lookup of A8 in A2:A6 with the result returned from B2:B6. However, the result returned is a little crude. The value being looked up is 21 and this is part way between the 20 and the 22 entry in the table but the lookup returns exactly 25, i.e. the value corresponding to 20 degrees. In many cases it is more reasonable to work out an estimate part way between the entries 20 and 22, i.e. between 25 and 28.

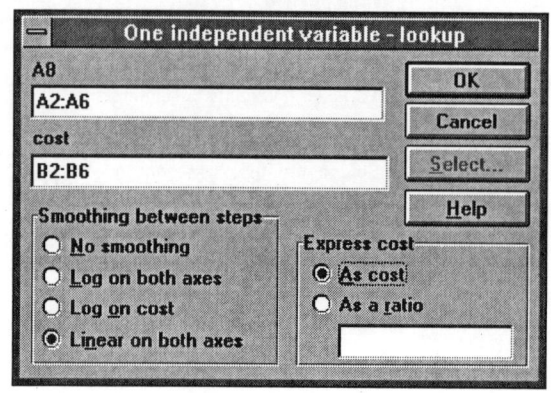

```
┌─ One independent variable - lookup ─┐
│ A8                          [  OK    ]│
│ [A2:A6            ]         [ Cancel ]│
│ cost                                  │
│ [B2:B6            ]         [ Select..]│
│ ┌Smoothing between steps─┐  [  Help  ]│
│ │ ○ No smoothing         │┌Express cost┐│
│ │ ○ Log on both axes     ││ ⦿ As cost  ││
│ │ ○ Log on cost          ││ ○ As a ratio││
│ │ ⦿ Linear on both axes  ││[         ] ││
│ └────────────────────────┘└────────────┘│
└───────────────────────────────────────┘
```

You can do this using Curve Builder by selecting one of the smoothing options. If you select Linear on both axes then a straight line is drawn between the two points given by the lookup table and this is then used to give a more accurate estimate of Y by looking up X using the line. Notice that this is not the same as fitting a line to the set of data points used in the lookup table by regression.

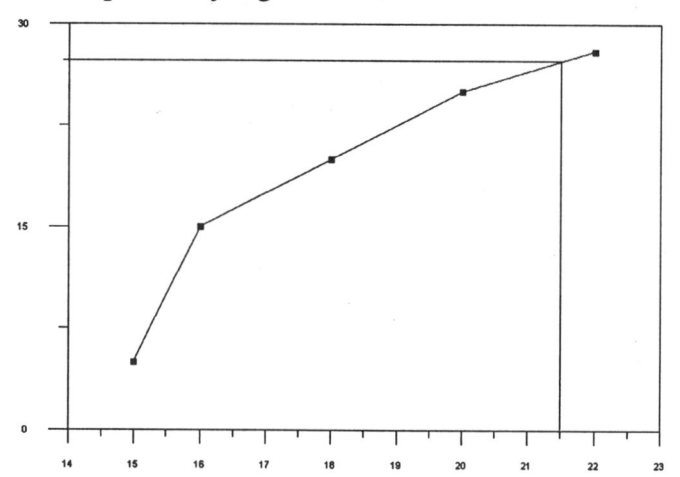

In this case each pair of points is joined by their own individual straight line which is used for X values between the points. Now you will find that the estimate of Y for X equal to 21 is 26.5 which seems more reasonable.

The actual formula used by this Curve Builder option is not based on LOOKUP but LINLINS, a function that is discussed later in this chapter:

=LINLINS(B2:B6,A2:A6,A8)

As well as straight line smoothing you can also select LogLinear and LogLog smoothing if you think that this is appropriate. In each case the points of the lookup table are joined by LogLinear or LogLog curves as specified. The functions used are LINLOGS and LOGLOGS respectively.

## » S-shaped curves

Another very common type of relationship encountered is the S-shaped curve. The reason why this curve occurs so often in practice is that "saturation" effects come into play. For example, if you are trying to market a product then at first a given amount of "effort" will increase market share by the same amount. That is, the relationship between marketing effort and share is initially a straight line but later a given amount of effort produces an ever smaller increase in market share. The reason is, of course, that the market tends towards saturation and eventually no amount of extra effort will sell any more product. The characteristic shape of such a relationship is like a long S with the top tending towards the saturation value.

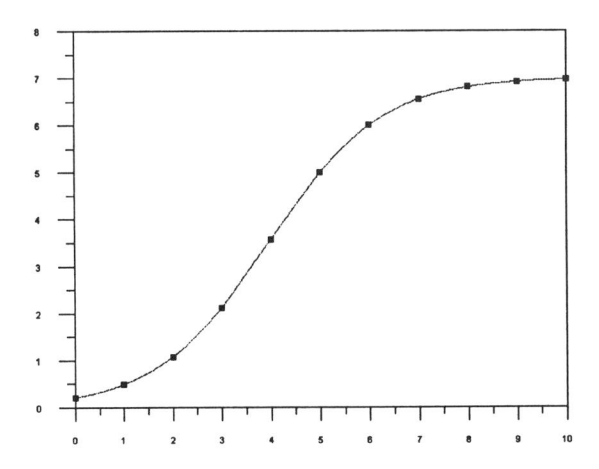

You can use an S-shaped curve to estimate a new value of Y given a known value of X using the Curve Builder. The procedure is the same as for the other types of curve and in this case is especially simple as there is only one way to specify the curve - two points and a saturation value. If you select the S-shaped curve option then you are forced to select the Two points option. In the dialog box that appears you have to give two points that you know lie on the curve and the saturation value.

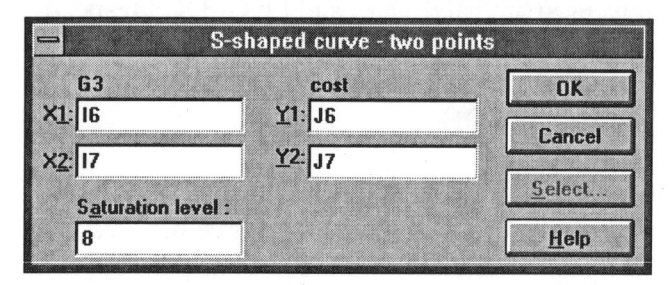

```
┌─────────── S-shaped curve - two points ───────────┐
│      G3                  cost          ┌────────┐ │
│  X1: │I6  │           Y1: │J6  │       │  OK    │ │
│  X2: │I7  │           Y2: │J7  │       ├────────┤ │
│                                        │ Cancel │ │
│  Saturation level :                    ├────────┤ │
│  │8    │                               │ Select │ │
│                                        ├────────┤ │
│                                        │  Help  │ │
└───────────────────────────────────────────────────┘
```

The resulting curve is adjusted so that it passes through the two points specified and flattens off at the Y value specified as the saturation point. The S-shaped curve option makes use of the SHARE function, which is described later.

# » Fixed and variable components

A very specialised type of curve is provided by the Fixed and variable components option. This assumes that Y is given by two components - a fixed cost and a variable per item cost. The terms "fixed" and "variable" are a little misleading because both components can depend on the value of X via a lookup table. What happens is that the value of X is looked up in the list of values specified and then a value for the fixed cost F is returned and a value for the variable cost V is returned. The two costs are then combined to give Y using

$$F+V*X$$

*Fixed and variable components* **233**

In other words, the variable cost is multiplied by X to convert it from a per item cost to a total cost. As X was used to look up the variable cost you might think that you might as well store V*X in the table or even the total cost for each value of X. However, keeping the per-item cost separate allows estimates for values not in the table to be created, see below.

For example, suppose the cost of starting up a machine to produce a number of items is given in columns A, B and C showing the fixed startup cost for each batch size and a per-item production cost. To estimate the total cost of producing a batch of 7500 as specified in A7 you can use the Curve Builder with the Fixed and variable components option. In this case you have to specify the curve using a lookup table.

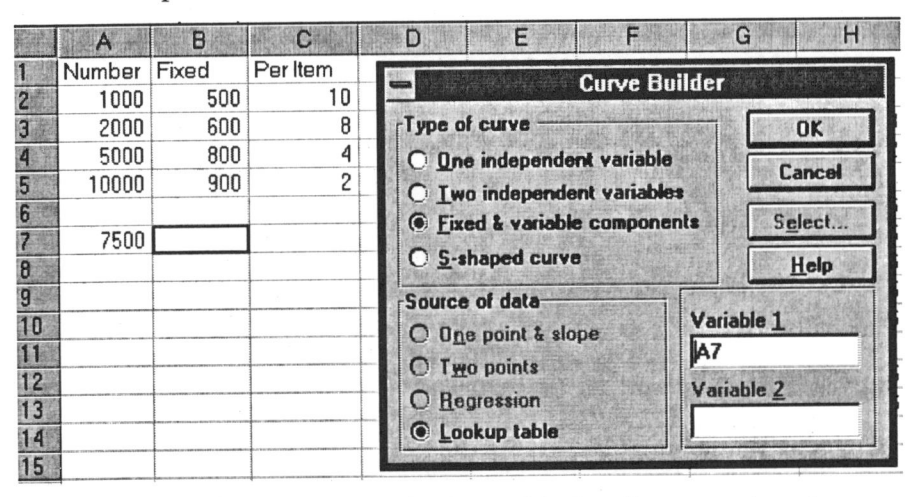

|   | A | B | C |
|---|---|---|---|
| 1 | Number | Fixed | Per Item |
| 2 | 1000 | 500 | 10 |
| 3 | 2000 | 600 | 8 |
| 4 | 5000 | 800 | 4 |
| 5 | 10000 | 900 | 2 |
| 6 |  |  |  |
| 7 | 7500 |  |  |

**Curve Builder**

Type of curve:
- ○ One independent variable
- ○ Two independent variables
- ● Fixed & variable components
- ○ S-shaped curve

Source of data:
- ○ One point & slope
- ○ Two points
- ○ Regression
- ● Lookup table

Variable 1: A7
Variable 2:

[OK] [Cancel] [Select...] [Help]

The specification of the lookup table involves entering the ranges for the three lists of values - A2:A5, the X or lookup variable; B2:B5, the fixed cost; C2:C5 the per-item cost.

**Fixed & variable components**

Variable: A7
A2:A5

Fixed component of cost
B2:B5

Variable component per A7
C2:C5

[OK] [Cancel] [Select...] [Help]

Curve Builder then inserts the formula

=LOOKUP(B2:B5,A2:A5,A7)+
A7*LOOKUP(C2:C5,A2:A5,A7)

Although the Fixed and variable components cost estimation is a useful tool, it is important to check that it works in the way you want when there isn't an exact match in the table. For example, the cost of producing 7500 items isn't actually in the table. The fixed cost for setting the machine up and the per-item cost corresponding to 5000 items is used by the LOOKUP function instead. This still gives a reasonable estimate because the per-item cost is multiplied by 7500 and not 5000 as would be the case if you stored the total cost in the table.

## » Two independent variables

The final Curve Builder option takes us into new territory in that it allows you to estimate a value of Y that depends on two independent variables. In theory there is no reason why you should not estimate Y using any number of independent variables but Curve Builder stops at two variables as a practical upper limit. (See Regression later in this chapter for ways of working with more than two independent variables.)

When you move to two independent variables the principles are more or less the same as in the one independent variable case except that now the curve is a two-dimensional surface. The two independent variables X1 and X2 now fix a point in two dimensions and this determines the Y value by the height of the surface above this point.

As in the single independent variable case, simple curves, or in this case surfaces, are easier to work with. The simplest surface is a flat plane which is of course the two-dimensional

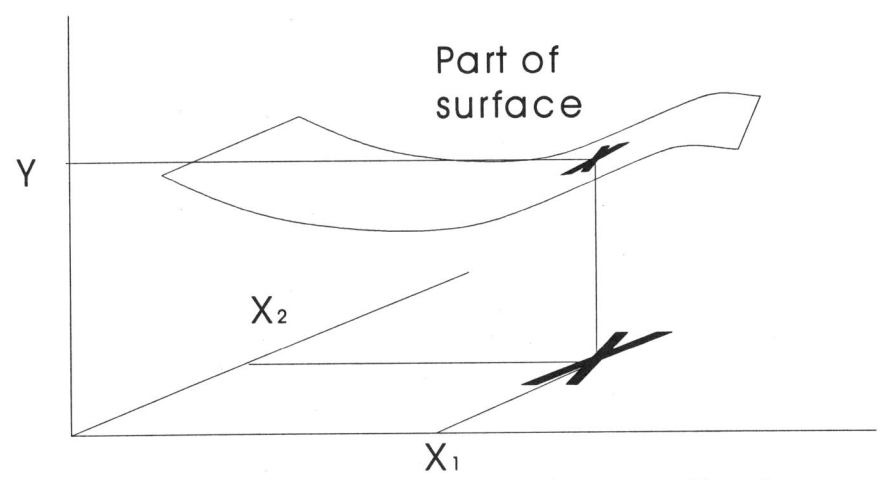

![Figure showing a 3D surface with axes Y, X1, X2, labeled "Part of surface"]

generalisation of a line. You can also generalise the LogLinear and LogLog curves to surfaces.

You can use Curve Builder to estimate a Y value based on a pair of X values in the usual way. The only real difference is that you have to select the Two independent variables option and supply two X values, or cell references, to be used in calculating Y. The only options for specifying the surface are a point and two slopes, three points or regression. Notice that for a surface you do have to supply a point that it passes through and two slopes - the change in Y when you alter X1 keeping X2 fixed and the change in Y when you alter X2 keeping X1 fixed. Similarly, it takes three points to fix the position of a plane. If you want to make use of the regression option then you need three lists of data corresponding to known values of X1, X2 and Y.

For example, if you have a column of known X1 values in A, known X2 values in B and Y values in C then you can use the Curve Builder to estimate the value of Y corresponding to an X1 value in A9 and a X2 value in B9 by first selecting cell C9, where you want the estimate, and the using the Tools, Curve Builder command. Select Two independent variables

**236** *Estimation and Prediction*   *Chapter 11*

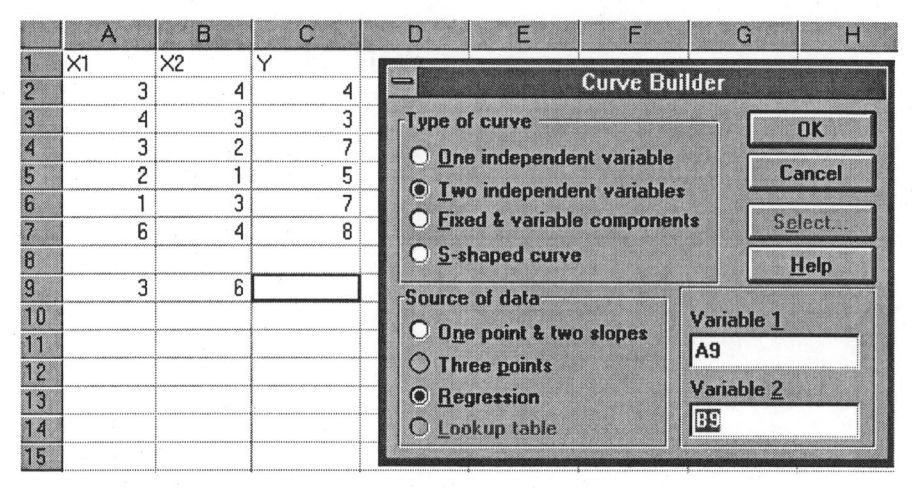

|   | A | B | C |
|---|---|---|---|
| 1 | X1 | X2 | Y |
| 2 | 3 | 4 | 4 |
| 3 | 4 | 3 | 3 |
| 4 | 3 | 2 | 7 |
| 5 | 2 | 1 | 5 |
| 6 | 1 | 3 | 7 |
| 7 | 6 | 4 | 8 |
| 8 |   |   |   |
| 9 | 3 | 6 |   |

[Curve Builder dialog: Type of curve — One independent variable, ● Two independent variables, Fixed & variable components, S-shaped curve. Source of data — One point & two slopes, Three points, ● Regression, Lookup table. Variable 1: A9, Variable 2: B9.]

and the Regression options. Enter A9 as the specification for variable 1 and B9 as the specification for variable 2.

Next you have to specify the location of the data to be used to estimate the plane using regression. The X1 data is in A2:A7, the X2 data is in B2:B7 and the Y values are in C2:C7. Finally select Both Linear and click on OK.

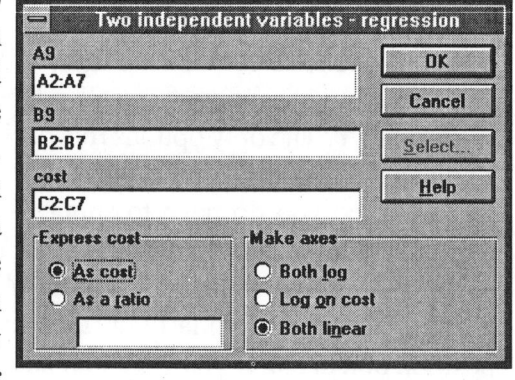

[Two independent variables - regression dialog: A9: A2:A7, B9: B2:B7, cost: C2:C7. Express cost: ● As cost, As a ratio. Make axes: Both log, Log on cost, ● Both linear.]

Curve Builder inserts the formula

$$=\text{TREND2}(C2:C7, B2:B7, A2:A7, B9, A9)$$

into C9. The TREND2 function is the two independent variable version of the TREND function. This is one of the statistical functions discussed later.

> ### Bug Box - Two independent variables
>
> The bug in the point and slope specification described earlier in connection with one independent variable also applies to the two independent variable case. In the Linear case the second point should be calculated as
> $$2*X_1, X_2, S_1*X_1+Y_1$$
> and the third point should be
> $$X_1, 2*X_2, S_2*X_2+Y_1$$
> where $S_1$ and $S_2$ are the slopes specified for $X_1$ and $X_2$. In the LogLinear case the points should be
> $$2*X_1, X_2, Y_1*S_1{\wedge}X_1$$
> and
> $$X_1, 2*X_2, Y_1*S_2{\wedge}X_2$$
> In the LogLog case the extra two points are correctly calculated as
> $$2*X_1, X_2, Y_1*S_1$$
> and
> $$X_1, 2*X_2, Y_1*S_2$$

## » Summary

This completes the description of the Curve Builder. Once you have seen its basic principles of operation each of the options should seem logical. However, the range of curves that you can specify can seem overwhelming and difficult to select between. In each case you have to think about what the curve means in terms of the basic relationship between X and Y. The following types of curve can be used to estimate Y:

» Straight line - a unit increase/decrease in X always produces the same increase/decrease in Y.

» LogLinear curve - a unit increase in X produces a percentage increase in Y.

- » LogLog curve - multiplying X by a factor, e.g. doubling it, produces a percentage increase in Y.

- » Lookup table - any relationship between X and Y (possibly using smoothing between values) in the table.

- » S-shaped curve - a relationship that is linear in its mid range but which flattens off to a saturation value for large values of X.

- » Fixed and variable costs - a lookup table method of estimating a Y value that depends on a fixed cost and a per item cost.

- » Two independent variables - generalisation of one independent variable using either a plane, LogLinear or LogLog surface.

## » Forecasting

Forecasting is much like estimating a quantity and many of the techniques discussed in the first part of this chapter apply. The main difference is that in forecasting the independent variable X is time and the dependent variable Y is thought of as a "time series" of values. Generally you will have a set of values for Y for a sequence of times and the problem is to predict the value of Y at some future time or times. For example, suppose you have the sales figures for a product for each of 18 months stored in column A. Your problem is to forecast the sales for the next month i.e. the value of sales that will be recorded in A20.

|    | A     |
|----|-------|
| 1  | Sales |
| 2  | 205   |
| 3  | 206   |
| 4  | 206   |
| 5  | 207   |
| 6  | 207   |
| 7  | 207   |
| 8  | 207   |
| 9  | 207   |
| 10 | 208   |
| 11 | 208   |
| 12 | 208   |
| 13 | 208   |
| 14 | 209   |
| 15 | 209   |
| 16 | 209   |
| 17 | 210   |
| 18 | 211   |
| 19 | 212   |
| 20 |       |
| 21 |       |

The simplest way of doing this is to use the Tools,Forecast command - although you could make direct use of the functions that it uses. First select the column of data, including the cell that you want the forecast, A2:A20 in this case. Next select the Tools,Forecast command. The Forecast dialog box that appears allows you to specify the type of forecasting method.

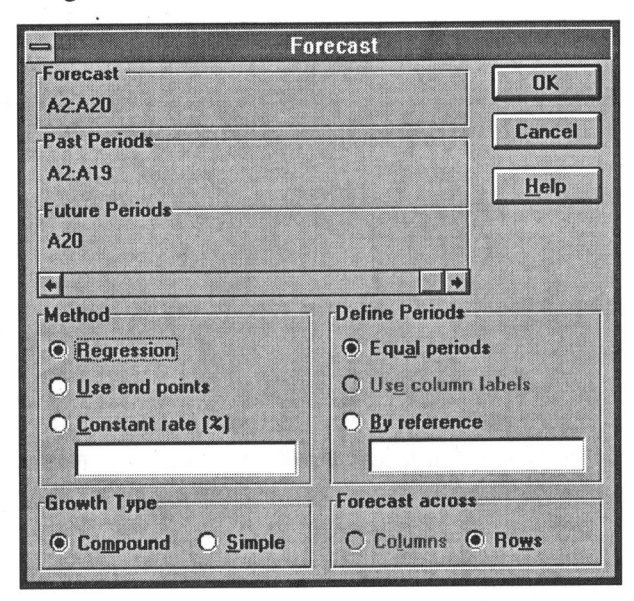

The Forecast box shows the range that you selected and this is divided into two parts - Past Periods and Future Periods. The Past Periods are used to forecast the Future Periods. You can alter which periods are considered to be Future Periods by moving the slider bar. Notice that Future Periods are always at the bottom of the column or right of the row and if they already contain data this will be overwritten by the forecast.

Once you have selected the Future Periods the next step is to decide on the forecasting method. There are really only two forecasting methods on offer because the Constant rate option is really a way of generating a data series based on certain assumptions. The two methods are regression and end points. The regression method finds a best fitting line to all of the data. The end point method simply fits a line to the first and last available data values. In other words the regression option attempts to take account of all of the data in finding a best fitting line but the end point option only takes notice of the first and last values. Which is better? The question is a very difficult one to answer in general. The regression option is less likely to be influenced by a single abnormal value but the end point method gives you an estimate of the change over the longest period of time. If the data in the time series really does fit a line as opposed to any other shape of curve then regression is likely to be better than simply using the end point method.

As in the case of estimating the Y value using Curve Builder, you can use the LogLinear form of regression or the end point forecast. In this case the values are assumed to increase by a percentage of their previous size. For example, a deposit earning compound interest at I% grows in this this way by increasing by I% of its value each time period. For this reason LogLinear growth is often called "compound growth" and Forecast gives you a choice between simple, i.e. linear, and compound, i.e. LogLinear, growth.

In the case of the sales figures example regression using simple growth seems appropriate. Using these options the Forecast tool inserts the formula

=TREND(A2:A19,ROW(A2:A19),ROW())

into A20. The TREND formula fits a line to the Y data in A2:A19 and the X data given by the row numbers of the range. It then predicts the Y value for an X value given by the current row number. This is simple enough but why are the row numbers used as the independent variable? The answer is that often the time values are left out of the forecasting data and as long as the values were obtained at equal intervals you might as well use 1,2,3, etc. as the X variable.

If the time intervals were not equal then you have to specify them. To do this you should select either the Use column labels option, which is only available for models or the By reference option. The By reference option expects you to specify a row or column containing time or date values that can be used as the X variable in the forecast. It is very important that if the values you are trying to predict were measured at unequal time intervals you specify these using one or the other of these two options.

Whenever you attempt to forecast a value it is worth constructing a chart that allows you to look at the shape of the time series. In the case of the sales figures example you can see that the regression forecast isn't unreasonable.

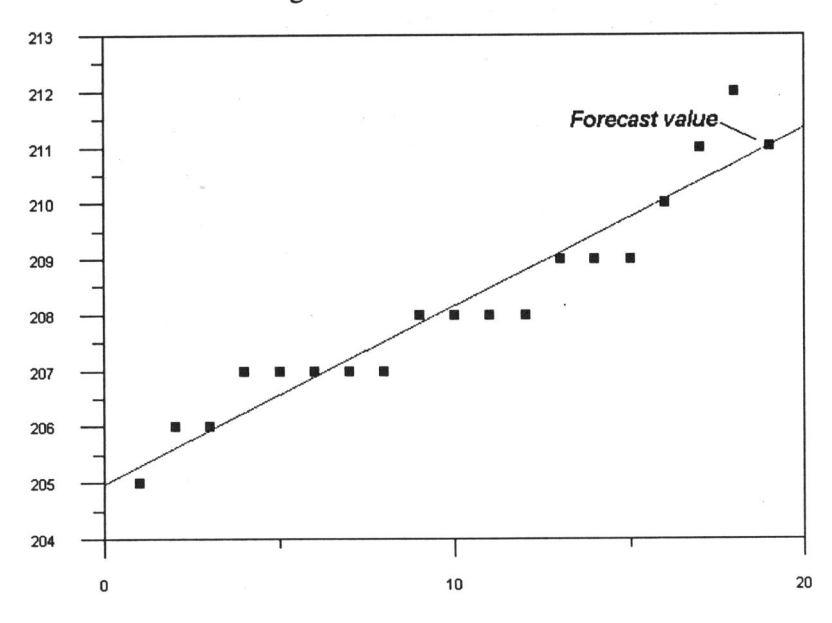

Notice, however, that if the Use end points option had been chosen the line joining the first and last Past Periods values would have given a much higher forecast.

If you select Constant rate or Constant increment then what happens is that the entire forecast range, apart from the first value, is filled with a series generated using the first value. If you select Compound growth and specify Constant rate the series will grow using compound interest at the rate you specify. If you select Simple growth then the values will change by the specified percentage of the first value. Clearly this isn't so much forecasting as generating a series of values that correspond to applying compound or simple interest to a starting value.

## » The statistical functions

Both the Curve Builder and Forecast tools rely on the use of SCW's wide range of statistical functions. Although these tools have been provided so that users do not need to encounter these functions directly, they are not difficult to understand and there are some that can only be used directly.

There are two functions for each type of curve - one allows you to estimate a new value of Y and the other provides details of the curve itself.

So, in the case of a straight line the TREND function will estimate the line using regression on a set of known x and known y values and then estimate a value of y given a value of x. That is,

> TREND(known ys, known xs, new x)

gives the value of y corresponding to x.

The second function associated with a line, LINLINEST, returns the specification of the line, its slope and intercept with the Y-axis, given a set of known x and known y values. That is,

> LINLINEST(known ys, known xs, type)

gives the slope of the line if *type* is 0 and the intercept if *type* is 1. To use this information you need to know the equation of the line. It is

$$y=S*x+C$$

where S is the slope of the line and C is the intercept with the Y-axis otherwise known as "the constant". If you use LINLINEST to find S and C you can estimate y values corresponding to any value of x using this equation.

Once you have seen what TREND and LINLINEST do the rest of the statistical functions are easy to understand because they do the same two jobs but for curves of different types.

To summarise: if X and Y are lists of known values, x is a value for which you would like to calculate the corresponding y value then

» Line - equation y=S*x+C

        y=TREND(Y,X,x)
        S=LINLINEST(Y,X,0)
        C=LINLINEST(Y,X,1)

» LogLinear - equation y=C*(S^x)

        y=GROWTH(Y,X,x)
        S=LINLOGEST(Y,X,0)
        C=LINLOGEST(Y,X,1)

» LogLog - equation y=C*(x^log$_2$S)

        y=COST(Y,X,x)
        S=LOGLOGEST(Y,X,0)
        C=LOGLOGEST(Y,X,1)

There are also statistical functions for the two independent variable versions of the line, LogLinear and LogLog curves, but in this case there is only a single function in each case which estimates the value of y given a value of x. That is, if X1, X2 and Y are lists of the first and second independent variables and their corresponding Y values then:

» Two independent variables linear relationship

   y=TREND2(Y,X1,X2,x1,x2)

» Two independent variables LogLinear relationship

   y=GROWTH2(Y,X1,X2,x1,x2)

» Two independent variables LogLog relationship

   y=COST2(Y,X1,X2,x1,x2)

There is also a single function for the S-shaped curve:

» S-shaped curve

   y=SHARE(x1,y1,x2,y2, s,x)

specified by the two points x1,y1 and x2,y2 and the saturation level s.

Finally, there are four functions concerned with using a lookup table in estimation. The simplest form involves no smoothing between values while the other three employ alternative smoothing methods:

» no smoothing

   y=LOOKUP(Y,X,x)

» linear smoothing, i.e. a line between each pair of points

   y=LINLINS(Y,X,x)

» LogLinear smoothing, i.e. a LogLinear curve between each pair of points

$$y=\text{LINLOGS}(Y,X,x)$$

» LogLog smoothing, i.e. a LogLog curve between each pair of points

$$y=\text{LOGLOGS}(Y,X,x)$$

# » Curves and charts

As well as the statistical curve fitting functions used by Curve Builder and Forecast, you can also make use of the CurveFit command within the Chart menu. When you plot a chart such as a line chart or scatter diagram you are plotting a series of Y values against a series of X values and SCW will perform a regression on these values to fit a curve of your choice.

If you create a chart and double click on it you will see the Chart menu replace the usual sheet or model menu. To fit a curve to the data you have to select Curve Fit menu item.

This gives you four choices of curve. The Simple curve corresponds to a straight line and the Exponential curve corresponds to the LogLinear curve that is available in Curve Builder. However, the Polynomial and Logarithmic options correspond to new curve types not available in Curve Builder.

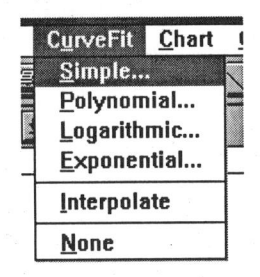

A polynomial curve is a smooth curve with an equation that involves only powers of X. The highest power that occurs is called the degree or order of the polynomial.

For example, the polynomial of degree one is

$$y=aX+C$$

because the highest power is $X^1$. You may recognise this as the equation of a straight line and indeed a straight line is a special case of a polynomial.

The polynomial of degree two is

$$y=aX^2+bX+C$$

which is the equation of a quadratic. Similarly a third order polynomial is a cubic and so on.. SCW allows you to fit a polynomial up to the fifth degree. The higher the degree the more turning points the curve has. In simpler terms the higher the degree the more changes of direction the curve can have. This makes it possible for the curve to exactly fit one more points than its degree. For example, a line, degree 1, can always be arranged to pass through two points. A curve of degree 2 can always be arranged to pass through three points and so on. You need to keep this in mind as you fit increasingly high degree polynomials to data that has only a small number of values. For example, getting a good fit to six data points using a line is interesting - getting an exact fit with a fifth degree polynomial is what you would expect!

The logarithmic curve option fits a curve with equation

$$y=a*\log(x)+c$$

This makes the characteristic relationship between x and y such that repeatedly doubling x produces the same increase or decrease in y. Many physical quantities behave like this. For example, perceived loudness goes up by one unit each time you double the power output of a loudspeaker.

When you select a curve fitting option the equation of the curve, complete with the values for the slope and the constant, are shown on the chart. You will also find a quantity $r^2$ or

R squared. This is the square of the correlation coefficient between x and y. In more practical terms this is a measure of how well the curve fits the data. You can think of it as the percentage of variation of y that is explained by the curve. For example, if you have an r^2 value of .9 then you can interpret this as meaning that the curve accounts for 90% of the variation of y. Conversely this must mean that 10% of the variation is due to error or random effects not accounted for by its relationship with the x variable.

The final curve fitting option is Interpolate. This isn't really a curve fitting in the same sense as the others. An interpolation procedure is used to place a smooth curve through each of the plotted points. In other words, the fit is guaranteed to be perfect! Fitting a curve by interpolation is really only useful as a cosmetic treatment - that is it might make your chart look better but it isn't usable as a method of prediction or forecasting.

As an example consider the sales data used earlier. If you plot a simple scatter diagram and fit a simple curve, i.e. a line, the result is very impressive.

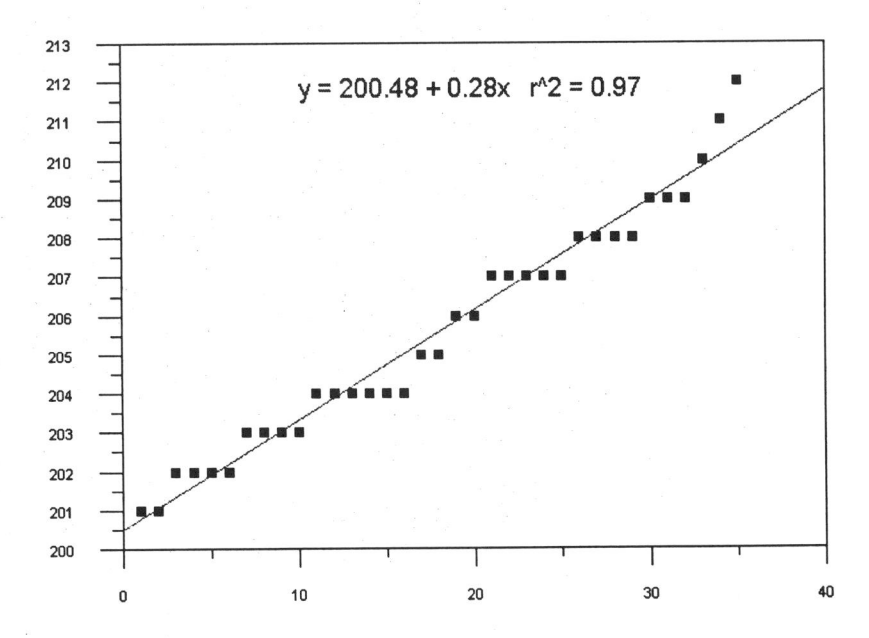

$y = 200.48 + 0.28x \quad r^2 = 0.97$

With an r^2 value of .97 there only remains 3% of the variation in y unaccounted for. In most cases you would be well advised to accept the simplicity of a line given this level of goodness of fit. But if you do try a higher order polynomial you may be even more encouraged by the increase in r^2. For example, fitting a third order polynomial gives an r^2 value of .98 leaving only 2% of the variation in y unexplained.

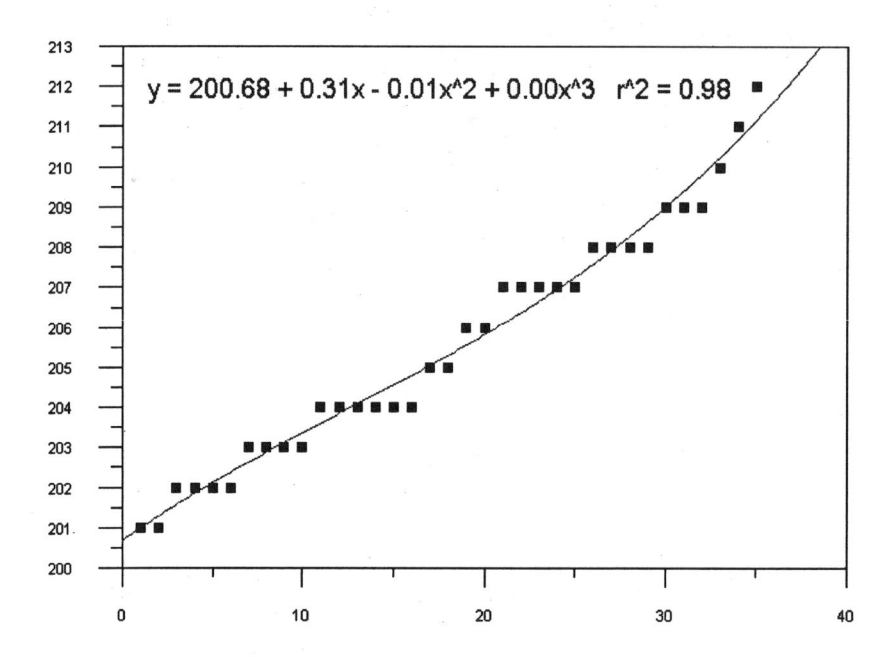

$$y = 200.68 + 0.31x - 0.01x^{\wedge}2 + 0.00x^{\wedge}3 \quad r^{\wedge}2 = 0.98$$

However, if you examine the chart you can see that the polynomial really only fits better at the end of the range. Also, as you increase the order of the polynomial you expect the fit to get better i.e. r^2 increases as you increase the order. In this case a 1% increase in explained variation is hardly worth the complexity of having to use a cubic rather than a line.

In short

» beware of overfitting a curve to data that is well explained by a simpler curve.

## » Regression

All of the Curve Builder, Forecast and chart options are restricted to one or at most two independent variables. SCW provides a powerful curve fitting command that will work with up to 87 independent variables. The Data,Regression command only works with sheets and you have to structure the data so that the known X values are listed in columns of a single block. The known Y range has to be a list of the same number of values as there are X values. You also need to specify an output range where SCW can store the values that specify the fitted surface. If you use the Regression command with a single independent variable then you are fitting a line to predict Y and this is equivalent to the action of the TREND or LINLINEST functions. In this case you can also opt to fit a Quadratic or a Cubic and this is the equivalent of the Polynomial curve fitting in the chart menu.

When you work with two independent variables you are fitting a plane to the data and this is the equivalent of the two independent variables option in Curve Builder. However, the Regression command will give you the details of the equation of the plane whereas Curve Builder will not. After two independent variables you cannot imagine what the surface looks like because it goes beyond what can be seen in normal 3D space. However, this doesn't matter because the equation of the surface always has the same form. Each independent variable is multiplied by a slope before being added together along with a constant. That is, if there are three independent variables Y is given by

$$Y = aX1 + bX2 + cX3 + d$$

with four independent variables you would just add a term in X4 and so on.

## 250  Estimation and Prediction                     Chapter 11

As an example of the use of the Regression command consider the data shown below with three independent variables.

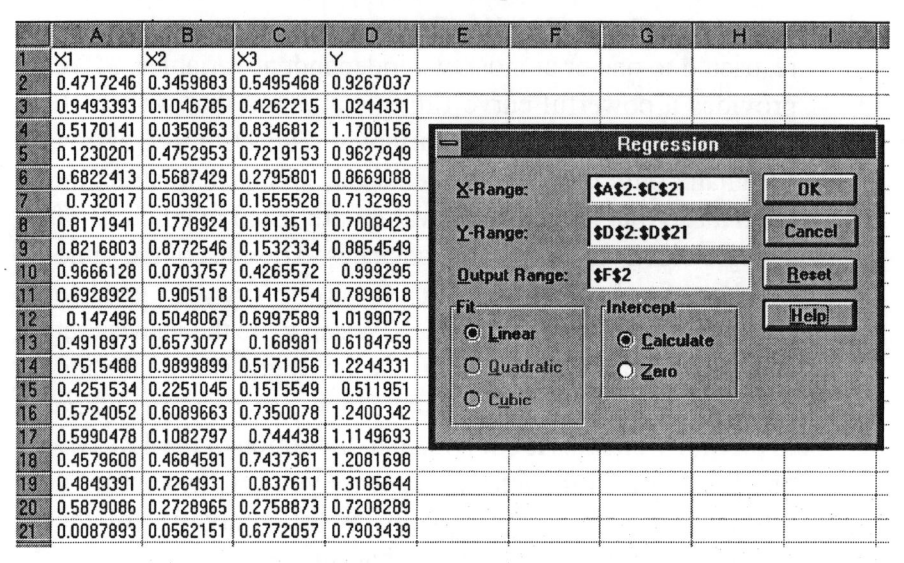

|    | A | B | C | D |
|----|---|---|---|---|
| 1  | X1 | X2 | X3 | Y |
| 2  | 0.4717246 | 0.3459883 | 0.5495468 | 0.9267037 |
| 3  | 0.9493393 | 0.1046785 | 0.4262215 | 1.0244331 |
| 4  | 0.5170141 | 0.0350963 | 0.8346812 | 1.1700156 |
| 5  | 0.1230201 | 0.4752953 | 0.7219153 | 0.9627949 |
| 6  | 0.6822413 | 0.5687429 | 0.2795801 | 0.8669088 |
| 7  | 0.732017  | 0.5039216 | 0.1555528 | 0.7132969 |
| 8  | 0.8171941 | 0.1778924 | 0.1913511 | 0.7008423 |
| 9  | 0.8216803 | 0.8772546 | 0.1532334 | 0.8854549 |
| 10 | 0.9666128 | 0.0703757 | 0.4265572 | 0.999295  |
| 11 | 0.6928922 | 0.905118  | 0.1415754 | 0.7898618 |
| 12 | 0.147496  | 0.5048067 | 0.6997589 | 1.0199072 |
| 13 | 0.4918973 | 0.6573077 | 0.168981  | 0.6184759 |
| 14 | 0.7515488 | 0.9899999 | 0.5171056 | 1.2244331 |
| 15 | 0.4251534 | 0.2251045 | 0.1515549 | 0.511951  |
| 16 | 0.5724052 | 0.6089663 | 0.7350078 | 1.2400342 |
| 17 | 0.5990478 | 0.1082797 | 0.744438  | 1.1149693 |
| 18 | 0.4579608 | 0.4684591 | 0.7437361 | 1.2081698 |
| 19 | 0.4849391 | 0.7264931 | 0.837611  | 1.3185644 |
| 20 | 0.5879086 | 0.2728965 | 0.2758873 | 0.7208289 |
| 21 | 0.0087893 | 0.0562151 | 0.6772057 | 0.7903439 |

Regression dialog:
- X-Range: $A$2:$C$21
- Y-Range: $D$2:$D$21
- Output Range: $F$2
- Fit: ● Linear  ○ Quadratic  ○ Cubic
- Intercept: ● Calculate  ○ Zero
- Buttons: OK, Cancel, Reset, Help

You can see that the X range has been defined to be the block A2:C21 and the Y range is D2:D21. The output range has its top left-hand corner at F2. All of the results of the regression will be stored in the output range block - overwriting anything already there.

| F | G | H | I | J |
|---|---|---|---|---|
| | Regression Output: | | | |
| Constant | | | 0.085062 | |
| Std Err of Y Est | | | 0.0252138 | |
| R Squared(Adj,Raw) | | 0.9877232 | 0.9896616 | |
| No. of Observations | | | 20 | |
| Degrees of Freedom | | | 16 | |
| | | | | |
| Coefficient(s) | | 0.4871002 | 0.2562784 | 0.9941309 |
| Std Err of Coef. | | 0.0256542 | 0.0196878 | 0.0256836 |

There are a great many results reported in the output area. The fitted surface is defined by the Constant and the row of Coefficients at the bottom of the output area. These are listed in the order X1, X2, X3 and so on. The remaining values give statistical information on how good a fit the surface is. The R Squared value is the percentage of the variation of Y that the regression has accounted for. The standard error on Y is the error that you would expect in a Y value estimated using the equation. The number of observations is self explanatory and the number of degrees of freedom is used to look up the significance level of the R squared value. Notice that each of the coefficients of the equation is also accompanied by an estimate of the error. So given these results the regression accounts for nearly 99% of the variation in Y and the equation to predict Y from X1, X2 and X3 is

$$Y=0.487*X1+0.256*X2+0.994*X3+.085$$

rounding the coefficients to three decimal places. The error on the predicted Y value is roughly plus or minus .025.

If you need to know more about regression than this simple introduction then see a standard text on statistics.

# Key points

» Curve Builder can be used to construct a formula that will estimate y given x.

» You can select the type of curve or relationship that is appropriate - linear, loglinear, loglog, S shaped curve or a lookup table.

» You can specify the curve either by giving two points, a point and slope or by regression using known x and y values.

» The Forecast tool works in a way that is very similar to the Curve Builder but it uses a curve to predict new values in a time series.

» Both Curve Builder and Forecast use SCW's range of statistical functions. These allow you to estimate new values of y and the exact form of the curves.

» The Chart menu also contains a range of curve fitting options.

» The Data,Regression command, which is only available in sheets, allows you to fit multiple independent variables to a single dependent variable.

# Chapter 12

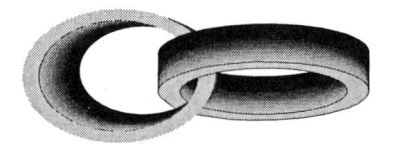

# What-if? Sheets, Links and Models

SCW's two major components - models and sheets - are designed for two very different tasks. The sheet is ideal for ad-hoc work. The model is ideal when there is a regular and strong structure in the data. Real data tends not to fall clearly into the ad-hoc or structured categories and so you often need the qualities of the model mixed with the sheet. This is quite possible using SCW's and Window's ability to form links between applications. One of the most important uses of model-sheet links is in presenting the results of a model. If the model is functional then a sheet can also be used to present it with a series of values and collect its results as a What if table.

## » Links

You can create links between sheets and models just as easily as between sheets. The subject of linking in its broader context is discussed in full detail in Chapter 6 of *Mastering CA SuperCalc for Windows* but to recap:

You can enter a reference to another sheet or model in the form

>*'name'!'ref'*

where *name* is the filename of the sheet or model as it appears in the title bar of a window displaying it and *ref* is any valid cell reference. If you are linking to a model then *ref* has to be valid for that model and if you are linking to a sheet then it has to be valid for a sheet. For example, to link to the cell in the top left-hand corner of a sheet called Sheet1 you would use

>='Sheet1.MDS'!'$A$1'

And to link to the cell in the top left-hand corner of the default view of the default model you would use

>='Model1.MDM'!'A1.B1.C1.D1'

This can seem a little odd at first because you are using the sort of cell reference that belongs in a sheet within a model and vice versa.

You can also use links within formulae in the form

>*'name'!'formula'*

or

>*formula(link range)*

where *formula* has to be valid for the sheet or model you are linking to.

For example,

    ='Sheet1.MDS'!'SUM(A1:A10)'

or

    =SUM('Sheet1.MDS'!'A1:A10')

will sum A1:A10 in Sheet1.MDS and return the result to the cell it is stored in.

The only difference between sheets and models with regard to formulae with links is that in a model you can make such a formula global. As a global formula it behaves in the usual way and you can associate it with a scope, apply it to cells and globally update it.

Although you can enter links by simply typing in the appropriate formula, it is much simpler to point to the ranges concerned. As long as you have the sheets and models involved in the links open you can start entering the formula as usual and then click on the sheet or model that contains the cell or range you want to reference. SCW will automatically make an appropriate link formula for you. Notice, however, that you cannot change fixed items or pivot a model while you are pointing at a range that it contains.

You can, of course, manage the links formed between sheets and models using the File,Links command in the usual way and you can disable the updating of links using the Options,Calculate command to disable the updating of links. For a large model with a global link formula it can take some time to update all of the values so disabling the update until it is really necessary is a good idea.

Finally it is worth saying that creating and using a suitable workspace which includes all the sheets and models linked together is another good way to keep everything where you want it. A set of linked sheets and models organised in this way behaves as a single entity as far as saving and loading are concerned.

To summarise:

- » Link formulae for sheets and models have the same general form *'name'!'ref'*

- » The references or functions used have to be correct for the sheet or model that is being linked to.

- » Link formulae in models can be made global.

- » You can manage links using the File,Links command.

- » If link updating is taking too much time, switch to manual calculation and turn off link updates using the Options,Calculate command.

- » Use a workspace to keep all the linked sheets and models together.

## » The mailshot example

Links are not a difficult idea and putting them to good use is mainly a matter of noticing when they can be useful. For example, consider the mailshot model introduced in Chapter 10. The production cost part of the model used the simple formula

=-LABEL("Batch size")*1.5

which clearly assumes that the unit production cost doesn't depend on batch size. In most cases it does and the next question is how to build this into the model. The obvious method is to use a lookup table - perhaps even a fixed and variable cost lookup table as constructed by Curve Builder. Creating a lookup table for unit cost against batch size is no real problem but where should you store the data? You could store it in the model but this would mean inserting items, or worse a whole dimension, that really didn't belong just to hold the lookup table. It would be much better to create a new sheet to store the data in. Use File,New and create a sheet called PRODCOST.MDS or something similar. In this sheet you can store the production cost data using any convenient area. If you save the sheet on disk it can be used in future as a source of production cost data for any other sheet or model. If the production costs change then changing this one sheet will update all of the sheets or models linked to it.

|   | A | B |
|---|---|---|
| 1 | Batch size | Unit cost |
| 2 | 1000 | 2 |
| 3 | 2000 | 1.5 |
| 4 | 3000 | 1.4 |
| 5 | 4000 | 1.3 |
| 6 | 5000 | 1.2 |
| 7 |  |  |

Returning to the model the next step is to pivot it so that the global formula calculating production costs is visible. This has to be changed to:

=LOOKUP('PRODCOST.MDS'!'$B$2:$B$6',
    'PRODCOST.MDS'!'$A$2:$A$6',
        VALUE(LABEL("Batch size")))
            *LABEL("Batch size")

While this formula looks horribly long and complicated you should recognise it as nothing more than a simple lookup of the batch size to give the unit cost and then a multiplication by the batch size to give the total cost. The only reason that it looks long and complicated is the inclusion of the sheet name in each of the range references.

In practice you don't have to type this formula in. Just enter LOOKUP and point to the relevant ranges within the sheet. Notice that the formula has to be entered in this way with the sheet name repeated for each range because the VALUE(LABEL("Batch size")) part of it refers to the model and not the sheet. Once you have noticed this you can see that the formula is more sophisticated than you might at first think. It works something out using information from both the sheet and the model. As long as you remember to allow your changes to update the global formulae the results of all of the production cost calculations should be changed.

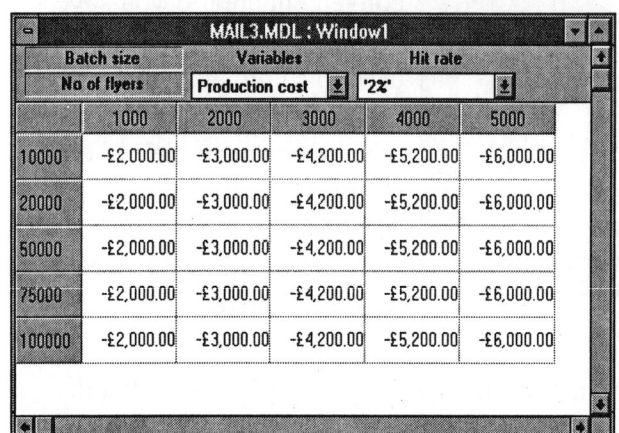

| | | MAIL3.MDL : Window1 | | | |
|---|---|---|---|---|---|
| Batch size | | Variables | | Hit rate | |
| No of flyers | | Production cost | | '2%' | |
| | 1000 | 2000 | 3000 | 4000 | 5000 |
| 10000 | -£2,000.00 | -£3,000.00 | -£4,200.00 | -£5,200.00 | -£6,000.00 |
| 20000 | -£2,000.00 | -£3,000.00 | -£4,200.00 | -£5,200.00 | -£6,000.00 |
| 50000 | -£2,000.00 | -£3,000.00 | -£4,200.00 | -£5,200.00 | -£6,000.00 |
| 75000 | -£2,000.00 | -£3,000.00 | -£4,200.00 | -£5,200.00 | -£6,000.00 |
| 100000 | -£2,000.00 | -£3,000.00 | -£4,200.00 | -£5,200.00 | -£6,000.00 |

| | PRODCOST.MDS : W | |
|---|---|---|
| | A | B |
| 1 | Batch size | Unit cost |
| 2 | 1000 | 2 |
| 3 | 2000 | 1.5 |
| 4 | 3000 | 1.4 |
| 5 | 4000 | 1.3 |
| 6 | 5000 | 1.2 |
| 7 | | |

You can use the same technique to take account of the decrease in the unit cost of printing the advertising literature with the number ordered. You could even include this second lookup table within the same sheet - it is all a matter of how you want to organise your data and whether the cost data is likely to be reused.

## » Sheets and constants

Using a sheet as the repository of data used in a lookup table is a very common use of links - but it isn't the simplest. If you examine the mailshot example you will find that there are a number of values which have been entered as constants, such as the product's price, which could be altered to give a different outcome. You could add an extra dimension called

Price with a range of items giving the product pricing. However, in this case increasing the dimensionality of the model is a little excessive in that you are not really interested in exploring the way the overall profitability of the mailshot changes with price. It is obvious that increasing the price will increase the profit in direct proportion! What you are interested in is in viewing the model correctly calculated for a specific product price. In other words, you want to be able to set the price level easily rather than see a range of prices.

There are two ways of tackling this problem. The first is to use a named constant. You can create names that apply to models exactly as you can in sheets. You can also create names that refer to constants. For example, if you use the command Formula,Define Name you can use the dialog box that appears to create a named constant for Price. Simply type in the value or expression that evaluates to give the sales price for the product.

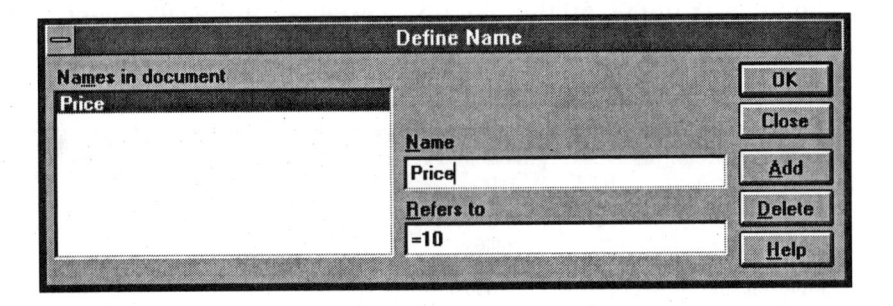

After you have defined the name you can use it in formulae within the model in place of the constant. In this case the formula giving the total income from the product sales is

=IF((LABEL("No of flyers")*LABEL("Hit rate"))>
    VALUE(LABEL("Batch size")),
      LABEL("Batch size")*Price,
        LABEL("No of flyers")*LABEL("Hit rate")*Price)

The only difference being that the sales price of £10 has been replaced by a reference to the name "Price".

The advantage of this method is, of course, that you can now change the price used within the model by redefining the name. The disadvantage is that it isn't particular obvious in the sense that you have to know that a name is being used before it occurs to you to change it! This situation is worse if you make extensive use of names to name ranges or single cells.

The alternative is to create a sheet which holds the values of constants used in the model. For example, in the case of the mailshot model we could create a sheet called Constants and store in it unit price, unit mail cost etc.. The formulae in the model could then be modified to refer to these cells. Unfortunately in early versions of SCW the IF formulae used in the Mailshot model are too complex to work with a reference to another sheet. The solution is to introduce a new item - Number sold - on the Variables dimension and calculate the income and mail costs separately.

| | MAIL2.MDL : Window1 | | | | |
|---|---|---|---|---|---|
| Batch size | No of flyers | | Hit rate | | |
| Variables | '10000' | | '2%' | | |
| | 1000 | 2000 | 3000 | 4000 | 5000 |
| Production cost | -£1,500.00 | -£3,000.00 | -£4,500.00 | -£6,000.00 | -£7,500.00 |
| Flyer print cost | -£200.00 | -£200.00 | -£200.00 | -£200.00 | -£200.00 |
| Flyer mail cost | -£200.00 | -£200.00 | -£200.00 | -£200.00 | -£200.00 |
| Number sold | 200 | 200 | 200 | 200 | 200 |
| Sales income | £2,000.00 | £2,000.00 | £2,000.00 | £2,000.00 | £2,000.00 |
| Product mail cost | £300.00 | £300.00 | £300.00 | £300.00 | £300.00 |
| Profit | £600.00 | -£900.00 | -£2,400.00 | -£3,900.00 | -£5,400.00 |

The new formulae are:

for Number sold

=IF((LABEL("No of flyers")*LABEL("Hit rate"))>
 VALUE(LABEL("Batch size")),
   VALUE(LABEL("Batch size")),
     LABEL("No of flyers")*LABEL("Hit rate"))
with scope   Batch size.Number sold.No of flyers.Hit rate

for Sales income

=Number sold*'10
with scope   Batch size.Sales income.No of flyers

for Product mail cost

=Number sold*1.5
with scope   Batch size.Product mail cost.No of flyers

With these changes the model can be altered further to use a sheet to supply the constants. The first thing to do is create a sheet called CONST.MDS which contains values for the product unit price, unit mail cost and unit printing cost.

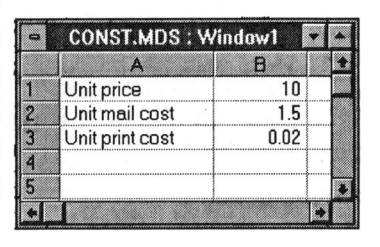

| | A | B |
|---|---|---|
| 1 | Unit price | 10 |
| 2 | Unit mail cost | 1.5 |
| 3 | Unit print cost | 0.02 |
| 4 | | |
| 5 | | |

Next the formulae in the model have to be edited to make use of these constants.

Sales income becomes
   =Number sold*'CONST.MDS'!$B$1
Product mail cost becomes
   =Number sold*'CONST.MDS'!$B$2
and flyer print cost becomes
   =-LABEL("No of flyers")*'CONST.MDS'!$B$3

Now you can change these values in the sheet and instantly update the model.

## » Sheets for presentation

Models can be too complicated to allow the conclusions which you reach by using them to be instantly understandable by others. One solution to this problem is to create additional windows onto the model so that multiple views can be seen. An alternative is to use a sheet to collect results as a report. At its simplest these report links will be just simple references to particular cells in the model but you can also make use of sheet functions to summarise the conclusions of the model.

For example, in the case of the mailshot it would be interesting to provide the maximum profit attainable. You could do this by creating a new sheet and entering the formula

=MAX('MAIL2.MDL'!'5000.Profit.
    (10000:100000).(1%:8%)')

or something very similar. This formula will find the maximum of the values in a two-dimensional range corresponding to the entire visible dimensions. You can only enter a 2D range by pointing because you cannot change the fixed items. However, after the formula has been entered it is easy enough to edit it to find the maximum in the entire model

=MAX('MAIL2.MDL'!
    'Batch size.Profit.No of flyers.Hit rate')

You can calculate any statistic on the values in a model in the same way and even construct tables and charts within the sheet.

## » What-if tables

Functional models are one way of tabulating formulae so that you can investigate the effects of changing particular 'input' values. Data tables or what-if tables are another way of creating tables of values but they only work in sheets. However, they can be used in ways that go well beyond their simplest description.

A data table tabulates a formula for a given range of values. There are two types of data table - one- and two-input tables. A one-input table will vary a single value in a formula and a two-input table will vary two. In the case of the one-input table the input values have to be presented as a list - either as a row or a column. The results of working out the formula using each of the input values in turn are listed in the column to the right or in the row below. The formula to be tabulated has to be at the start of the row or column of results. This may sound complicated but it fits in with the way you usually want to construct a table of values.

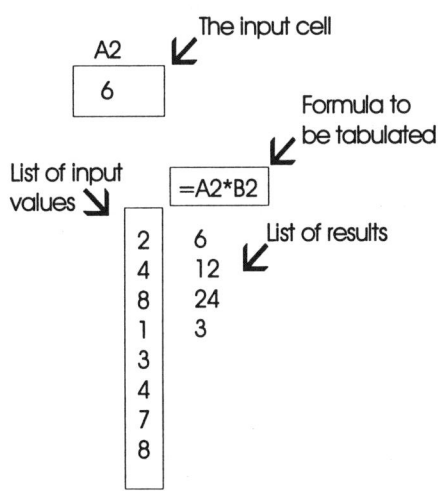

```
                     The input cell
         A2        ↙
        ┌─────┐
        │  6  │
        └─────┘          Formula to
                       ↙ be tabulated
List of input   ┌────────┐
values  ↘       │ =A2*B2 │
        ┌───┬───┴────────┘
        │ 2 │ 6      List of results
        │ 4 │ 12   ↙
        │ 8 │ 24
        │ 1 │ 3
        │ 3 │
        │ 4 │
        │ 7 │
        │ 8 │
        └───┘
```

The only missing detail is how the input values are actually used in the formula that is being tabulated. This where the power of the data table springs from so it is an important detail. You have to specify a cell in the sheet to be used as an input cell. When the data table is calculated the input values are placed one by one in this nominated cell, the entire sheet is recalculated, and the value of the formula is stored as the next result. Notice that it is the entire sheet which is recalculated not just the formula at the head of the results list. Indeed if the formula being tabulated doesn't depend on the input cell then it will not change as the table is built up. Of course in most cases it does change because it makes use of the value in the input cell - sometimes by a direct reference and sometimes very indirectly indeed.

## » A one-input example

For example, suppose you want to tabulate the function COMPBAL, which gives the value of a deposit after the effect of compound interest, for a fixed deposit and term and for a range of interest rates.

To do this you could construct a one input data table. The values of the interest rate that you want to tabulate the function over have to be entered in a row or column - A4:A8 in this example.

| | A | B | C |
|---|---|---|---|
| 1 | 1% | | |
| 2 | | | |
| 3 | | 1030.4417 | |
| 4 | 1% | | |
| 5 | 2% | | |
| 6 | 3% | | |
| 7 | 4% | | |
| 8 | 5% | | |
| 9 | | | |

Next you have to enter the function to be tabulated at the head of the results row or column - B3 in this case. The function entered into B3 is

=COMPBAL(A1/12,36,1000)

which gives the balance after 36 months of £1000 invested at an annual interest rate as specified in A1. This formula works in exactly the same way as any other formula that you might enter in that its result depends on whatever is stored in A1 at the moment you recalculate the sheet.

## A one-input example

The next step is to use the Data,Table command and fill in the dialog box that appears.

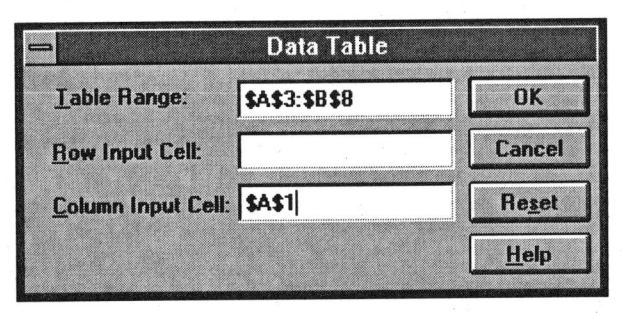

**Data Table**
- Table Range: $A$3:$B$8
- Row Input Cell:
- Column Input Cell: $A$1

The data table range is A3:B8 i.e. the entire data table including the formula in the top row. In this case there is only a column input cell, i.e. A1 - the cell that the column of data is copied to one by one. When you click on OK the result is a table of values.

There are a number of points worth commenting on. The first is that the formula and the value in A1 are not affected by the production of the table. That is, the values in A4:A8 are substituted into A1 one at a time while the table is being prepared but the original value in A1 is preserved. You can see that the formula in B3 still calculates a result based on what is currently in A1. The values tabulated are constant values and not formulae that will change when the sheet is recalculated. That is, if you change the formula in B3 you have to re-make the table using the Data,Table command.

| | A | B | C |
|---|---|---|---|
| 1 | 1% | | |
| 2 | | | |
| 3 | | 1030.4417 | |
| 4 | 1% | 1030.4417 | |
| 5 | 2% | 1061.7835 | |
| 6 | 3% | 1094.0514 | |
| 7 | 4% | 1127.2719 | |
| 8 | 5% | 1161.4722 | |
| 9 | | | |

That's all there is to one-input tables. The only extra detail is that you can tabulate more than one function at a time if you want to. The additional functions have to be entered at the head of each list of results that you want to calculate. For example, to tabulate a second function along with COMPBAL you would simply enter the formula into C3 and define the table so that this column was included. Notice that all of the functions being tabulated have to use the same input cell.

## » Two-input data tables

A two-input data table works in the same way as the single input table but now there has to be a row and column of values. The function to be tabulated has to be stored at the intersection of the row and column of values and, of course, you have to define two input cells.

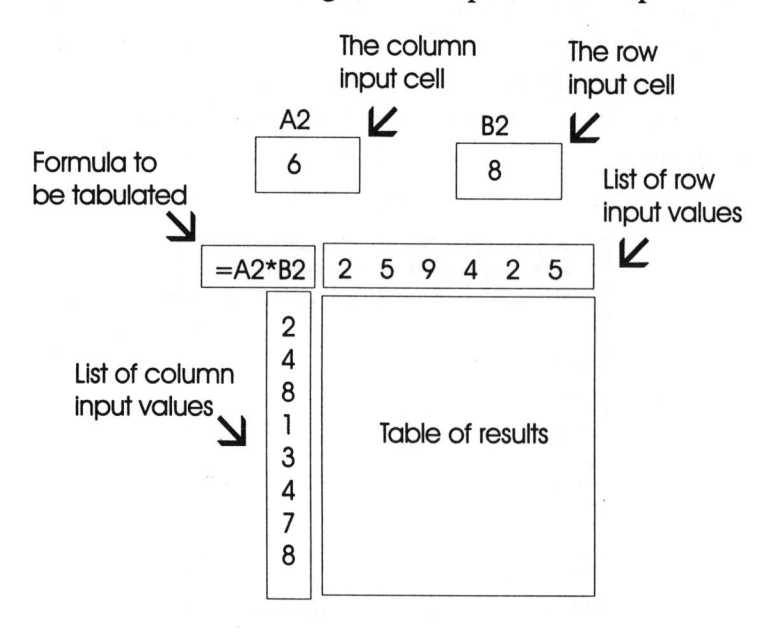

The single formula is tabulated for each of the row and column values in turn. Again it is important to keep in mind that what the Data,Table command actually does is to take each pair of values and store them in the input cells, recalculate the entire sheet and then store the value of the formula in the appropriate place in the table. Also notice that the original values stored in the input cells are not altered.

As an example of a two-input data table consider the task of tabulating the FV (Future Value) function for a range of interest rates and terms. The FV function calculates the value of a regular investment and, given that you have decided how much to save each month the question that you generally need answering is how much is the investment worth at the end of a number of likely periods and at a range of likely interest rates. To answer this question you need to construct a table with interest rates stored in the left-hand column and terms

|   | A | B | C | D | E | F | G |
|---|---|---|---|---|---|---|---|
| 1 | 1% | 1 | | | | | |
| 2 | | | | | | | |
| 3 | | 120.55153 | 1 | 5 | 10 | 15 | |
| 4 | | 1% | | | | | |
| 5 | | 2% | | | | | |
| 6 | | 3% | | | | | |
| 7 | | 4% | | | | | |
| 8 | | 5% | | | | | |
| 9 | | 6% | | | | | |
| 10 | | | | | | | |
| 11 | | | | | | | |
| 12 | | | | | | | |
| 13 | | | | | | | |

in the top row.

The FV formula is stored in the corner of the table, i.e. at B3, and it is

$$=FV(A1/12,B1*12,-10)$$

## Data Table dialog

| | |
|---|---|
| Table Range: | $B$3:$F$9 |
| Row Input Cell: | $B$1 |
| Column Input Cell: | $A$1 |

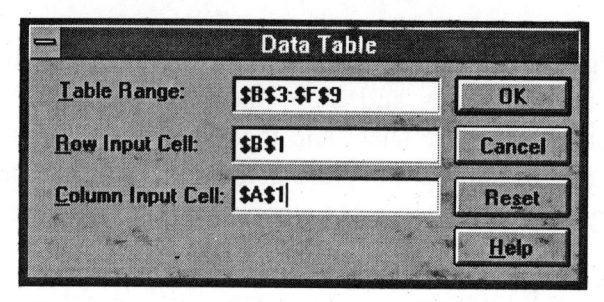

Buttons: OK, Cancel, Reset, Help

Notice that the rate is assumed to be stored in A1 and the term in B1. These are going to be used as the input cells for the column and row values.

The Data Table dialog box has to be filled in so that the Table is defined to be B3:F9, the row input cell B1 and the column input cell A1.

When you click on OK the values in the left-hand column and top row of the table are placed in A1 and B1 respectively one pair at a time, the sheet is recalculated and the result of the formula stored in B3 is stored in the appropriate place in the table.

| | A | B | C | D | E | F |
|---|---|---|---|---|---|---|
| 1 | 1% | 1 | | | | |
| 2 | | | | | | |
| 3 | | 120.55153 | 1 | 5 | 10 | 15 |
| 4 | | 1% | 120.55153 | 614.99049 | 1261.4987 | 1941.14 |
| 5 | | 2% | 121.10613 | 630.47356 | 1327.1966 | 2097.1306 |
| 6 | | 3% | 121.66383 | 646.46713 | 1397.4142 | 2269.7269 |
| 7 | | 4% | 122.22463 | 662.98978 | 1472.498 | 2460.9049 |
| 8 | | 5% | 122.78855 | 680.06083 | 1552.8228 | 2672.8894 |
| 9 | | 6% | 123.35562 | 697.70031 | 1638.7935 | 2908.1871 |

You should compare this tabulation with the one created using a functional model in Chapter 10.

## » Tabulating a model

To give you a clearer idea of just **how powerful the Data, Table command is, the following example creates a table** of values that were obtained by recalculating an entire model for each row of the table. The **model in question is the** modified mailshot example that uses a sheet to supply it with basic constants of the calculation.

We have already seen how it is possible to find the maximum value of the profit across all of the cells in the model using the MAX function in a linked sheet. Once you have a formula in a sheet there is nothing stopping you from attempting to use the Data,Table command to construct a data table using it. In this case the only complication is specifying the input cell.

The data table has to be entered into the CONST.MDS sheet. The values of Unit price that we would like the maximum profit tabulated for should be entered into B8:B13 and the formula that we require to evaluate should be put into C7 ready for tabulation.

| | A | B | C |
|---|---|---|---|
| 1 | Unit price | 10 | |
| 2 | Unit mail cost | 1.5 | |
| 3 | Unit print cost | 0.02 | |
| 4 | | | |
| 5 | | | |
| 6 | | | |
| 7 | | Unit price | 52000 |
| 8 | | 10 | |
| 9 | | 11 | |
| 10 | | 12 | |
| 11 | | 13 | |
| 12 | | 14 | |
| 13 | | 15 | |
| 14 | | | |
| 15 | | | |

In this case the formula is:

=MAX('MAIL4.MDL'
    'Batch size.Profit.No of flyers.Hit rate')

The next step is to fill in the Data,Table dialog box. The data table is B7:C13 and the column input cell is B1. When you click on the OK button the table is constructed in the usual

## Data Table

| | |
|---|---|
| Table Range: | $B$7:$C$13 |
| Row Input Cell: | |
| Column Input Cell: | $B$1 |

[OK] [Cancel] [Reset] [Help]

way. Each value in the column of the data table is loaded into B1 in turn, the entire sheet is recalculated and the value of the formula in C7 is stored in the table. Of course the clever part is that when the sheet is recalculated so is the model that it is linked to via the formula that you are tabulating and this uses the current value in B1 - hence the result is the maximum profit for each of the values in the table.

**CONST.MDS : Window1**

| | A | B | C | D |
|---|---|---|---|---|
| 1 | Unit price | 10 | | |
| 2 | Unit mail cost | 1.5 | | |
| 3 | Unit print cost | 0.02 | | |
| 4 | | | | |
| 5 | | | | |
| 6 | | | | |
| 7 | | | Unit price | 52000 |
| 8 | | | 10 | 52000 |
| 9 | | | 11 | 57000 |
| 10 | | | 12 | 62000 |
| 11 | | | 13 | 67000 |
| 12 | | | 14 | 72000 |
| 13 | | | 15 | 77000 |
| 14 | | | | |
| 15 | | | | |

In this particular case the table is of little practical interest because increasing the unit price of the item results in a very simple change in the maximum profit, i.e. it increases by £5000 for every £1 increase. In a more realistic model the percentage response from the advertising would be made to depend on the unit price and in this case the table would be a valuable way of summarising the results of the model. Using a sheet to provide input values to a model also allows you to tabulate any summary statistic you care to compute.

## » Goal seeking

There is another, and some might argue more direct, route to finding a maximum profit or minimum cost than creating a functional model or a table of values. The Tools,Goal Seek command will automatically change the value stored in an input cell in an effort to make the value in another cell reach a specified value. Goal seeking works with models or sheets and even with linked models and sheets.

Its principles are very similar to those of the Data, Table command. That is, the input cell is modified, everything is recalculated and the value in the target cell is compared with the goal value. If the target is close enough to the goal then the process stops and the value of the input cell is the value you are looking for. If the target cell is larger or smaller than the goal then a new input value that hopefully moves the target value closer to the goal is tried in the input cell. Of course there is no guarantee that the goal seeking process will find the desired value of the target in which case it is up to you to stop it manually by pressing the Stop button.

As a simple example of the use of the Tools, Goal Seek command consider the problem of finding the value of A1 that makes the formula A1^2+A1+3 in B1 equal to 15 - both the formula and the goal are entirely arbitrary.

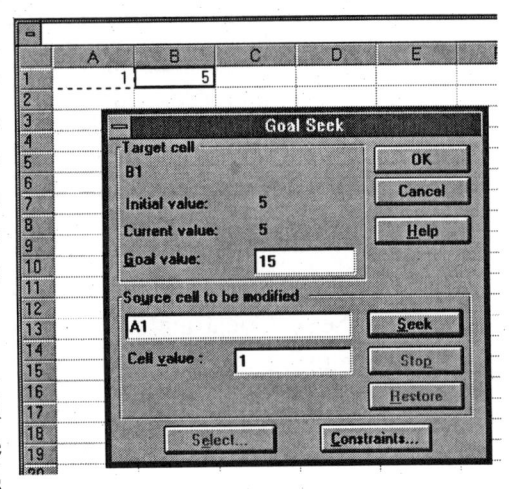

To do this select cell B1 and use the Tools,Goal Seek command. In the dialog box that appears enter 15 as the Goal value and A1 as the cell to be modified. When you click on Seek you will see the value in A1 change and the sheet recalculated until the value in B1 reaches 15. The solution is close to 3.

Although this is a simple example it contains most of the elements of using Goal Seek. However, sometimes you have to actually create a function specially to be the subject of a goal seeking exercise. For example, if you want to find a value of A1 that makes A1*A1 equal to the contents of B1 then you will need an additional function. In this case the function that you want to use as the target is B1-A1*A1 and the goal value is 0. If you look at this you will see that what we have done is to create a function that gives the error or discrepancy between the two values and then simply asked the goal seeker to reduce this to 0. This a common strategy.

The only complication is that the value that is being changed in an effort to make the target cell equal to the goal might be constrained to lie between given maximum and minimum values.

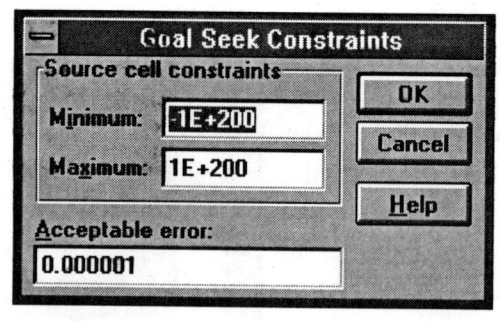

```
┌─────── Goal Seek Constraints ───────┐
│ ┌─Source cell constraints─────┐     │
│ │                             │  ┌──OK──┐
│ │ Minimum:  -1E+200           │  └──────┘
│ │                             │  ┌─Cancel─┐
│ │ Maximum:  1E+200            │  └────────┘
│ │                             │  ┌─Help─┐
│ └─────────────────────────────┘  └──────┘
│  Acceptable error:                  │
│  0.000001                           │
└─────────────────────────────────────┘
```

You can set the acceptable range for the source cell using the Goal Seek Constraints dialog box. In this you can set a maximum, a minimum value and the degree of difference between the goal and the target that you find acceptable.

## » Goal seeking mailshot

The biggest difficulty in using the goal seeking facilities is in seeing exactly when they could be useful. Although the simple example given earlier does help you to understand how goal seeking works it doesn't even hint at how powerful the method is. The important point is that, like the Data,Table command, the formula that you are using as the target can involve values obtained by the recalculation of an entire sheet, model or even a linked system of models. To give you some idea of how this works consider the mailshot example again.

Instead of using the Data,Table command to build a table of the maximum profits we can use the Tools,Goal Seek command to alter the unit price until the maximum profit as given by the model is equal to any specified value - £70,000 in this case. The target cell is C7 as this contains the formula that finds the maximum and the source cell is B1 because this is the cell linked to the model that gives the unit price. The goal seeking takes some time but eventually stops with a unit price of £13.60.

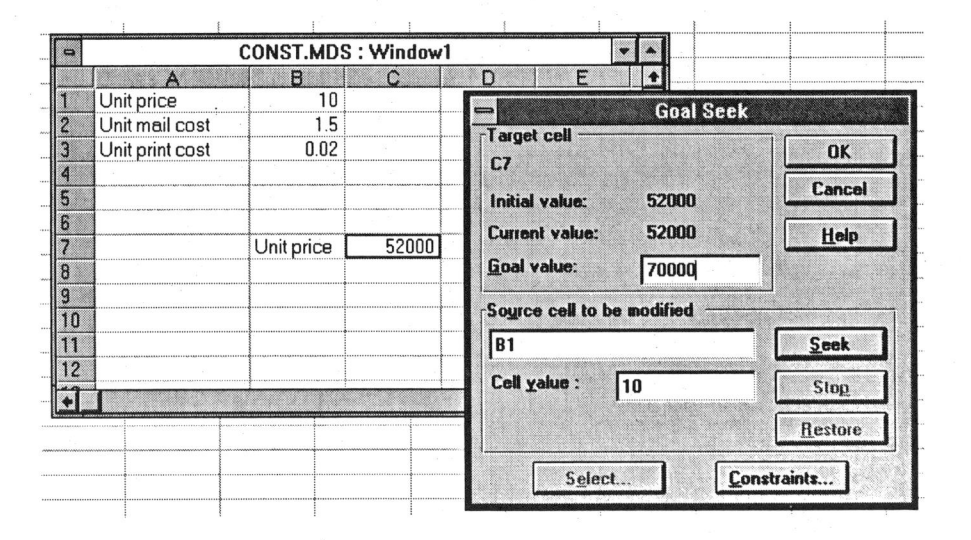

# Key points

» Links can be used to combine the best features of sheets and models.

» Links to a sheet are typically used to provide input values to a model and to display results and summary statistics.

» What-if tables are tabulations and as such are an alternative to functional models. However, they can also be used to tabulate the results of a model for a range of input values.

» Goal seeking is an optimisation tool that will automatically vary the value in an input cell until a specified output value is achieved.

# Index

## A
absolute 50, 115, 122
Add Dimension dialog 31
aggregation 151
alignment 75
ALLOC 176
Allocate dialog 180
allocation 175
Append 59
Apply Formula dialog 132
Apply formula to scope 63
Apply Names dialog 118

## B
background colour 75
backup 34
best fitting line 216
bold 76
Border 74

## C
categorical data 14
cell level formula 56
cell reference 39
centre justify 76
charts 195, 245
Chi squared 171
CHOOSE 190
clicking 33
colour 75
column dividers 87
column width 87
COMPBAL 184
compound growth 240
constant global formulae 105
continuous variables 140
converting labels to names 119
copying formulae 54
correlation coefficient 247
COST 243
COST2 244
Create Backup 34
creating global formula 68
crosstabs 10, 140
Ctrl-click 79
cubic 246
currency styles 102
Curve Builder 218
CurveFit 245
curves 212

## D
data tables 263
data types 144
Data,Regression 249
Data,Set Database 146
Data,Table 265
database 13, 140
dBase III 144, 147
DBF format 144
default item names 39
default model 23
Define Formula Scope 70
Define Name dialog 117
define style 77, 94
degrees of freedom 173
deleting 123
deleting fixed dimension 32
deleting items 27
dependent variable 213
deviations 167
dimension 11, 23, 88, 189
dimension index 128
dimension styles 89
DIMENSIONNAME 189
discrete variables 140
dragging 33
duplicate item names 127

## E
Edit Scope 58
Edit,Add Dimension 31
Edit,Copy 54
Edit,Delete Dimension 32
Edit,Delete Items 27
Edit,Insert Item 29
Edit,Move Item 31
Edit,Paste 55
Edit,Rename 24
Enter Cell-level formula 65, 70
equals sign 39
expected values 169
exporting a database 146, 149
external databases 144

## F

F9 193
File,Links 255
File,New 22
File,Open 34
File,Save 34
financial functions 184
fixed dimensions 15
fixed items 16
font 75, 95
Forecasting 238
foreground colour 75
Format All 81, 90, 94
Format, Label Style 89
Format,Column width 87
Format,Label Column Width 90
Format,Label Row Height 90
Format,Row Height 87
Format,Style 77, 94
formatting 74
formatting slices 80
Formula,Create Names 119
Formula,Define Name 117, 146, 259
Formula,Replace 119
Formula,Set Scope 57
Formula,Terms 200
fully crossed dimensions 159
Future Value 194

## G

Global button 57
global formula 56, 64, 65
Global Inheritance 130
Goal Seek Constraints 272
goal seeking 271
GROWTH 227, 243
GROWTH2 244

## H

hiding items 89

## I

Ignore relative/absolute box 119
imported page models 108
importing a database 145
independent variable 213
index 100
index notation 128
Insert Item dialog 29
inserting 123
inserting dimensions 31
inserting items 29
inserting items by dragging 30
Interpolate 247
intersection range 42, 54, 58
italic 76
item index 128
ITEMINDEX 188
ITEMNAME 189
items 12, 23, 29

## J

justification 75

## L

LABEL 184
large models 111
least squares 217
LEFT 187
left justify 76
line chart 245
links 254
LINLINEST 242
LINLINS 231, 244
LINLOGEST 243
LINLOGS 245
LogLinear curve 224, 225
LOGLOGEST 243
LOGLOGS 245
LOOKUP 244
Lookup table 228

## M

Make axes 220
marginals 160
missing values 18
Model bar 16
Model Bar dialog 91
mouse 25, 33
moving 31,125
multidimensional data 8
multiple indexing 109
multiple views 86, 262

## N

named constants 259
names 24, 117, 259
naming series 101
nested models 159
new file 22
numeric formats 75

## O

One independent variable curve 219
one-input data table 263
opening files 34
Options,Calculate 255
Options,Display 91
Options,Model Bar 91
Options,Workspace 34

## P

page models 99
patterns 75
pivoting 106
plotting row labels 199
point size 75
pointing 47, 117
polynomial curve 245
pop-up menu 76
precedence in formatting 85
predicted values 169

## Q

quadratic 246

## R

R squared 247
range functions 54
range references 40, 120
Recalc button 193
recalculation 111
regression 217, 222
regular data 100
relationships between variables 212
relative 50, 114, 122
Rename dialog 24
renaming 26, 126
Replace 60
right justify 76
right mouse button 25
rotation 12, 16, 26
row height 87
rulings 74

## S

S-shaped curve 231
saturation 231
saved windows 87
saving files 34
scatter diagram 245
scope 55, 57, 115, 120, 129
selecting ranges 79
self allocation 180

Set Scope dialog 57
SHARE 244
Shift-click 79
shortcut menu 25
significance level 172
single quotes 38
slice 74
slope 222
smoothing 244
sparse data 17
split range 43
statistical functions 242
string functions 187
structure 8
Style All 82, 96
Style Define dialog 77
style names 77, 94
styles 76
summary page 107

## T

terms 199
text functions 187
time series 238
Tools,Allocate 175, 180
Tools,Curve Builder 218
Tools,Forecast 239
Tools,Goal Seek 271
TREND 221, 223, 242
TREND2 244
true relative reference 116
TrueType fonts 75
two independent variables 234
two-input data table 266
type effects 75
typeface 75

## U

underline 76
underspecification 45, 54, 122
unhiding items 89
Update Global formula 65
user-defined function 154

## W

what-if tables 263
Window 86
Wrap Text box 75

# Other Books of Interest

**Mastering CA-SuperCalc for Windows**
by Janet Swift
CA-SuperCalc for Windows is a two-in-one product - comprising the familiar 2D spreadsheet as well as the multidimensional modelling component. In this book Janet Swift goes from the basics of using sheets to their advanced features - covering charts and reports, database facilities and macros using CA-ble. Whether you are upgrading from the DOS version of SuperCalc or are a completely new spreadsheet user you will find it contains the information you need to make best use of CA-SuperCalc for Windows.
**ISBN 1-871962-24-2**

**The Expert Guide to SuperCalc**
by Janet Swift
This book was written with reference to the DOS spreadsheet SuperCalc 5 but is equally relevant to the Windows version since it has lost none of its potential in the move to a more friendly operating environment - indeed CA have taken care to ensure that it has retained the very features that made it such a powerful analytical tool. Most users only ever take advantage of a fraction of what a spreadsheet like SuperCalc can do for them and in this book Janet Swift aims to introduce readers to a wider range of possibilities by introducing some new ideas, methods and techniques that she has developed over years of being a SuperCalc user.
**ISBN 1-871962-10-2**

**The SuperProject Expert**
by Andrew C Johnson
This book is about CA-SuperProject for Windows which is widely used in business, industry and the service sector. Project management is a sphere in which computers have revolutionised the way businesses operate - but the impact has not been as far reaching as might have been expected due to the complexity of the software itself. In initial chapters Andrew Johnson explores the basics of creating and viewing a model using CA-SuperProject. He then goes on to show methods and techniques in dealing with the complexity inherent in large projects. Later chapters deal with tracking and costing projects and allocating material resources, and include a discussion of rescheduling in the light of actual data, earned value analysis and inventory costing.
**ISBN 1-871962-23-4**

**For more information or a catalogue contact:**

I/O Press, Oak Tree House, Leyburn, North Yorkshire DL8 5SE
Tel: (0969) 24402 Fax: (0969) 24375

### The 386/486 PC: A Power User's Guide (Updated Second Edition)
by Harry Fairhead
Windows applications such as CA-SuperCalc for Windows require a computer based on a 368/486 processor. Harry Fairhead provides the technical information you need to make the most of this hardware, explaining aspects such as extended and expanded memory, LIM, hard disk seek rates, caching, memory interleave and shadow RAM. He also shows you how to configure and optimise your system for the applications you are interested in. The final chapter covers latest developments - the Pentium chip, the local bus, superscalar architecture and Windows NT.
ISBN 1-871962-22-6

### Desktop Publishing with PagePlus 3
by Andrew Marshman and Mike James
The Windows environment has increased the range of widely used applications and one of the "boom" areas has been that of DTP with more and more people producing their own advertising literature and promotional materials. This book relates to Serif's latest popular and competitive package PagePlus 3 and has a wealth of information for both beginners and experienced users covering basic principles through to the intricacies of pre-press and volume colour printing.
ISBN 1-871962-38-2

## In Preparation

### Financial Functions Using a Spreadsheet
by Mike James and Janet Swift
Calculations concerning percentages and interest rates are at the heart of every financial decision. Most spreadsheet users are unaware that there is a complete financial calculator built into their software. You can work out repayments on almost any type of loan and determine the interest earned on almost any type of investment. Starting from simple ideas this book shows how you can quickly master financial calculations and get to grips with seemingly impenetrable financial functions. Each is explained and illustrated with working templates dealing with practical problems.
ISBN 1-871962-01-3

### Programming in CA-Realizer and CA-ble
by Mike James and Janet Swift
Realizer 2.0 is a complete development language for Windows and OS/2. It is easy to use, powerful and the language that is the basis for CA's application macro language CA-ble. If you are interested in writing macros for CA-SuperCalc for Windows or for CA-SuperProject then you will find all the help you need in this title.
ISBN 1-871962-37-4